650

THE GLOBAL
BRAND CEO

BUILDING THE ULTIMATE MARKETING MACHINE

THE GLOBAL BRAND CEO

BUILDING THE ULTIMATE MARKETING MACHINE

MARC DE SWAAN ARONS

FRANK VAN DEN DRIEST

AIR/TREAM™ New York

THE GLOBAL BRAND CEO

BUILDING THE ULTIMATE MARKETING MACHINE

© copyright Marc de Swaan Arons &
Frank van den Driest, 2010

AIRSTREAM° New York
First published in 2010
Airstream International
816 Broadway, Suite 4, New York, NY 10003

ISBN 978-0-615-38708-6

De Swaan Arons, Marc & Van den Driest, Frank

DESIGN Van Marcus, Amsterdam, The Netherlands

SECOND EDITION, OKTOBER 2010

Printed in the Netherlands

For our Families

Contents

CASE STUDIES INCLUDED IN THIS BOOK

Acknowledgements

Over the last decade, many special people have supported us. We would like to thank them for their trust, time and encouragement.

First and foremost, we'd like to thank our families for their never-ending support and encouragement. EffectiveBrands, and everything we've built over the last decade, wouldn't be what it is today without you.

Secondly, we would like to make a special mention of our partners-in-crime, Stef Gans and Helen Duce. Without you, EffectiveBrands would be a much smaller and less successful company (and a whole lot less fun, too).

Then there are all our colleagues at EffectiveBrands with whom we work daily to help make the EffectiveBrands vision a reality. In New York, London, Amsterdam, Singapore, Paris, and Tokyo, we recognize your support and are privileged to count you as colleagues.

A special thank you to all our clients who have allowed us to share our project work in case studies, as well as to the other global marketing leaders who participated in our Leading Global Brands interviews and helped forge our thinking over the years. And especially to Silvia Lagnado and the first Dove Global Brand Team. Our work together going back to the first days is something we will forever be proud of.

Jan Peelen, Fergus Balfour, and Wim Dik deserve a special mention for the early confidence they showed in us and for all the energetic coaching and support over the years.

And finally, for over five years we've wanted to write and publish this book. It would probably have taken us another five years without the support of David Shaw, Meghana Rao, Halle Darmstadt, Peter Smith, Lisa Sanders, Barbara Dijkhuis and Auke Vleer.

Thank you all.

Contributors to this book

We would like to thank all the global marketing leaders who made themselves available for interviews.

You helped shape the final contents with your ideas and examples.

JENNY ASHMORE - Global Marketing Capability Officer, *Mars Incorporated*

DUNCAN BLAKE - Director of Brand, *BP*

KERRIS BRIGHT - CMO, *British Airways*

JAMES CALI - SVP Gum and Candy Global Category Team, *Kraft Foods*

SIMON CLIFT - CMO, *Unilever (2008 - 2010)*

LEE ANN DALY - CMO, *Thomson Reuters*

JENNIFER DAVIDSON - Global Senior Marketing Director, *Molson Coors International*

NICK FELL - Marketing Director, *SABMiller*

DAVID GERSHON - Founder and CEO, *The Empowerment Institute*

NIGEL GILBERT - Group Marketing Director, *Lloyds Banking Group (2008 - 2009)*

PHILIP GLADMAN - SVP Global Marketing, *Smirnoff*

TEX GUNNING - Board Member *AkzoNobel responsible for Decorative Paints*

NIGEL HOLLIS - Chief Global Analyst, *Millward Brown*

LENNARD HOORNIK - Corporate VP and Head of Global Marketing, *Sony Ericsson Mobile Communications*

FOLKERT KAMPHUIS - Global COO of Animal Health, *Novartis*

NICK KENDALL - Group Strategy Director, *Bartle Bogle Hegarty*

PETER KIRKBY - VP Global Marketing Excellence, *GlaxoSmithKline Consumer Healthcare*

KARIN KOONINGS - VP of Brand and Marketing, *Starbucks Coffee International (2004 - 2008)*

SILVIA LAGNADO - CMO, *Bacardi*

BOON LAI - Area Marketing Officer, *VP Greater China, Philips Electronics*

MIKE LINTON - CMO, *Best Buy* (1999 - 2006) and CMO, *Ebay* (2007 - 2009)

ANTONIO LUCIO - CMO, *VISA International*

SØREN LUND - Senior Director PG1 Marketing, *LEGO System A/S*

AMANDA MACKENZIE - CMO, *Aviva*

ROB MALCOLM - President Global Marketing, Sales and Innovation, *Diageo* (1999 - 2008)

MARC MATHIEU - SVP Global Brand Marketing, *The Coca-Cola Company* (2003 - 2008)

PHIL MIRVIS - Fellow at Boston College Center for Corporate Citizenship

JONATHAN MOORE - Marketing Director, Household & Body Care U.K., *Sara Lee*

MARIEKE DE MOOIJ - Cross Cultural Communication Consultant

ANN NESS - VP Corporate Brand Management, *Cargill*

PIETER NOTA - Executive Board Member Marketing, Research & Development and Sales, *Beiersdorf*

NEIL PUNWANI - Global Brand Director, *Fanta (2005 - 2009)*

STEPHEN QUINN - EVP and CMO, *Walmart*

MARTIN RILEY - CMO, *Pernod Ricard*

ALINE SANTOS - VP DIG Global, *Unilever*

MARIANNE SCHOENAUER - Director of Global Marketing Knowledge Management, *Unilever*

JOHN SEIFERT - Chairman and CEO, North America, *Ogilvy & Mather Worldwide*

JIM STENGEL - Global Marketing Officer, *Procter & Gamble (2001 - 2008)*

EGBERT VAN ACHT - CMO, *Philips Consumer Lifestyle (2008 - 2009)*

PETER VAUGHN - SVP Global Brand Management and Marketing, *American Express*

GREG WELCH - Global Practice Leader, Consumer Goods & Services, *Spencer Stuart*

DAVID WILKIE - Managing Director, *Marketing 50*

TIM WRIGHT - President, Future Group, *GlaxoSmithKline Consumer Healthcare*

KHALIL YOUNES - SVP Group Sales, Marketing & Innovation, *Carlsberg Breweries A/S*

THE GLOBAL BRAND CEO

BUILDING THE ULTIMATE MARKETING MACHINE

Introduction

In September 2000, the two of us met for the first time in the American Hotel in Amsterdam to discuss the key challenges brands were facing in a rapidly converging, interactive and globalizing economy. We were both passionate, buzzing with new ideas...and the sparks started flying.

Three months, and many e-mails, phone calls, and PowerPoint presentations later, we met again, this time in New York. That same week we flew down to Brownsville, Texas, kicking off a week-long coast to-coast trip in an Airstream trailer to thrash out what it would take to build a new consultancy that could add value in this exciting field, and make us happy, too.

We spent the first two days of the trip thinking through how we would want to work together, and deciding what kind of company we wanted to build. Today, these values and operating principles still guide every single one of our team members.

It took us another year and a handful of big projects with founding clients to zoom in on what has become our sweet spot and business obsession ever since: *How to increase global marketing effectiveness.*

Looking back now, a decade later, we have a lot to celebrate.

Ten years ago, we started EffectiveBrands based on the insight that global marketing leaders new to the job had few resources to turn to for support on *how* to do their job well. There was no book to read, no peer council to join, and no specialized consultancy to turn to.

Today, to our knowledge, we are still the only marketing consultancy specifically focused on increasing global marketing effectiveness.

We are incredibly proud of the team of over 50 consultants all over the world that now work with us.

Eight years ago, we started the *Leading Global Brands* study to identify what it takes to win in global marketing. To date over 250 global brands, 2,500 global brand leaders and 21,000 global marketers and their colleagues have contributed to this study.

Five years ago, we co-founded the *Global Brand 50*, a council that allows the leaders of global marketing organizations to share best practices and exchange insights with peers in a non-competitive environment.

And this September we are celebrating our anniversary with nearly 20 EffectiveBrands Directors, and many more clients at the World Expo in Shanghai, China.

With this book, our goal is to share our vision on what it takes to win in global marketing, and to offer a practical approach to help the global marketing leaders of today and tomorrow become Global Brand CEOs.

New York, Amsterdam, July 2010

Marc de Swaan Arons
Frank van den Driest

The Rise Of Global Marketing

Do We Really Need Another

Book about Brands?

DIAGEO

ROB MALCOLM - PRESIDENT GLOBAL MARKETING,
SALES AND INNOVATION, DIAGEO (1999 - 2008)

Over a marketing leadership career spanning 35 years, Rob Malcolm, *President, Global Marketing, Sales and Innovation, Diageo,* has been a student, practitioner and teacher of global marketing to everyone around him. Rob has maintained a tireless curiosity for learning and a passion both for sharing his insights and participating in searching discussions.

In the course of his tenure as President, Global Marketing, Sales and Innovation of Diageo, Rob helped transform the world's largest drinks company into one of the premier marketing - and marketing training - companies in the world.

Under Rob's leadership, Diageo grew rapidly and developed arguably the world's strongest drinks brand portfolio, including category leaders like Guinness, Johnnie Walker, Smirnoff, Captain Morgan, Baileys, J&B, Tanqueray and Jose Cuervo. Until his retirement in 2009, Rob had oversight of more than 70 brands in 170-plus countries. His overall marketing budget was more than $2.5 billion annually. Along the way, he helped Diageo garner countless awards for its advertising, direct and digital marketing, design and innovation, from numerous Effies to Cannes Gold Lions to the U.K.'s prestigious IPA Advertising Effectiveness Award.

After receiving his Bachelor's and MBA degrees in Marketing, Rob began his career with Procter & Gamble in Brand Management (as have so many of today's most successful marketing leaders). During his 24 years at P&G, he progressed through both marketing and general management assignments in the U.S., the Middle East and Europe. Eventually, he would work on approximately 75 brands in some 40 countries. P&G provided Rob with a strong foundation in all disciplines of marketing, and honed the keen strategic discipline and analytical rigor that are among the legacies of this marketing veteran's extraordinary career.

Central to Rob's, and Diageo's, success is the proprietary disciplined marketing approach that Rob helped develop and implement, and which he led for almost a decade – 'The Diageo Way of Brand Building.' Developed and taught internally by senior Diageo leaders, this program is aimed not only at marketers but all company employees. The Diageo approach ensures that everyone in the room speaks a common business and marketing language; that all brands share common marketing processes; and that Diageo employees can swiftly leverage whatever lessons they learn (good and bad), across the entire global organization.

When Rob retired from Diageo, he left in perfect operating order one of the world's most successful global marketing machines. Diageo's marketers can switch from brand to key market and from category to region without missing a note or a beat. And if and when they leave the company, other global organizations snap them up overnight.

Since retiring from full-time corporate work in 2008, Rob remained active in a range of business and marketing endeavors, including sitting on several company boards, serving as an advisor to MDC Partners, Diageo, and also teaching marketing at the Wharton Business School. Rob also serves on the board of the AMA.

Rob's passion for marketing, and in particular the need to combine highly rigorous analytical discipline and creative flair, has been reflected in numerous lectures, speeches, articles and interviews over the years.

Clearly, Rob is an uncommon marketing leader. He's also among the very first marketers to recognize and embrace the importance and opportunity of global brands and the priority of building an effective global marketing machine. By pursuing both he has helped develop formidable competitive advantage for Diageo.

WHY DO WE NEED ANOTHER
MARKETING BOOK?

There are two short answers to this admittedly good question. The first is based on our own experience of continuously reviewing key globalization changes from multiple perspectives – consumer, competitors, customer, technological and of course, brands and marketing.

We believe that something really *has* changed in marketing over the last decade. Essentially, there's too much today that's too different for any of us to keep on doing *business as usual.*

The second reason is more flattering. Our clients, colleagues and just about every other marketing stakeholder we've spoken with has suggested, prompted, urged, and in some cases challenged us to give them the lay of the land as *we* see it. Not to mention that a lot of our marketing colleagues, past and present, have asked us to refer them to a simple, practical guidebook about the implications for marketers in today's rapidly globalizing world market.

Sorry, we said, our hands are tied. No such book exists. That is, until now.

ALMOST EVERY MARKETER TODAY WORKS
FOR OR COMPETES AGAINST A GLOBAL BRAND

Think about it for a second – just ten years ago, things looked very different. The dawn of the 21st century kicked off with global brands leading and redefining many of the world's biggest markets. Today, in almost every major product category, contemporary global brands drive innovation. They sculpt consumer expectations around value and solutions.

Sure, back in 1983, Theodore Levitt confidently proclaimed that, *'Gone are accustomed differences in national and regional preferences.'* Still, it wasn't until much more recently that global brands gained the stature and muscle Levitt predicted. Years before that, when most of today's marketing leaders were in business school, few professors or textbooks even *mentioned* global brands. Then, the most celebrated marketing textbook case studies and the fight for market leadership revolved around local and – no two ways around it – mostly American brands.

If business today is primarily global, you might expect support materials to have followed in step. No such luck. No marketing or business books on the shelves take aim specifically at how to develop a winning global marketing *strategy*, build an effective global marketing organizational *structure*, and – while we're still on the subject – create wining global marketing *capability*.

Which is why we decided finally to make the time to write this book.

Over the past decade, we have had the privilege to advise and learn from marketing leaders in nearly every conceivable type of organization. It could be Profit or Non-Profit. It could be CPG or Telecom. It could range from Healthcare to Personal Care, from Electronics to Service, from Finance to Beverages. Again, our experience has shown that across every industry, and without exception, global brands today play a significantly more important 'Smartphones' role than they did only a decade ago.

Still in doubt? In 2002, as part of our *Leading Global Brands* study, we reached out to global brand leaders with a simple value exchange proposition: *Give us 90 minutes of your time. Be ruthlessly honest. Now – what are the most important opportunities and challenges you run into on a daily basis? What works? What never works? What do you wish you'd done during day one of your global marketing leadership role? Alternatively, what do you wish you'd never done?* In return, we promised a full debrief presentation in which we'd synthesize what we learned into a roadmap of guiding principles and recommendations.

Gratifyingly, the *Leading Global Brands* (LGB) study turned out to be a runaway hit. In the first six months alone, over 25 global marketing leaders volunteered to participate. A few years later, our LGB study tacked on a quantitative assessment. We also decided to start almost every new project with a quantitative assessment to measure what was working, what wasn't, and how best to remedy it.

To date, over 250 global brands, 2,500 global marketing leaders and roughly 21,000 marketers and their colleagues have contributed to our study. As we expected, our proprietary research among global marketing leaders finds that global brands today play an increasingly critical role in almost every worldwide market for products and services. For every CMO, global marketing effectiveness has become *the* contemporary hot-button issue.

But what's really changed out there in the world? What are its implications? What should every global marketer leader be thinking about, strategizing over, pondering? In this chapter, we'll review today's altered landscape from the perspective of a marketer within a global marketing organization. We'll also review the key consumer, customer, technological and organizational trends and developments that we predict will shape future strategies and approaches. We'll also share some of the most striking findings of our *Leading Global Brands* study.

But first let's start by defining what we mean by *'global brands'*.

This book is all about increasing global brand effectiveness and efficiency across *multiple markets*. The vision and approach presented by us address the specific opportunities and challenges faced by marketing leaders working with brands that are sold in *multiple markets*. The brand can have the same name everywhere or be marketed under a different brand name. We include B2C Brands like Dove, Starbucks and Coca-Cola, but also B2B brands such as ING Bank, Cisco and WebEx.

It is our experience that the opportunities and challenges faced when marketing across multiple international markets get bigger as the number of markets increases. So the more international markets your brand is exposed to, the more relevant this book may be to you.

The Market Is Globalizing

Not that he asked us, but Thomas Friedman couldn't have said it better. Today, a pack of Shanghai teenagers shares more of the same interests and obsessions with counterparts in Paris, Barcelona and New York City than they do with their own family members living only an hour away.

The World Really Is Flat

Case in point: Valentine's Day. Ten years ago, this heart-thumping, card-roses-and-chocolate-giving celebration was exclusively an Anglo-Saxon practice. Today, China recognizes and welcomes Valentine's Day across practically all social networks. What's more, thanks to mass media, the typical Asian consumer knows everything there is to know about Christmas. In both cases, hearts, chocolates, wreaths and reindeer are becoming more popular every year.

Technology, and the explosion of the Internet, are creating a sense of collaborative ownership and shared community. Thanks to the Internet, even a small firm can radically increase its reach. All across the web, a pebble-slinging David can act like a swaggering Goliath. The Internet almost instantly endows a small business with stature, credibility, consistency and capability. It also dramatically lowers and even eliminates traditional barriers to market entry. Today a company in Mumbai can easily market its products or services to a potential customer base in Brazil. A marketing campaign targeted for Spain can be adjusted to serve the Argentinean market. And anyone equipped with a computer can buy goods and services, and respond to advertising and/or marketing with a simple mouse click.

Corporations can also harness the Internet to deepen their internal collaboration. With the right technological infrastructure, a company can simultaneously conduct videoconferences with any number of other remote locations. It can facilitate a digital conversation among the far-flung advocates of a company's signature product. It can roll up global sales figures from a hundred different markets onto a dashboard splashed across every employee's PC, hours after the quarter ends.

But connectivity and transparency have their flipsides as well. A local misstep can no longer be contained, glossed over, or ignored. The Internet has handed every consumer a podium and a megaphone. If a media report accuses a company of exploiting child labor in its Indonesian factory, French customers may respond by boycotting its products. Overnight, the oil spill in the Gulf of Mexico resulted in BP petrol station boycotts across Germany – news that, thanks to social media networks, instantly flooded the globe. In the last few months, we've seen Apple on the defensive about high suicide rates in a Shengzhen factory that supplies nearly every technology provider; Honda reversing a pay freeze for workers employed in some Asian production plants; and Pampers coming under question in the U.K. and the U.S. in the wake of a controversial new product design.

Says Phil Mirvis, Fellow at Boston College Center for Corporate Citizenship, *'The public increasingly expects organizations and their brands to take responsibility for their complete global footprint and dealings with society. The problem is that most firms are not internally organized to do that holistically.'*

In short, like it or not, by circumstance if not by choice, for good or for bad, we believe that every brand is now performing on the global stage. So what happens next?

The Connected Consumer

Technology has also introduced an unprecedented number of new distribution systems that deliver knowledge to consumers via more channels than ever before, from mobile phones and e-commerce sites, to blogs, wikis, tweets, podcasts and more.

As of early 2010, an estimated 1.78 billion individuals across the globe were glued to the Internet. The Radicati Group reports that in 2009, users sent 90 trillion emails. Netcraft researchers claim that the Internet today comprises a mind-bending 234 million websites. Led by the iPhone, Smart

Phone penetration is doubling annually, and has already lassoed in over 14 percent of all U.S. mobile subscribers in the space of just a few months. In Asia the numbers are much higher. Many experts predict that Smartphones will eventually become the dominant source of information for consumers, trumping traditional media like TV and radio. How can they not if they provide users with everything from live TV and news broadcasts and instant stock trading to discounts on groceries?

Media is converging – and globalizing. Back in 1983, there were 50 dominant media corporations. Today media is owned and operated by nine giant firms, the five largest being Time-Warner, Disney, Bertelsmann, Viacom and Rupert Murdoch's News Corporation. When we consider what consumers across the world watch, read, and listen to, the combined influence of these media behemoths almost defies description. Global news and entertainment channels like CNN, BBC World and Discovery – not to mention Al Jazeera and MTV – reach countless millions across the globe daily. Social networking websites and push channels like Facebook, Twitter and FourSquare allow users instant access to friends (and complete strangers); while LinkedIn leverages the power of personal and professional networks to facilitate career success.

Says Pieter Nota of Beiersdorf, *'The changes are fascinating. We are seeing consumers using media in totally new ways. People really want to be connected with many other people at the same time. The younger generation interacts with media in a different way from the older generation. And we have to learn to work with these changes.'*

Easy access to volcanic amounts of data has also altered the way consumers interact with brands. Rob Malcolm himself deftly frames the challenge: *'The consumer is in control. Their access to information and the stimulus and power through all kinds of new media represent the most fundamental and exciting challenge to marketers across the world.'*

And consumers are becoming intolerant of messaging that companies neglect to tailor to their needs. Recent research carried out by Verdict finds that online consumers now expect to be offered personally relevant and appropriate products and services, as well as an 'edited choice.' One recent example? The introduction of apps for Smartphones that shoppers can use to scan product barcodes. In return, they receive key decision-making data about both the product and the manufacturer. For example, does the company support sustainable farming? What about equal rights for its gay workers? Does it lobby against fair trade? The (dirty) truth is all right there on your phone to help you make better informed choices.

In an effort to harness their technological power, online retailers are learning to understand the various 'need states' of their customers. What do consumers really want from their online experiences? K-Mart, for one, has seen enormous success with its dedicated 'Father's Day' and 'Hanukkah' shopping mini-sites. These 'sitelets' require next to no changes in product assortment or physical distribution, yet consumers experience them as personally tailored and targeted.

Globally Converging Consumer Needs

For us, one thing is clear: every one of our clients is seeing a significant convergence of consumer needs across the categories they serve. Sure, this perspective may be in some cases self-serving. Then again, consider these *Leading Global Brands* study findings: sixty-nine percent of the global marketing leaders we pulsed agreed that their consumers are more global than they were a decade ago. And a whopping 72 percent believe that globalization will continue throughout the next decade.

The increasing influence of television, travel, and structural emigration has resulted in a growing similarity of global values and tastes that can't help but affect customer desires and expectations. From Sweden to Scotland, more and more customers across the world share identical or similar needs in a product or service category – which indicates that today's consumers are more than willing to accept standardized global products.

Even in the food and beverage arenas, where national preferences historically predominate, the velocity of change in eating habits is striking. The Japanese are now eating doughnuts. The British are shunning their beloved pints of beer for cold American and European-style lagers. Health-minded consumers from the nation of Georgia to the state of Georgia begin their day with yogurt. And Burger King is as popular in Paris as it is in Peoria, Illinois.

Fact: there will remain huge differences across markets. During an interview, a food marketer once told us that the global brands in her portfolio were expanding at 30 to 40 percent growth rates, but that her base remained small. In fact, her brands represented only 3 to 4 percent of the total food markets in the Asian markets. By contrast, some of our technology clients tell us they no longer bother printing multilingual product manuals. They simply emboss the product's website on the packaging of a globally harmonized product and let consumers take it from there.

In general, the rule of thumb seems to be that the newer the product category, the greater the capacity to harmonize the mix upon launch. Mobile phones have no antecedents (Walkie-Talkies notwithstanding). Therefore, Nokia, Samsung, Sony Ericsson, and Apple can seed the playing field as they develop the category together. The same goes for 'new' foods like snacks and energy drinks. Companies like Unilever and Kraft, who operate in more traditional food categories, look on enviously as Frito Lay and Red Bull roll out single mixes globally.

Jennifer Davidson, Global Senior Marketing Director, Molson Coors International, says, *'Consumer needs from a functional point of view are very consistent in the beer category. Consumers in cosmopolitan cities have a lot in common; and I think their cultures are strongly influenced by each other.'*

In many categories, it's the macro drivers that are really, truly converging. Wired-up, wised-up consumers know more than they ever have about what's taking place beyond their front yards. Traveling is easier. Communicating is handier. TV channels are proliferating. Consequently, people are opening their minds more rapidly for a simple reason: they're exposed to more.

As markets develop, many of the marketers we work with acknowledge these precise same trends. For example, the increase of women in the workforce crunches the time a working mother has to prepare meals. This has led to dinners she can prepare quickly, as well as to convenience foods.

A trend like this is global (though naturally, the 'fast' foods consumers seek vary depending on the market).

Not everyone agrees. In her book, 'Global Marketing and Advertising, Understanding Cultural Paradoxes', author Marieke de Mooij argues that as economies develop, their populations use their newfound wealth to manifest their cultural diversity:

'The drive for cross-market advertising consistency is often counterproductive. The innate need for cross-situational consistency of Western marketing managers induces them to develop consistent brand identities and uniform advertising across countries. This is a fundamental error that may limit cross-cultural success.'

Our conclusion? Well, we can state with assurance that there are many more markets today in which consumers expect, or at least accept, products that have been harmonized globally. It could be that the packaging is the same everywhere, or the product itself, or even the advertising. Companies are responding not only because they want to. In today's global economy, if they want to survive, companies quite simply *have* to.

Globalizing Customers And Competitors

Retail and professional customers are globalizing at a fast pace too. Our prediction? The flight from the middle will continue. The big will get even bigger. The small will disappear or become inescapably niche. Witness the spread of Walmart , Tesco, and Carrefour across the world's retail landscape.

Says Jim Stengel, former Global Marketing Officer, Procter & Gamble: *'Retail customers around the world will get bigger and agglomerate. The trend will continue. But at the same time many new potential customers are appearing from nowhere. What you've got to do is not be myopic – or you might miss other opportunity channels.'*

The competitive landscape has changed dramatically in many markets – and continues to shape-shift at an ever-increasing rate. Tex Gunning, Board Member AkzoNobel responsible for Decorative Paints, notes that, *'As companies globalize, they meet new competitors, not old ones.'* Quality private labels and discount alternatives flourish in Europe, and increasingly in the U.S., traditional household names like Coca-Cola, Apple, Sony, McDonald's, Nokia, GE and Disney are today joined by giant challengers like HTC, Google, Lenovo, LG and Samsung.

Consider this: ten years ago, few people took Samsung seriously, especially its rivals. Samsung products were considered clunky and way behind the curve. Today the company is the design and technology leader in the TV industry, as well as a close competitor for the pole position in the mobile telephony market. All this and more in a decade or less! If that's not enough to make anyone anxious, a whole new crop of players is lurking in the wings. Many are 'awkward teenagers' who clearly need more experience before they get it right. Many lack the 'polish' that successful global brands require. Many are inexperienced branders, or offer product quality that's more inconsistent than not. But make no mistake: others are future Steve Jobs and Bill Gates. And the fact is, while these players may resemble awkward teens, *all* of them do things faster, cheaper, and often *better* than current market leaders.

And what about these brands? Haier, Tata, MTN, Huawei, Geely, Kaspersky. Chances are you won't have heard of some of these companies. Don't say we didn't warn you. Keep a sharp eye on the business section. Or ask one of your colleagues about their new Asian competitors.

Crunch this all together – the commoditization of products; the geyser-like rise of the Internet; the globalization of media; the transparency of markets; consumers' increasing sophistication; the rationalization of investment behind star brands – and you'll appreciate why, in the words of Scott Bedbury, former CMO of Nike, *'It's a new brand world.'*

We couldn't agree more. Over the last decade, the market share of global brands has shown unparalleled growth in almost every market. Isn't it time we understood how to harness this growth?

Marketing Is Globalizing

Of course marketers have not been sitting on the sidelines, idle. The field is clearly in a state of supreme flux.

Marketing Organizations Are Going Global

It comes as no surprise that companies today are all wrestling with the challenge of how to become global in outlook, approach and business strategy execution. It's a worldwide challenge that has spawned the rise of the *global marketing organization* and the role of the *global marketer*.

The marketing role as we traditionally know it is poised for reinvention. In recent years no other function within an organization has undergone such a profound sea change in the ways we conceive, structure and measure what it is exactly we do.

An Economist Intelligence Unit survey in 2009 found that more and more firms are working and reorganizing to establish truly global brands. They're also providing their customers with a consistent brand experience across disparate regions.

In today's digital and global economy, fiercely competitive firms are dramatically decreasing product lifecycles while rapidly absorbing lessons from one another. Which has led to commoditization in many categories, as well as fast-increasing costs of innovation.

Example: J.C. Penney Co. the fashion purveyor, has used digital technologies and a revitalized global supply chain to shrink its product cycles for women's fashion from *70 weeks in 2000, to 50 weeks in 2005, to just under 17 weeks in 2010* for some major collections. According to the retailer's top executive for procurement, Peter McGrath, *'You can go into a runway show and have a designer interpreting the fashion on a factory floor in China within three hours.'*

Today, many companies have established near-seamless synchrony between trend spotters and designers. Trend team members may continue to attend fashion shows and study store windows, but subscription-only websites deliver Milan's runway shows and Bergdorf Goodman's Christmas windows to Internet users in real time. Why wait five months to pick out a color scheme? Today a photospectrometer can scan colors digitally and circulate them around the world via the web. Cutting-edge, high-resolution technology spits out such uncannily precise computer images from which designers can determine minute details and alterations without leaving their offices.

The cost of differentiation has exploded. To stand out, companies have to invest at significantly higher levels than they've had to in the past to develop 'real' innovation. They've had to differentiate their brands on a basis other than price. And all the big players find it financially necessary to roll out their products globally to recover these higher costs of innovation and gain cost efficiencies in their R&D, supply chain and marketing investments.

BMW has aggressively separated from the pack by improving its connections with suppliers. BMW was among the first companies ever to set up a dedicated process (including a website) to seek out ideas from suppliers. To date, BMW has put into practice almost one-third of over 10,000 supplier-provided suggestions from all over the world. The company saves time and money. Best of all, innovation is in the hands of people whose intimate knowledge of the product has helped improve acceptance rates and reduce speed-to-market times.

Once the preserve of consumer packaged goods companies, today almost every industry, and at the highest echelons of management too, considers brand management, and particularly *global* brand management, integral to their success.

They're right, too.

Formerly in charge of marketing at AkzoNobel, Kerris Bright, CMO British Airways says, '*At AkzoNobel we spent significant energy into taking a much more global approach because there were huge advantages. When we put the global business up for grabs with agencies and other partners, we clearly noted a lot more interesting reactions versus what we would get if we did this six times over locally. You get more of a budget, stable ideas; you get better quality people and a spirit of...let's go on this journey together.'*

Jennifer Davidson of Molson Coors agrees: *'As our business model becomes more complex, as our business becomes more global and as our brand portfolios get more diverse, we need more of a global marketing focus - more of a global brand focus - in order to be successful.'*

Brands Are Going Global

Martin Riley, CMO, Pernod Ricard, and a former competitor of Rob Malcolm at Diageo (though everybody is pretty friendly with one another across the drinks industry), has this to say: *'I clearly see the role of global brands increasing. Just looking at the drinks industry - which is very local, actually - you can absolutely see that global brands are becoming more important to all the key players.'*

John Seifert, Chairman and CEO, North America, Ogilvy & Mather Worldwide agrees: *'In this fragmented marketing and media environment, clients recognize that to have a well-defined, compelling global brand helps them cut through a lot of the clutter.'*

Witness the imprimatur that is the Interbrand annual ranking of the world's top 100 global brands – arguably the most closely watched barometer of brand health on the planet. In 2009, the asset value of the world's top-10 brands accounted for almost 70 percent of the value of those organizations (in case you needed even more conclusive proof that a global brand often creates significant economic value for the business it serves).

Here again, the findings from our *Leading Global Brands* study are convincing. More than two thirds of all respondents confirm that global brands have become more important over the last five years and concur that they manage their global brands more centrally than they did just three years ago.

Another reason why global brands are becoming more important? Organizations are putting their resources behind a few star brands.

Folkert Kamphuis, Global COO of Animal Health, Novartis, notes that, *'About 10 years ago, we had very few global brands, which generated 20-25 percent of our turnover. Nowadays we're looking at 80 percent of our turnover being in global brands. We deliberately work with 12 focus brands. We forced that priority down to every market, except for the emerging growth markets where we have a slightly different model. But in most markets, the focus brands are the same.'*

Marketers Are Going Global

As many markets globalized over the last decade, organizations struggled to keep pace. Many attempted to respond by building competitive advantage with more global, efficient, yet locally responsive marketing management. They sought to uncover just the right balance between local relevance and global leverage. Along the way, an essential new position emerged: the global *marketing leader*.

The global brand marketing leadership community is growing fast. In 1999 we estimate that there were only some 25,000 marketers worldwide with the descriptor 'global brand' or 'global marketing' in their job titles. Today, on LinkedIn, the number (which includes global marketers at every level) tops 540,000. If we zoom in exclusively on the leaders within this community, we still find almost 70,000 VP level and up senior global marketing executives – individuals like Silvia Lagnado, CMO of Bacardi and the former head of Dove, who are redefining what cutting-edge global marketing leadership success really means.

We believe this new cadre of global marketing leaders represents the new elite of marketing – the *Champions League*, as it were, now and for the foreseeable future. The group includes not only the CMO, but the top 200 marketers at companies like Procter & Gamble, GSK, Diageo and Unilever; the top 100 marketing leaders at companies including Nike, Sony and Ford; and arguably, the top 25 marketers at Cargill, Citibank, Starbucks and Molson Coors.

'Clients are increasingly asking us to help them reconcile their brand portfolios and

focus on the brands with the highest potential for global and sustainable growth.

And they are delisting the brands they feel they have neither the financial capacity nor the strategic will to maintain.'

JOHN SEIFERT - CHAIRMAN AND CEO OGILVY NORTH AMERICA

While these leaders' roles and responsibilities vary from company to company and between industries – and their official titles range from *Chief Marketing Officer (CMO)* to *Global Brand Director* to *Global Head of Category Marketing* to *Vice-President of Global Marketing* – the big questions they struggle with daily show a surprising degree of convergence.

The new global marketing leaders face a daunting task because they are now responsible not just for developing the marketing strategy, but now also building the marketing organizational structure and developing training and knowledge management systems. We refer to these three areas as *strategy*, *structure*, and *capability*. This isn't to say the new global marketing position lacks cachet, opportunity or a lofty combination of the two. Far from it.

Says Jonathan Moore of Sara Lee, *'I remember when I was first asked to work on a global team, I was excited as it seemed that that was the pinnacle of marketing.'*

Getting Global Marketing Right

Companies – and consumers – can barely keep abreast of today's changes. Says Greg Welch, Global Practice Leader, Consumer Goods at Spencer Stuart, *'The world has changed – but organizations simply haven't been wired or set up to deal with that change.'*

Our own *Leading Global Brands* study concludes that less than 15 percent of today's organizations fully agree that they believe their own global brands are effectively leveraging their scale. Even fewer believe that their organizations excel at expeditiously rolling out successful global brand initiatives.

The truth is, some organizations have never successfully managed to 'crack' going global. Renault is an intriguing example of a prestigious car company that has introduced a significant number of innovative car designs in Europe (Twingo, Scenic, Espace), but has never made much headway outside its European home market.

Walmart, the world's largest retailer, was forced to retreat out of both the German and South Korean markets. Analysts claimed that Walmart failed to localize and customize its stores to meet the preferences of local consumers, but other companies came up against the same problem. Within the space of a month, France's Carrefour, the world's second largest retailer, also quit the South Korean scene. Other international brands like Nokia, Nestlé, and Google still struggle there.

You might wonder: if global brands are *that* important, why are so few companies successfully managing to build and operate them (and reap the benefits)? In the pages ahead, we'll look at the global marketing landscape: what will remain 'business as usual' for marketers as they go global? What are the new challenges they face? What's the best way to overcome these challenges?

Global Marketing = Marketing

Let's be clear about one thing. Obviously, the market has, and continues to change radically – some might even say beyond recognition. Marketers' demands have changed just as dramatically. But in the end, we think it's important to recognize that the basics of marketing *haven't changed one iota.*

We continue to innovate, develop positioning and brand products. Moreover, the principles of portfolio management and world-class packaging aren't going anywhere either.

What *has* changed is the following. Tomorrow's organizations must be sufficiently equipped to efficiently and effectively develop global market strategy, structure and capability. Which, we're the first to admit, is easier said than done.

The next chapters focus on the biggest challenges these global marketing leaders wrestle with daily.

Questions like: *What should the role of global marketing be? And what is the appropriate global marketing structure and operating model for the first few years of going global? And, how do we leverage our marketing learning quickly from one place in the world to the others, and adequately involve the key local markets in marketing strategy development without turning the whole thing into a committee exercise?*

We will also look at how to create one common language and approach in marketing, and raise overall marketing skill levels across the organization. Of course these are just *some* of the challenges that new global marketing leaders face. In the next chapter we'll be revisiting these and exploring others, as well as focusing on what makes this increasingly relevant role so exhilarating.

We feature case studies and examples from brands like Sony Ericsson and Dove and focus on what motivates marketing leaders about their global role.

It's worth repeating: Global marketing effectiveness has become a defining hot-button issue for almost every business and, most definitely, for every CMO. And so that's what this book is all about.

We genuinely believe that today the question is no longer *whether* to go global ... but *how* to do so effectively and efficiently.

JOHNNIE WALKER'S GLOBAL 'PROGRESS'

As the top Scotch brand for Diageo – the largest multinational wine and spirits company in the world – Johnnie Walker remains the preferred drink of sophisticated, accomplished businessmen.

Smooth though the Scotch may be, its business history has been admittedly bumpy.

After a decade of steady growth that lasted until the mid-1990s, the brand's fortunes took a tumble from 1995 to 1999, when sales contracted by a whopping 9.5%. The culprit? Years of murky management. Late 90's marketing was tactical, with a short-term, promotional focus. Between 1997 and 1999, the company ran roughly 27 different advertising campaigns for Red Label and Black Label across the world. In short, as a brand, Johnnie Walker was here, there, everywhere, and nowhere.

The key to revitalizing Johnnie Walker, Diageo recognized, lay in transforming Johnnie Walker's staid, traditional image. Which is when Rob Malcolm came aboard, creating not only a new global marketing team but also a new framework, the *Diageo Way of Marketing*.

Diageo's new global brand executive team commissioned London-based advertising agency Bartle Bogle Hegarty (BBH) to come up with a fitting marketing and advertising campaign. Recalls Rob Malcolm *'How do you actually run brands, with the kind of scale that exists in multiple markets? Recognizing it simply won't work to just jam one thing down everybody's throat but at the same time, if all you did was go to the lowest common denominator, there is no way that you can make money and run a business and make any sense out of it. So, that's when my curiosity about finding a better way, a good way of doing this, began to occupy my mind.'*

In collaboration with BBH, Diageo developed a strong, sure-footed brand idea that would again propel Johnnie Walker to market-leader status. Their first challenge? To capture thought leadership by expanding the competitive field beyond Chivas Regal and Dewar's, and reframe Johnnie Walker as a World Cup-level 'icon brand' poised to shoot it out with other globally legendary brands.

After analyzing the world's most famous brands, BBH concluded that all of them had two key things in common. First, each was founded on a fundamental human truth that could potentially unite people all over the world; and second,

Post-war Lebanon

each transcended geography, culture and language via a universally recognized icon symbolizing everything the brand represented.

Johnnie Walker needed to develop these same assets in order to *unify* the world – not splinter or fracture it.

Diageo and BBH uncovered the first truth by digging deep into the brand's history, gleaning one single insight into what would become a defining brand property. The insight had to do with success. What did success mean? Previous generations had defined it materially. But a new generation of men was quietly rewriting the old paradigm. For them, life wasn't only about the destination. Getting there mattered too, a *lot*.

Sure – guys still wanted to make money, particularly in the new and aggressively developing Asian markets. But a deeper, more fundamental truth had emerged. Diageo and BBH realized that no matter his age, life-stage, or situation, every man has in common a hard-wired desire to move forward, to improve himself in some way. This innate, universal need to advance and progress morphed into the universal truth the team would eventually use as the foundation for the Johnnie Walker global brand.

Once the team had grasped this insight, another knocked on the door. Johnnie Walker had long been associated with cartoonist Tom Browne's well-known brand symbol of entrepreneurial success: a striding cane-wielding man clad in boots and a hat. In an inspirational flash, BBH updated the image by laterally inversing the figure. Now it strode from left to right, implying continuous personal progress. With its updated, yet still familiar icon, plus a campaign tagline – 'Keep Walking' – that was symbolized with the new striding man, the brand now had a universally meaningful icon.

The new campaign, a smashing, contemporary combination of legacy and dynamism, emphasized every man's determination to follow his dreams and pursue his agenda.

Since that launch, 'Keep Walking' has run in more than 120 countries. Did we fail to mention 30 TV commercials, over 150 print executions, radio ads, websites, sponsorships, internal awards, consumer awards, and a charitable fund in support of the brand's purpose, all on the back a modest media budget estimated at US$40m annually?

As for the twin imperatives that have guided Johnnie Walker's media behavior – to reinforce stature and demonstrate pioneering spirit.

The team challenged countries to work with the agency in developing locally relevant progress manifestations. From the U.S. stock market to the Nelson Mandela Bridge in South Africa to Lebanon's post-war reconstruction, every piece of communication came together to stimulate and bring to life the brand's global concept in a locally recognizable manner.

This global approach – which managed to juggle disciplined freedom, focus, control, flexibility and local sensitivity – allowed Diageo to create a balance between global and local priorities, and has since been replicated not only by Diageo brands by but many brands across the world.

After a relatively tightly controlled launch period, and allowing increased local interpretation while keeping a tight grip on the core campaign platform, the campaign proceeded to further lionize the striding man, showing him conquering challenges on his ongoing journey of progress. It was a trailblazing media strategy that amplified the brand's core message by placing executions in surprising and meaningful places – whether leaping across buildings or adjacent to apt editorial content.

Needless to say, the campaign was extraordinarily successful. Within three months of launch, brand recall jumped from 22 percent to 50 percent, with a dollar-sales increase of 3.7 percent and a volume-sales increase of another 3 percent. Research agency Millward Brown found that the 'stopping power' of the print advertising registered at 84 percent – significantly above the original goal of 60 percent.

It's worth recapping. Evolving from 27 brand campaigns (at its most fragmented) to a unified worldwide campaign gave Diageo and Johnnie Walker unsurpassed global brand consistency over the space of 15 years. Even better, the campaign offered a sophisticated way of assessing growth across various markets.

Beyond the immediate impact on generating sales, the brand campaign also won accolades on the qualitative front. When all was said and done, managing a focused campaign across the globe helped Diageo create a far more unified organization. The team was now working much more productively across borders and the ways of working were better aligned. Motivation was way up.

Says Rob Malcolm: 'Global brand management is all about figuring out the sweet spot and the nuances behind what's global and what's local. And unlike what a lot of people say, I believe it's about thinking local, and acting global…. With Johnnie Walker, we worked hard to get the right strategy, and once we nailed it we activated it the right way at scale across the globe. To see the transformational value of that when you get it right is fantastic.'

What Keeps Global Marketers *Awake At Night*

...And What Gets Them Up Again

In The Morning

BACARDI.

SILVIA LAGNADO – CMO OF BACARDI

Silvia Lagnado, the CMO of Bacardi, was voted one of the Wall Street Journal's '50 Women to Watch' in 2009. Her global work with Dove, *'Debunking the Myth of Real Beauty'* is widely recognized as instrumental to the brand's phenomenal growth over the last decade.

With 20/20 hindsight, it's now easy to see why Unilever considered the Brazilian native the best possible person to fill the role of the company's first Global Brand Director. Silvia's directness, passion and transparency about what she knew – and also willingness to admit what she didn't know – quickly convinced her colleagues she was the 'real deal.'

When this engineer-by-training joined Unilever marketing in Sao Paolo, she rose swiftly through the ranks with jobs in high-growth categories such as Deodorants and Hair. Appointed in 2001 to the newly created position of Global Brand Director for Dove, Silvia, whose vitae at this point comprised 15 years working mostly in local or regional positions, had no idea what to expect.

Unilever, the US$50 billion consumer goods conglomerate that owns Dove as well as brands such as Lipton, Vaseline, and Ragu, was pursuing a 'Path to Growth' strategy. This entailed a company-wide focus on a handful of high-value core brands. The company's goal: To reduce the total number of brands from 1600 to 400 – and all over a period of five years no less.

Silvia's 2001 brief from Unilever read as follows: She would have full global brand responsibility for Dove yet regional directors would continue to report up their regional lines. Among Silvia's responsibilities was to align the Dove brand worldwide while continuing to drive annual growth of over 20 percent.

In the wake of a preliminary round of visits to some of the biggest country markets, and candid conversations with regional marketers overseeing these regions, Silvia was understandably apprehensive. Everyone she met was accustomed to operating under the rules of the 'old' Unilever. That company was a decentralized environment in which leaders encouraged country managers to make autonomous marketing decisions. Even more troublingly, some off the local marketers refused even to speak to her. Others were obviously leery of how Silvia's new position would affect the old way of doing things.

Silvia got the message in a hurry: a massive task lay ahead. Dove alone was running over 400 innovation projects from disparate locations. Many were duplicative. The brand had at least four conflicting positioning statements in use around the world and lacked any global consensus on where the brand was going, and how it should get there.

While daunting, the opportunity was also intoxicating. Imagine lining up all of Dove's global resources – not to mention 600 marketers and advertising agency support staff – behind a handful of clear-cut, highly focused goals. It would be a struggle, Silvia knew, though certainly not the first she'd squared off against during her career. So how was she going to get everyone to play along?

The story of how Silvia Lagnado faced down one challenge after another to attain an audacious triumph (which you'll read more about later in this chapter) forms the backdrop for a generation of global marketers who have successfully followed similar boulder-strewn paths. The obstacles Silvia and her team faced, and the principles they adopted to overcome these hurdles, mirror a genre that has emerged to drive unprecedented business growth in the 21st century: Marketing on a Worldwide Stage.

NEW GLOBAL MARKETING
FRONTIERS

If you're a marketer of a global brand, you probably recognize the following queasy scenario:

Let's imagine you're the head of a big brand's marketing team based in Thailand. Revenues exceed several hundred million Baht. You've probably put in 15 to 20 years of hard work in various marketing and sales roles. Just last year, you were appointed Head of Marketing for Thailand. From your perspective, and that of the people around you, the promotion feels well-deserved. In fact, for a Thai-based marketer, it's the ultimate recognition, especially when several Thai trade marketing magazines make note of your new position.

Then one day, a member of the global brand team pays a visit. Though he's canny enough to hedge his intentions, he nevertheless makes it clear that your current advertising campaign – the one that's been doing quite well, thank you very much – needs to be taken off-air. The replacement? A new global film featuring exclusively blonde kids. Before leaving, he guides you through a sexy-looking 'global roll out activation strategy' that completely lacks relevance for Thailand. The parting shot comes when he tells you to focus your team on 1, 2 and 3 for the rest of the year.

That night, you drive home in a funk. You try to reconstruct what just happened, and why it all went down so badly. Why was the conversation basically one-way? What happened to the serious discussion you were hoping to have about Thai local competitors, and recent retail developments? Why did the global brand leader ask you so few questions? Why didn't you insist that before anything else, the global team member grasp the realities of the Thai marketplace? And – just a quixotic fantasy here – what would happen if you pretended the visit never took place?

Cut to the global marketing leader sitting alone in the restaurant of his

Bangkok hotel. He feels equally as dark-spirited as the Thai-based marketer. He didn't feel at all welcome today. Throughout his visit, the team gazed blankly at him (even though *they* were the ones who'd asked him to visit). He couldn't shake the distinct feeling they wanted him to leave, ASAP. Moreover, they showed no enthusiasm whatsoever for the new global story. Didn't they realize how difficult it was to align the marketing teams of the U.S., Germany and the U.K. for the first time ever? Why did he even bother to come here? Surely it's the responsibility of regional brand leaders to visit countries that represent less than 5 percent of sales apiece? Why do these visits always feel so disingenuous and forced?

Also: How did it happen that he's no longer doing the part of marketing he loved so much – developing marketing mixes; collaborating with customer management to develop killer launch packages that make even Walmart do cartwheels; constructing advertising campaigns that inspire consumers to double their use of products? How and when did his marketing career slide off into a diplomatic and political role? Most of all…why is he on the other side of the earth, solo, separated from his family on a day that happens to be a public holiday in the U.S., but – of course! – is just another Monday everywhere else in the world?

If you recognize anything in this scenario, please read on.

NEW MARKETING OPPORTUNITIES AND CHALLENGES

The titles, roles and responsibilities of global marketing leaders vary widely among companies and industries. That said, the opportunities and challenges with which these leaders struggle daily (and that bring on regular bouts of 3:30 A.M. insomnia), are intriguingly similar.

These days, marketing is among the most invigorating, head-spinning, vexing functions in business. With the possible exception of Information Technology, we can't think of many other disciplines that have evolved so rapidly over the past decade. Regardless of whether we're looking at how today's consumers are organizing themselves, how the media landscape continues to converge, how brands have begun to interact with their users, or how new markets and competitors are springing up as if out of nowhere, the marketing function is more dynamic, exciting and nerve-shredding than it's ever been.

Thanks to our longstanding consulting work with a remarkable array of clients, we are privileged to have the perspective and background we do. In the pages ahead, you'll make the acquaintance of 45 of today's most important and influential global marketing leaders. Their words and opinions are revealing, inspiring, thought-provoking and – we hope – transforming.

The rise of interactive marketing and sustainability are well-known challenges familiar to just about everyone, not just global marketers. At the same time, if you're leading a global marketing organization, these issues can be infinitely more pressing and complex. Other future challenges we've identified are specific to marketers in charge of a global brand or global marketing organization. It's an intricately connected world out there. Beyond their effect on marketers, these challenges zing to the heart of what properly belongs under the umbrella of 'marketing', and what doesn't. In addition, some complicate the never-easy-to-resolve interplay between marketers and their colleagues.

As Lennard Hoornik, of Sony Ericsson, says, *'I think we as marketers are going through a redefinition phase of what we are responsible for. Nothing seems like it was before anymore. There is little agreement on what is in and what is out these days, and if we cannot agree among ourselves as marketers, how can we expect our colleagues on the board to understand?'*

To echo a recent Spencer Stuart report, is it any surprise that average CMOs in the U.S. last in their positions only 18 months?

Many of the global marketing dilemmas we've unearthed are behind the dramatic, tough-to-surmount, and ever-changing environment of present-day marketing itself. At the sharp, pointy tip of the stick? Global marketing.

What Keeps Marketers Awake At Night

So what are today's key global marketing issues? This chapter examines the TOP 10 challenges that keep global marketing leaders twisting wide-eyed under their bed covers...as well as the TOP 5 reasons why, if asked, and despite the bags under their eyes, these leaders wouldn't trade their jobs with anyone they know. To a man or woman, all the CMOs we spoke with feel confident they're playing at the top of their game, and that despite the daily mayhem going on around them, they still get a rush as they define the adrenaline-pumping future of marketing, both today and tomorrow.

1 - Consumers Are Taking Control

Today's companies perch riskily at the edge of a cliff. Why? Because marketing – that is to say, how companies create demand, lure in consumers and enable sales – has been flipped on its head.

No longer can companies depend on the marketing messages they send out or, more critically, presume that consumers will respond to them as usual, namely passively or co-operatively. Best of luck force-feeding information down the throats of contemporary consumers! They'll purse their lips, shake their heads and move along. Almost every CMO we spoke with in this book agrees that today's consumers are not only in charge of how they interact with brands, they're assembling reference points from wherever they wish, whenever they like, and in whatever form they choose. Moreover, they're leading the pack in, well, packs, calling on the power of the collective to drive down prices and negotiate solutions as needed.

Consider the iPhone application Red Laser. For $0.99, a user can download an ingenious little app that transforms your iPhone into a dedicated barcode scanner. How? Simply scan the barcode of the book, chicken soup or shampoo you're considering buying. Seconds later, the iPhone screen displays a list of competing nearby and online stores where, and at what price, you can buy the exact same item. (A London store manager recently busted one of the authors of this book for using Red Laser to pre-screen products for other shoppers, especially after he found the store was consistently overcharging its customers by roughly 25 percent.) In a connected world, markets are more and more transparent. Consumers can suss out quality or price differences with the flick of an app.

Is it any coincidence consumers are becoming far more discriminating and demanding? Of course, they're still searching for brands that will improve their lives, and at the lowest possible prices. Today though, their purchase decisions extend beyond the old-fashioned definition of 'value', and focus also on a brand's values. Tex Gunning of AkzoNobel Consumer Paints remarks that consumers want their brands *'to be more like human beings, to be socially responsible citizens, doing the right thing.'*

We like the sports analogy one CMO made recently: *'Ten years ago, marketing was like bowling. You held in your hand the ball, and the marketing message, and you could look down the lane and see the target you wanted to hit. You had the ability to take the ball and roll it with the speed and spin necessary to knock down the target and deliver your message. Today, it's more like pinball. You have a ball that you get to play with, and you pull back the lever, and all of a sudden the ball goes off and starts getting zapped around. You have almost no control over what happens with the ball.'*

Thus, marketers are scrambling to give up their old-fashioned 'push' model of communication, in favor of abiding by consumers' 'pull'. They're moving from Interruption to Engagement. The Era of the Empowered Consumer will profoundly affect the way products and services are sold, and how business is done...for the foreseeable future.

2 - The Role Of Marketing Within The Organization

Given: Consumers are changing the way they interact with brands. Which means? Well, the need for greater coordination within the company across all touchpoints becomes crucial. Any organization or brand is only as strong as its weakest touchpoint. Brands, as we all know, are about trust, and reducing risk in consumers' minds. Therefore, any inconsistency or below-par delivery of a brand promise can easily bring down the whole house. Which means that someone inside the organization – generally a marketer – must be responsible for coordinating across all of these touch-points. Where traditional marketing was once mostly outward-facing, this new internal coordination role demands not only crack internal interaction, but often the creation of new roles and responsibilities.

The interaction between marketing and the rest of the business is a challenge we see many CMOs hesitatingly taking on. It's hardly helpful that inside more than a few organizations, CMOs are battling marketing's legacy reputation among their peers as 'spenders' who bring little connectivity and even less accountability to daily business realities.

A recent Spencer Stuart study of CEOs and CMOs reveals that although peers and colleagues often perceive marketers as 'creative, passionate, inspiring and hardworking', they're also regarded now and again as 'undisciplined, un-commercial and not accountable.'

Lennard Hoornik of mobile phone supplier, Sony Ericsson, weighs in: *'I think a key challenge for marketing today is to get closer to the day-to-day business. When I took the role of head of marketing I said to my team, 'The first thing you do every time you meet with me is report the business health of your products and key markets.' 'How are our programs succeeding in market?' 'What is the forecast?' 'And what are the actions we are planning to improve results?' The focus quickly became more about the current business health and less of just overly brand-skewed. We need to make sure that everyone in the company understands that we feel just as accountable as they do for building our overall business strategy and making money.'*

With a near-constant stream of new media and sales channels available to today's consumers, the need to coordinate, collaborate and partner up *internally* is more crucial than ever. No longer can Marketing, Sales, PR, CSR, Internal Communications and Investor Relations work independently on their separate initiatives and touchpoints.

But with the necessity for increased collaboration also comes the challenge of matching responsibility with accountability. Websites, which are typically under the realm of brand marketing, are becoming critically important contact points for direct sales. So who's responsible for Internet-based customer service and messaging consistency? Who screens consumer response emails, which can be a significant source of new or improved product ideas and insights? Who manages the consistency of retailer partner marketing programs? In short, who's minding the store?

These and other questions are butting heads with our old definitions of 'marketing'. Yes, most can be easily addressed. But arriving at workable answers demands honest dialogue and negotiation among department heads.

3 - Demonstrating The Value
Of The Brand And Marketing

Among the knottiest new challenges that keep marketers (especially global marketers) awake at night are those to do with metrics, accountability and return on marketing investments. The easy answer? Well, we're still scratching our heads.

For over half a century, marketers have mostly managed to deflect detailed scrutiny of their spend by falling back on John Wanamaker's oft-quoted remark that half the money spent on advertising is wasted, but the problem is that no one knows which half. Let's put aside for a moment what Wanamaker said. Today, as spend migrates from push to pull to interactive media, companies can accurately measure results, effectiveness, and ultimately, Return on Investment. Firms can now even precisely calibrate the success of differing campaigns, messages and even website content.

But measurability brings with it its own set of challenges, ranging from responsibility, to an organization's accountability to confront, correct and improve any and all interactions with consumers. The result? Almost every organization we know is investing heavily in models and tools (not to mention people) that can measure, analyze and modify the efficacy and efficiency of marketing budgets.

Boon Lai, Area Marketing Officer, VP Greater China, Philips Electronics: 'A *key challenge is continuing to justify the importance of what we do in marketing.*

Particularly in the current economic situation, it's even more essential that we demonstrate the Return On Investment across our marketing programs and any other brand related activities such as internal training.'

That said, the issue of what constitutes the best effectiveness metrics is a critical topic not only among marketing leaders but also between marketing and the rest of the organization. Greg Welch, Global Practice Leader, Consumer Goods & Services at Spencer Stuart, recalls sitting in on a recent closed-door conference with a handful of senior U.S.-based marketers. He was amazed when they couldn't reach a consensus on the most critical metrics that should appear on a marketing dashboard. Says Welch, *'How do you justify your spend inside the organization? How do you communicate to your peers inside the company that this is the right number, this is the anticipated effect, and here's how we're going to measure it? I can't name another functional leader within the organization that faces such fundamental questions.'*

Put another way, measurability has unveiled an entirely new internal question: How much do you spend on marketing versus all other options? For example, versus customer management? What about on product development? All of a sudden, the traditional 'holy' ratio of spending between 7 to 15 percent of revenue on marketing in Consumer Goods is up for grabs. Which means that divisions maybe once a little jealous of marketing's large advertising budgets can today lay claim on these same budgets by comparing results per dollar spent.

Says Folkert Kamphuis of Novartis, *'Proving the marketing value for the business is a hot topic here, and not just because I want it to be. It has become a real topic we discuss at board level. I want my teams to always think about measuring return margin per invested dollar. How much margin do I get back for every dollar of marketing spend that I invest, and how do I prove that? That's my single biggest focus because it will really drive the focus on where we invest and how we invest.'*

4 - Differentiation

Once, marketers could make product claims that competitors were hard-pressed to duplicate. The differences among products were very real, and consumers knew why, and under what circumstances, they were paying a premium price. Take peanut butter. Only a decade ago it was easy for consumers to identify the high-quality brands versus the less prestigious ones. Many brands had a quarter-inch of oil floating atop a rock-hard mound of peanut butter, indicating that the product had separated. Not exactly a sight that cried out, 'Buy me.' Whereas *always smooth* was both a differentiator and a functional benefit that consumers recognized and appreciated. These days, all peanut butter brands are smooth and taste great. If you run into a jar of peanut butter with oil on top, it's most likely 'organic' and 'natural' and costs a small fortune!

Sad to say, the number of brands that can genuinely boast a hard functional differentiator, or even a Unique Selling Proposition (USP), has dwindled dramatically in recent years. Countless new competitors with no legacy costs to speak of have invaded practically every market, and today offer high-quality, lower-priced alternatives to familiar brand-name products.

As if all these new competitors weren't posing enough challenges, marketers in almost every category are today competing with private labels that imperil their own existence. Moreover, these labels are marketed by their own trade customer 'partners'. Whether it's 'Tesco's Finest' food products in the U.K., or in the U.S. Walmart's generic OTC drugs, branded generics are gradually chipping away at branded goods across the board.

Again, these competing brands once offered little more than functional parity. They lacked any emotional benefits. Those were the days! The new start-up brands on the block are cannily marketed. They're unshy about building their own competing brands. Consider HTC, the mobile phone handset company. Five years ago, HTC manufactured private label phones for operators. Today, Nokia, Motorola and Sony Ericsson are glancing nervously over their shoulders as HTC steadily gains ground. Who would have suspected?

The reason is actually simple. In the U.K., over the last 20 years many retailers have hired veteran marketers from Unilever and Procter & Gamble to develop and market their own private label brands. The results speak for themselves. The average share of private label in the U.K. has skyrocketed to over 50 percent in many categories, compared to less than 20 percent in the U.S.

At the same time, the cost of developing truly revolutionary new products is rising. As we know, the failure rate for new products is legendarily high and genuine innovation usually has its R&D price. In the old days, when a company found itself with a successful technology in its hands, the manufacturer knew it had a few years to recoup its costs and construct a competitive advantage. But as technological advances push forward in leaps and bounds, global market developments are almost completely transparent. As for those fabled functional differentiators? More and more, they're being copied and commoditized.

5 - Transparency & Convergence

Let's kick off with a small disclaimer: No marketer in his or her right mind would suggest that we now live in a world of homogenous global consumers. Despite round-the-clock chatter about universal congruency, cultural values and consumer interests vary significantly across the world, and always will.

That said, we *do* see strong transparency across, and convergence between, a whole lot of markets.

Earlier, we mentioned how contemporary Shanghai teenagers share the same interests and spending habits as adolescents in Paris, New York and London. Along with youth and its discontents, more and more companies are succeeding in building brands consistently across borders by appealing to universal needs such as motherhood and the urge to win, or by building brands in new categories that transcend culture. Some good examples? Apple's iPhone, Sony's PlayStation, even Pringles Potato Chips.

In a transparent market, if there's a better alternative solution (or price) to what your brand offers, you can bet consumers will know about it, and in minutes or hours, too. New global brands are bubbling up from nowhere, without any national legacy mindset or burdensome infrastructure to hold them back.

Consider the beer market. The brands you see across markets may be very local, but the infrastructure behind them is definitely not. According to

Jennifer Davidson of Molson Coors, 'We have enormous transparency in our market. If you sneeze in the beer market, everyone globally will know it in a matter of hours. Marketers can subscribe to a bulletin issued daily listing trade news, new campaigns, promotions and products launched all over the world.'

In response, marketers are scrambling to search for scale to increase competitive advantage, leverage resources and drive down costs. In order to maximize competitive advantage, they're driving innovations across as many markets as possible, and as swiftly as possible, too. Almost all companies feel the economic urgency to fast-track the roll out of their products globally. That way, they'll recover their costs more quickly, and also maintain a competitive edge. They're globalizing for the simplest of reasons: to drive down costs and increase efficiencies across Research & Development, Supply Chain, and, naturally, Marketing.

6 - Brand Consistency Across Markets

Among the most fiercely debated of all the challenges facing global marketers today: How much of a centralized brand expression should they exert in each of the company's markets? Put another way, how do global marketers uncover that ideal (and elusive) balance between showing sensitivity to a brand's culture *and* to the culture of each market the brand inhabits?

Ignore the first, and you'll have a fragmented mess of a brand that lacks any global identity and no financial advantage. You'll also cede control of your market messages. Ignore the second, and you'll surrender both connection and traction on the ground.

In the words of Simon Clift, CMO, Unilever, 'You want to be neither mindlessly global nor hopelessly local.'

Far too many of today's brands are not only ill-equipped to travel, they're also managed by people who don't understand how to help them go international. We all know the funny examples of brands getting it just wrong like Kentucky Fried Chicken's slogan, 'It's finger lickin' good!' that was translated into Chinese as 'You'll be eating your fingers!' and Purdue Chicken's slogan 'It takes a tough man to make a tender chicken.' that translates into Spanish as 'It takes a sexually excited man to make a chicken sensual.'

If marketers want their brands to gain in stature, and maintain a reasonable consistency around the world, brands have to balance a unified positioning with local activation programs that embrace as many diverse qualities as possible. That way, consumers from Dubai to Brazil can dig out elements of durable, relevant appeal within the same brand personality.

Hey – this isn't easy. It takes skill and forethought. How do we 'glocalize' a brand campaign in such a way that respects the product but also values and esteems those individuals who market and buy it locally? From her perspective, Silvia Lagnado sees, *'We still see a lot of marketers at all levels who struggle a lot with listening. Not because they don't know how to listen, and not because they're arrogant, but because they're scared of the complexity of the problem once they've listened to all the stakeholders.'*

Peter Vaughn, SVP Global Brand Management and Marketing, American Express highlights a companion challenge: *'A lot of people see local marketing roles as executional in nature; the challenge is to make those roles more than just execution, critical in the translation of a strategy for a local market, and giving enough flexibility to make that happen.'*

The key, according to Rob Malcolm of Diageo? *'Thinking local, acting global. Competitive advantage lies in figuring out how to do this global-local thing better than anyone else.'* We agree with Rob when he goes on to say, *'...when people inside the company actually get how to fit the pieces together, it unleashes alignment, speed, trust, and constructive challenge.'*

From our standpoint, brands need to tread cautiously and take care not to overkill in their quest for global consistency. In reality, we find it's really only the company Chairman who notices that a brand is marketed somewhat differently across markets. Not counting the multitude of business-to-business categories that cater to global business travelers, there are actually very few consumer markets where the target consumer gets to directly compare and contrast advertising across markets.

7 - Differing Levels Of Market Maturity

Among your charters as a global marketer? Define brand standards, and win internal adherence to these same benchmarks. Especially in the embryonic stage of a brand's development, marketers often operate on a short leash. They play 'logo cop' in each of the brand's domains, hauling up local teams, franchisees and channel partners who 'stray off the reservation'.

But when a brand has been around the block a few times, it's actually more appropriate to expand the brand's 'circle of acceptability'. That way, consumers have more possible localized touchpoints, channels and facets through which they can engage with the brand.

In Chapter 7 we'll discuss how some of the best global marketing organizations are developing models and tools for framing consistency, clustering markets (if you will), and then allowing flexibility within that framework. Many leading companies have now coalesced all their markets into development stages, e.g., nascent, fast developing, and highly competitive mature markets. Once brand teams have agreed on and grouped the relevant clusters, they can learn what it takes to move from one market development level to the next or grow within that development stage.

8 - Clarity On Roles And Responsibilities

Organizational complexity often conspires to undo and derail strategic intent. To avoid this, teams need to align themselves across time and space, roles have to be clearly defined, and attention must be paid to developing well-coordinated handoffs among global, regional and local teams. That said, our *Leading Global Brands* study finds that the above is more the ideal than the norm.

Over the years, we've also found that organizations are traditionally skilled at giving people responsibilities (who's going to do what), but chronically deficient at taking away those responsibilities (who's no longer going to do what). Leaders typically focus on the front end of initiatives, where visibility and enthusiasm are peaking. They ignore the unsexy necessity of tying up loose ends by telling people that their input has become unnecessary.

Often, the result is overlapping roles, resource duplication and unnecessary reworking at a program's local level – for instance, a local company that doles out research money merely to 'check' the new global brand campaign.

Everyone agrees that eliminating redundancy in overlapping roles is a good idea. At the same time, companies have to be mindful of finding a sensitive balance between influence and responsibility. A good example of responsibility without influence? A regional or local manager who receives centrally-produced work, and who then must vouch for its effectiveness across the region, or in-country, to colleagues in sales and across the rest of the company. That's nothing more than a recipe for misery. Marketers obliged to work under these conditions for any length of time will find little job satisfaction. Many will fly the coop to pursue other opportunities. Others stay on, suffering from the chronic condition we call 'presentee-ism' – an insidious affliction that drains vitality from any company culture. Caught uncomfortably between local and global, and with no real control, many regional marketers find themselves stuck.

If this sounds familiar, it's because marketers at all levels report that this same absence of alignment and control counts among their greatest frustrations. Picture an organization with a global footprint and 60,000 bright-minded employees scattered around the world. How do you align individual goals and aspirations in the service of a common objective? Structure and operating model are both key. Successful companies always expend time and energy to tweak and readjust their organizations in order to increase their speed-to-market and improve their traction on the ground.

Yet as we've noted, the game (and the rules) have both changed radically, and most organizations aren't yet set up to respond the way they should. John Seifert of Ogilvy passes this indictment: *'When you have geographical mechanisms like a local P&L, versus a global brand or category P&L, you create friction. I find that the single biggest challenge that undermines either existing global brands or the ability to build new ones among our clients is just a lack of organizational alignment. I'd say one of the biggest challenges we're facing every day is around the navigation of issues relative to structure, staffing and mechanisms for operating within the client organizations themselves.'*

Seifert's observation contains one of the knotty challenges facing global marketers. Our work with many leading global marketing reorganizations always uncovers a couple of plain realities: the above conundrum can't simply be solved with better organograms. Marketers' actual mindsets and behaviors all across the organization drive ultimate success. Is it any wonder we've devoted a whole chapter to this topic?

9 - Internal Focus And Vanilla Mixes

The bigger the organization, the greater the internal focus. Which may seem like an easily avoidable condition, but as anyone who's ever spent time in a multinational corporation can attest, change is easier said than done. Organizational structure, role confusion and alignment and stakeholder issues all deplete precious company-wide energy, and leave marketers and their work weakly focused on and connected to external market realities.

Lennard Hoornik of Sony Ericsson identifies the telltale signs of an overly internal focused department: 'When you see a lot of people talking about other people in the company, when people overanalyze stuff, when they're not taking decisions or reviewing actions, those are signals that you need to change: You need to be more open, more proactive, more keen on an outside-in view of your brand.'

In many organizations, the very existence of multiple marketing teams at global, regional and local levels creates a huge distraction from market reality and competitive dynamics. Here, we're reminded of the story of the small, sparsely populated Western town with just one lawyer who sat at his desk all week, bored out of his mind. Yet the moment a rival lawyer opened up shop across the street, the lawsuits came out of the woodwork. Over the years we've sat inside far too many global marketing organizations where, on the surface at least, the goal of winning outside in the market was temporarily replaced by the urge to prove the other, e.g., regional or global, marketing teams wrong.

This situation shows its face in various ways. Hiring competing consultants to develop innovation ideas, re-doing market research simply to prove a point, selling up with competing strategies – we could go on and on, but why bother? It's painful to observe, wastes money, creates friction and diverts the organization's gaze from where it should be directed.

Do you know what's even more subtly dangerous – and hard to notice if you're inside the organization? Surrendering. Agreeing to accept middle-of-the-road compromises, such as using gummy, generic customer insights to drive product innovation and communication strategies. Slide down *that* particular slope, and the results emerging from innovation and communication pipelines will be flat, compromised, vanilla brand solutions that fail to deliver on the full potential of the brand promise. We call this *Global Bland.*

10 - Pockets Of Excellence

In any global organization, there are bound to be great country teams that always get programs right...as well as markets lacking in expertise. This is especially true in organizations that lack a traditional protocol for leveraging learning and best practices from one market to the next. Even when a brand mix is cogent and incisive, it still faces challenges ranging from 'looking for differences' to 'not invented here' – namely, an entrenched, we-can-do-it-ourselves mindset eager to reject anything that was developed beyond local shores, or that seeks differences rather than commonalities.

(Simon Clift of Unilever warmly recalls how in his early days as a brand manager in Austria, all he simply needed to do was mention that Germany was also planning this or that initiative...and his marketing director would automatically grant him license to develop another approach. Talk about this dilemma writ large.)

These extraneous debates not only create hurdles and hinder roll out speed and implementation excellence, but they strike at the heart of a global brand's competitiveness. Every CMO in a global marketing organization knows about, and fears, this dynamic. As Karin Koonings, VP of Brand and Marketing, Starbucks Coffee International, says, *'Of course you're often going to have to rethink the problem definition and solution if there are really fundamental market differences that the brand faces. But more often than not, there's a way for programs to work across markets – it's just that you need to get the teams to look for similarities instead of differences.'*

'I think many people underestimate the complexity of managing what is ultimately a very consistent brand around the world. *It takes a strong strategy* as well as *strong leadership* and collaboration between local and global marketing teams.'

PIETER NOTA - HEAD OF MARKETING, RESEARCH & DEVELOPMENT AND SALES FOR BEIERSDORF

What Gets Marketers Out Of Bed In The Morning

Thus far, a reader might be tempted to believe that the role of global marketing leader is way too challenging for any one person – that it's all but impossible to fill. Not true! The cerebral challenge that requires a global marketing leader to win at three-dimensional chess while suffering under the weight of a dazed-and-confused 14-hour jet lag hangover – not to mention the rewards of leading a global marketing group in such a dynamic area – *always* trump the disadvantages. Not one CMO and global brand head we know would swap jobs with anyone else, *ever*. When asked to explain why they love their jobs so much, their answers are strikingly similar. Ready for the short list?

PURPOSE

Okay, it may sound lofty – and these global marketing leaders are fully aware they're not the Dalai Lama – but *purpose* is a recurrent theme that many of today's global marketing leaders often aspire to achieve.

For some, it may be an attendant symptom of a midlife crisis. Others may have found success early on in their careers and wonder now, *Is That All There Is?* Realizing they don't want their gravestones to read, 'She sold a ton of laundry detergent,' or otherwise eager to translate success into significance, many CMOs and global brand leaders we know are considering the role that they, their organization and their brands play in today's world.

Says Simon Clift of Unilever, *'When I think of the fact that our products touch the lives of over 2 billion people every day, I get excited about the opportunities that brings. Of course I don't get grandiose, that's not appropriate; but I do really wonder how we can make a difference. And often I wonder, for example specifically about sustainability, will my grandson look at me and say 'Why didn't you do more?'*

Whether it's Dove pursuing real beauty, Knorr recognizing the sacred moment when a family sits down to eat dinner together, or AkzoNobel-manufactured paints seeking to ignite the human spirit as they improve the look and feel of entire communities, an element larger than profit tends to drive these global marketing leaders.

Jenny Ashmore of Mars sums it up: *'One of the important responsibilities of the CMO role is the opportunity to step back and ask some of the most fundamental questions about what role the brand is playing in consumers' lives; to take the time to dig in and consider how you can make a meaningful impact.'*

INSPIRING OTHERS

No matter whether it's a global brand team made up of 50 marketers working on the same brand across the world, or a 5,000-member global marketing organization inside a company like Nestle, Mars, GSK, or P&G, global marketing leaders are responsible for the business success and personal development of some of the world's smartest marketers. The most successful global marketing leaders talked to us at length about the kick they get out of recruiting the right team, developing talent, and building the organizational capability that leads to global marketing success.

Says Jim Stengel of Procter & Gamble, *'When you realize that as the leader, you're playing a very important role in someone's life for some period of time, it elevates your game because it elevates your inspiration. There is nothing more motivating than helping people develop. I saw amazing ideas at P&G come out from everyday categories, and it's because we were able to help people develop their ideas, their skill level, and their ability to get things done.'*

DOING *BIG* THINGS

It's a fact – scale motivates. The potential to do *big* things *does* make an impact. Many of the marketing leaders we observe, talk to and study get a major buzz from knowing that what they do has wide-ranging impact across the globe. It could be directing the activation of a global sponsorship across all regions. It could be driving a new innovation that hits supermarket shelves in 33 countries on the same day. In short, influence and influen*cing* others is, frankly, a major kick.

Jonathan Moore of Sara Lee, *'The honest truth is that there are quite a few things we are working on today that we just could not do in the past because we* did not have the scale. *Just knowing that you will be able to introduce products into 30-plus markets on the day of launch makes the best people available and wanting to work with you, and makes the company excited, more willing to invest in the future, and more patient for us as marketers to get the mix right. Yes, it's a huge responsibility, but it spurs me to work at the top of my game!'*

BEING GLOBAL

Every one of the global marketing leaders cites their connection to consumers all over the world – and their capacity to connect to universal human needs – as one of the critical facts that make the job so satisfying (even if they're talking about, say, toothpaste). To wit:

'I think global marketers are privileged to have a job that is based around people and how they behave,' says Simon Clift of Unilever. *'I've always loved the fact that this job lets you sit down one day with a Mexican housewife talking about how she looks after her family and then a week later takes you to a slum in northern Brazil and the next week puts you in China, always talking to people wherever you are. I love the connection with humanity. I love the privileged position of seeing how people behave and how that behavior changes according to how you change the stimulus.'*

Adds James Cali, SVP Gum and Candy Global Category Team, Kraft Foods, *'I get a kick out of the diversity of experiences. I've lived in three countries and I'm pretty familiar with probably 15 or 20 markets. I enjoy them and embrace the diversity within the markets, the different challenges, the different routes of markets and the different consumer experiences.'*

PASSION FOR BRANDS

Every one of these global marketers is both a leader within a large organization and a skilled, veteran professional marketer. For them, it is primarily about the brand, and uncovering the mix of functional, emotional and societal levers that will drive it to greatness.

'From a global brand leadership perspective, I get incredible satisfaction from creating excitement and passion for the brand within the organization,' says Duncan Blake, Director of Brand, BP. *'And then seeing it being replayed as people take ownership of the brand, as they defend it and build it and nurture it as if it*

were their own. To be able to provide that kind of inspiration that enables people to lift the brand and bring it to life is immensely rewarding.'

WINNING AT THREE-DIMENSIONAL CHESS

By now we hope you agree with us that the global marketer role is among the trickiest positions extant. Toss in all the new challenges around measurement, new channel management, partner management, capability development and knowledge management, and the job description is formidable. Yet apart from the adrenaline rush many CMOs describe getting as they deal with today's complex challenges, another prime motivator is that few of today's rules and standards are set in stone.

Nigel Gilbert of Lloyds Banking Group puts it like this: *'The CMO role today is so much more complicated than it was just ten years ago. When I think back, and compare it then to today, I sometimes wonder how my teams keep up. It is intellectually challenging and extremely stimulating to play at the top of the league. I know that many of my team members are motivated by the challenge to do this better that our competitors. To just analyze better, get to better insights, develop better solutions and implement with superiority.'*

UNLOCKING THE VALUE OF THE GLOBAL MARKETING ORGANIZATION

And finally, perhaps *the* reason for why today's global marketing leaders are such critical figures in an organization's future, and many CMOs love what they do. Tapping into a source of value that is there for the taking: Great global marketing leaders know that if they get this right, they can *'unlock'* the value of their organization, and drive better performance.

We wouldn't have begun focusing on this topic a decade ago if we didn't passionately believe that unlocking the potential value of global brands and marketing organizations is inherently exciting. Nearly every global marketing leader rants about his or her job frustrations. These leaders are obsessed and focused on the exhilaration of making the whole bigger than the sum of its parts.

Unlocking the value of a global brand is all about building global marketing capability, leveraging ideas across geographies and functional silos, and motivating an organization to collaborate in new ways as never before.

It's about connecting people to build global brands that deliver bigger and better solutions to consumers everywhere in ways that are satisfying on a personal level and which make sense financially. The most successful global brand leaders today instinctively understood that it's about getting this mix right.

As Kerris Bright puts it, *'The big motivation for me is about being able to help unleash the potential in the organization and allow us to be faster, quicker, better, and a much more exciting place to work because we talk to each other, thinking of our consumers, about market trends and developments, building bigger ideas together. I get a buzz just thinking about the possibilities.'*

Jim Stengel agrees *'I always did consumer immersions when I travelled. I loved seeing magic taking place in different cultures and trying to understand what was happening behind that magic, and extracting and sharing those principles so that we could make more magic happen in more cultures.'*

Adds Jennifer Davidson of Molson Coors, *'The connections that people have made within the organization, the dialogue that's going on between the team members not only at the meetings, but people picking up the phone and calling each other across time zones for advice, to share ideas, emails where people are just jamming and building on an idea... that for me is extremely rewarding.'*

In our experience, the most successful global marketing leaders enjoy bringing people together. It's as simple as that. In their personal lives, our guess is they're the ones who enjoy arranging a party, then looking on as their guests enjoy one another's company. Make no mistake – there are some not-insignificant egos at work in these senior marketing roles. But time and again, we've found that the most successful global marketing leaders believe it's less about being the centre of the party than it is about bringing people together and accomplishing their goals.

BUT BEFORE WE GO ONE STEP FURTHER...

Reviewing these opportunities and challenges might make a reader fail to see the forest from the trees. Over the past decade, we've conducted many senior leadership 'challenging' or 'coaching' work sessions that probably looked and felt like psychotherapy counseling sessions. And it's undeniable that the new global marketing position is complex, exhausting, at times lonely, unfit for the faint of heart – and on a difficulty scale, right up there with the role of Middle East peace treaty negotiator and a guy in a white smock trying to find a cure for the common cold.

But don't resign yet!

As we hope these pages have shown, today's global marketers are exhilarated and highly motivated. When you think about it, what could be more satisfying and empowering than paving the way toward a new reality? Rewriting the rules for a world whose future shape hasn't even been fully imagined yet? In the world of global marketing, there are no Michelin or Fodor's guides, no maps, no itineraries. But we hope that by now you've gotten a rough sense of the destination.

MAKING DOVE FLY HIGHER

Dove is a superlative example of a brand that embraces its global presence and increases its global marketing power daily. How? By leveraging both global scale and local relevance.

The story of Silvia Lagnado and the first Dove Global Brand Team (GBT) brings to light many of the opportunities and demands that brands face when addressing global growth opportunity.

DOVE'S CAMPAIGN FOR REAL BEAUTY

Over the last few years, the Dove Campaign for Real Beauty (CFRB) has received enormous attention both from consumers and the global press. It's also brought home numerous awards by raising awareness around Dove's mission to make women (not supermodels) feel more beautiful every day. How? By thumbing its nose at stereotypical views of beauty and inspiring women across the globe to take great care of themselves. Launched in over thirty countries, the Dove campaign has led to unsurpassed consumer recognition and sales growth.

The question remains: How did Silvia Lagnado and her team pull off a massive step-change initiative that transformed not just consumer thinking, but every which way the brand worked internally?

It's worth noting that Dove was the very first Unilever brand to be assigned a dedicated Global Brand Team. It all started when roughly twenty-five regional, local and global team members attended an intensive leadership course. After many soul-searching team sessions, the recurring question boiled down to, 'What is Dove's philosophy on beauty?' Mining this question further, an unsettling trend emerged: only 2 percent of all women felt comfortable proclaiming that they were 'beautiful.' So where did that leave the remaining ninety-eight percent?

The global team realized that as a long-term strategy, the 'One-Quarter Moisturizing Cream' claim alone couldn't create sufficient competitive advantage. In order to create a genuine impact on society, Dove needed to build a purposeful proposition that would connect with real people. Dove couldn't just be another brand that perpetuated billboard stereotypes of skinny, flawless, impossible-to-obtain 'professional' beauty.

By creating the Campaign for Real Beauty (CFRB), Lagnado and her team aimed to address and rebalance shopworn public ideals of female attractiveness. The team also recognized that the CFRB gave them an opportunity to positively affect society, reconnect with Dove's original roots, and further grow the brand by forging a stronger emotional bond with consumers.

ARE YOUR SEATBELTS FASTENED?
In Silvia Lagnado, Jim Collins would have found a kindred spirit. Years before the publication of From Good to Great, Silvia's primary focus was getting the right people on the bus. Recognizing that her original multi-disciplinary and multi-regional Global Brand Team needed clearer leadership, she created the 'Dove Board' consisting of marketing colleagues from the key regions as well as finance and development members.

The new Board members swore an 'oath of allegiance' to the brand's global agenda, while also continuing to report up to their regional business heads. Lagnado's unconventional brand 'Board' made many across Unilever – including the corporate Chairman – uneasy. Still, Silvia recognized the importance of making an internal statement of intent. Realizing that members wouldn't be able to push through ideas randomly, the Board immediately set out to win over the trust of key stakeholders inside and outside the company.

The brand team commissioned an internal benchmarking study to ensure that all global stakeholders contributed their ideas and concerns about Dove's new direction and preliminary global strategy. The fact that the team was taking the trouble to ask these questions helped improve its relationship with many country teams. It was a clear signal that Dove was fully aware that global branding needed to drive local business growth.

The study had another effect, too. By providing a real understanding of what the team needed to focus on, the Board was able to swiftly develop a new brand vision, mission and strategy, fast dubbed the Dove 'One-Pager' – a document that every participant in the Dove world would eventually live, breathe, eat, drink and murmur in their sleep.

Creating the right balance between consultation and direction? The Board was right on it. Lagnado's small team knew it needed to present a cogent, non-negotiable strategic direction for the brand, while addressing genuine market differences by listening to, and understanding, both genuine concerns and practical needs.

Done. Having established the first global positioning, the Board next made a concerted effort to inspire Dove marketers around the world to throw their support behind the work that lay ahead. Brand stewardship workshops on every con-

new Dove Firming.
As tested on real curves.

Dove
Firming Range

Dove Campaign for Real Beauty

tinent ensured that the word was out. The Board, whose members were spread out all over the world, also set up weekly conference calls devoted to discussion and alignment, regular web conferences to communicate with important marketers in key countries, and last but not least, 'Planet Dove' – an Intranet site that gathered and circulated best implementation practices from all over the world.

TAKE-OFF

Lagnado and her team supported the first Campaign for Real Beauty pilots in three smaller countries. Next, Dove Board members worked closely to convince senior stakeholders across the company that it was time to graduate from pilots and move into a full scale roll out. The initial mixed results improved quickly and dramatically as local marketers, fired up about the campaign, developed state-of-the-art local activation programs to bring the Dove campaign to life.

Did anyone say 'wildfire'?

By abandoning the conventional method of portraying 'perfect' women as female role models – and inspiring 'real' women along the way – Dove's campaign completely overturned conventional advertising beliefs of who and what defines female beauty. Not only did the campaign attract grassroots-level panel discussions, school programs and countless television, but Unilever created The Dove Self-Esteem Fund to increase awareness among young girls about the links between beauty and body-related self-esteem.

The profoundly simple message of 'real beauty' helped to rally people behind the cause – but Lagnado's primary focus was to instill women with its social and emotional import. In the U.S., the team considered using the same advertising that ran in the U.K., but in the end, decided they would use American women in the campaign (this not only made the ad come across as more 'real' to American consumers, it also created local 'celebrities').

The strong, more interdependent relationship between the global and the local marketing teams paid instant dividends. For one thing, it allowed for an open and honest debate on the pluses and minuses of developing a new commercial specifically for the American market. Ultimately, the global team opted to support the U.S. proposal. The upshot? Some of the most important television in the U.S., including 'The Oprah Winfrey Show', interviewed and highlighted the American women featured in the commercials – a feat that never would have never happened if Dove had chosen to use the original U.K. campaign in the U.S.

HIGH-FLYING, ADORED
Success begat success, but this time it was on a global scale. Almost every global media featured – or debated – the new Dove campaign. According to PRWeek, the publicity surrounding CFRB generated more than 650 million imprints during the first summer alone. Competitors and other brands recognized Dove's global marketing approach as groundbreaking (which it was), inspiring countless global brands to follow suit. More importantly, CFRB improved business results and success in practically every country – and showed for the first time how a brand could align globally, take an outspoken public stand on an important, controversial topic, and grow its business everywhere.

PART TWO

What Global Brands *Do Best*

(They Didn't Get Big By Accident)

SIMON CLIFT - CMO UNILEVER (2008-2010)

Throughout his 30-year career Simon Clift has been called everything from the bête noir of Unilever to *'Best International Marketer of the Year'* and *'CMO of the Year'*.

He is not someone you will likely forget meeting, nor will you ever be confused about what he really believes. With an infectious passion for the potential of brands, a zero tolerance for mediocrity, and a razor sharp mind that can vilify an ambivalent brand positioning statement in seconds, he has a reputation that makes even the most senior leaders nervous about debating any serious topic with him.

A less known side to Simon is his passion for cultivating great ideas and talent. All the way up to his role as Chief Marketing Officer (CMO) of Unilever, Simon has been the nurturer and protector of nascent brands and marketers that he felt needed the air time to blossom. The results include an impressive array of multi Billion dollar global brand successes that include AXE and Omo and a huge personal following of market-ers who trust his judgment blindly. Weary of personal publicity, 'he once famously called his P&G counterpart a 'Media Whore' – immediately explaining that he meant it in the nicest possible way of course.

Simon started as a marketer at Unilever straight out of University in 1982, perhaps not quite the logical choice after having read Modern and Medi-eval Languages at Cambridge in the U.K.. He came up through the ranks and held various marketing positions in the U.K, Portugal, Austria and Mexico. His love affair with Latin America, and particularly Brazil, where he now owns three homes, started when he was made Managing Director of Unilever's Personal Care business in Brazil and then Chairman of Uni-lever's Latin American personal care category for 3 years. Forced to move back to London for the role of Marketing President of Unilever's Home & Personal Care Division, and subsequently Group Vice President for Personal Care, he was ultimately directly responsible for the worldwide strategy, marketing, innovation and advertising of Unilever's €12 billion Personal Care business.

In June, 2008 he relinquished his category P&L responsibilities to be-come Unilever's first global Chief Marketing Officer, responsible for how

Unilever develops and executes its core function of marketing across all categories – incorporating worldwide advertising agency policy, marketing research, media planning and buying, and also responsible for developing Unilever's overall marketing capability and talent.

Having lived both sides of the marketing and business equation, Simon knows what it takes to successfully develop and then market a brand across multiple continents, as well as how to build an effective marketing machine. He oversaw the re-launch of Unilever's Marketing Academy as well as the launch of a fundamentally new marketing operating model in 2003, stressing at the time that he did not want anyone in the organization to forget the fundamentals by either thinking or acting 'Hopelessly Local or Mindlessly Global'.

Simon has always had a passion for connecting to the people who use his brands, often making the time on international trips to visit focus groups or consumers in their homes to listen and learn. He starts with the premise that people want brands to be good for them and that they must always deliver on the brand promises. Demanding clarity and consistency in communications across regions and reaching marketing targets in the most effective manner starts with complete clarity about the target audience and their needs. Simon was one of the first senior marketers to fully embrace the concept of brands needing to deliver against a larger purpose and being innovative in tackling modern-day societal challenges.

Throughout his career as marketing leader Simon Clift has demonstrated an impressive ability to focus on both the 'what' and 'how' of marketing. In this chapter we will drill down particularly on what it takes to develop a winning global marketing mix.

CHARACTERISTICS OF WINNING
GLOBAL BRANDS

Over the past thirty years, Simon Clift has demonstrated a laudable ability to focus on both the 'what' and the 'how' of marketing. In this chapter, we'll dig even deeper to uncover what it takes to develop a winning global marketing mix.

Over the years, we've had the opportunity to study successful and not-so-successful brands across many categories and geographies. Along the way, we couldn't help but wonder: Which brands succeed? And why? What do these brands stand for? What do they promise consumers? How do they define success? How do they deliver it? So, if you want to become and remain a *winning* global brand, what does it take?

For starters, let's assume that these global brands didn't just stub their toes on fame and glory. For every successful global brand, countless individuals have tried, iterated, piloted and, as they say, 'worked very hard and paid the price.' Countless global marketers have devoted themselves to creating the perfect storm of *right*: The right fundamentals. The right product or service. The right positioning. The right value proposition. The right audience. The right price. The right time, the right place.

But aligning the planets – the *right* planets, that is – isn't easy. Insights, vision, skills, resources and systems aren't everyday qualities, which is why so few marketing organizations today have them in place. Thus, across wide-ranging geographies, few companies are able to attain consistent results with their brand or brands. Even marketing's Grand Dame, Procter & Gamble, which boasts 24 brands that have each racked up more than US$1 billion in annual sales (plus 18 brands each worth between US$500 million and US$1 billion in annual business volume), sometimes gets it wrong.

We believe the following three key characteristics of the global brands are critical contributors to their success:

1   BUILDING ON A UNIVERSAL CONSUMER TRUTH
2   TAKING A STAND WITH PURPOSEFUL POSITIONING
3   OFFERING A TOTAL BRAND EXPERIENCE

Let's take them in order.

Universal Consumer Truth

We like to say that with an unlimited budget you can buy or spend your way into five markets for five years – but you can't do this in twenty-five markets for twenty-five years. At the base of all successful global brands, the key to longevity is buried in a universal consumer truth – one so intuitive, and innately human, it needs practically no explanation or translation. An innate need that's handily recognized across the world that transcends culture, politics and the latest fashions.

Global 'End Values'

Consumers everywhere around the world understand and respond to certain inherent values. At their core, many if not all successful global brands personify a global truth. According to Marc Mathieu, SVP Global Brand Marketing, The Coca-Cola Company, *'at the root of every global brand is a universal need.'*

Let's revisit Johnnie Walker's positioning. Johnnie Walker appeals to the universal appeal of progress, which derives from the universal need for success. Unilever's Blue Band margarine (known across the world as anything from Rama to Blue Ribbon) appeals to the maternal instinct for nurturing healthy children, which links to an end-value, namely, family security. Nike pointedly addresses winning. All over the world, consumers understand these values instantaneously. Take true friendship, a global end value. Do Uruguayans define – or experience – friendship any differently than Croatians? No.

Which isn't to say a clearly-defined universal human truth buttresses all global brands. Many of our clients still have their work cut out for them. The reasons are various, but they invariably come down to too many transient brand managers, each making their mark by tweaking the brand's positioning. The cumulative effect is a wayward, confused, I-Don't-Know-What-I'll-Be-When-I-Grow-Up brand.

Often, after many years of up-and-down brand management, the brand's universal need has...well, where'd it go? It's lost. It's been watered down. It's been thinned out. It's in hiding. In some cases, it turns out other regions were given rope to 'do their own thing' – and now several 'consumer needs' are competing for recognition within the firm. If you want a challenge, try bringing these entities together. You'll find that behind every 'need' and positioning is an individual, a team, a huge research project and often a whole lot of ego.

Using A Common Language

Our work with global brand leaders typically kicks off with a journey. Our mutual goal is to rediscover and identify a brand's universal truth. Frankly, sometimes we hit a wall. Language, or bad translation, gets in the way of effective collaboration.

Case in point: A few years ago, we worked with a brand with a long history of delivering excellent value for money. When we came aboard, the brand was trying hard to consolidate many different brand visions around the world into one global brand positioning statement. We supported the global brand head as he worked with a new Global Brand Committee made up of key regional and local marketers to lock down this single global positioning. On the team was also his agency, like so many great positioning agencies, from the U.K. And as time went on, the agency came up with the phrase, 'Great performance without costing the Earth.'

You may understand this perfectly…but you'd be outnumbered by all the Huhhhs? in the audience. The Germans, for one, assumed the company had at last recognized their market's extreme sensitivity to eco-unfriendly products, and that the brand had come around to supporting an eco-friendly strategy. It took a few embarrassing conversations to clarify that 'costing the Earth' actually meant 'not costing too much money.'
The critical skill, says Philip Gladman, SVP Global Marketing, Smirnoff, who's responsible for the firm's vodka brands, including Smirnoff, is that, *'You've got to tap into the crux of what people hold dear – and that's not only just what is spoken, but perhaps even more important, what's left unspoken.'*

But when the language no longer is the challenge, interesting chemistry can happen, and the results can be electrifying. Take HSBC for example.

BUILDING THE GLOBAL HSBC BRAND

The HSBC Group is one of the largest banking and financial services organizations in the world. Headquartered in London, HSBC's international network comprises roughly 8,000 offices, serving more than 100 million customers in 88 countries and territories across Europe, Asia Pacific, the Americas, the Middle East, and Africa. Among the world's multinational banking or financial giants, few can match either HSBC's global reach or its financial fundamentals.

An aside: The HSBC Group is named after its founding member, the Hong Kong and Shanghai Banking Corporation Limited, established in 1865 to finance the growing trade between China and Europe. The Group's early penetration in Asia allowed it to make huge and immediate gains, thereby capturing a sizable chunk of the market.

HSBC's brand strategy and image have come a long way since the late 1990s. In those days, says Chris Clark, then head of marketing planning and brand strategy at HSBC Group, the multinational was '*a disassociated group of banks that carried completely different flags around world.*' In 1999, the HSBC brand was non-existent. Only five years later, its value was $8.7 billion.

So how did HSBC achieve this turnaround? Read on.

Companies build a great brand on the back of a universal insight that resonates with target consumers. At first glance, this challenge sounds impossible. There's no such thing as a 'global consumer' – just millions (make that billions) of individual ones. That said, what great brands do magnificently well is zero in on those consumers' sweet spots.

How does this relate back to HSBC? The organization acknowledged that while consumers appreciate the value of international organizations and services, understandably they question the prevailing '*one size fits all*' global model. Customers are individuals. They want companies to treat them as such. They want to feel as though companies care about them, recognize their needs, and understand what makes the community where they live special, different, or unique.

The organization based their global brand idea and campaign on this insight. It was a courageous move. It addressed head-on the 'global-local' conundrum: do you drive for global leverage, or do you strive for local relevance?

Early on, the core team decided to focus on the differences between people and cultures and not countries. It would avoid the solemn, product-led advertising so common within the financial sector. HSBC set about developing a conversation with its customers. Its goal was to make the brand more approachable, more human, more understanding. *Why do people use financial services? What are the different emotional attachments people have to their financial belongings?*

Launched in 2002, HSBC's worldwide advertising campaign defined the distinct personality of the group's brand by introducing HSBC as *'the world's local bank.'* The campaign was developed by teams led by Peter Stringham, then Global Head of Marketing for HSBC, and Nigel Gilbert who led the global team at their advertising agency. It honored HSBC's underlying philosophy – namely, that the world is a rich, diverse place that ideally should respect different cultures and people. The ad campaign was clear, powerful, and defining. It communicated the following: *Anyone who banks with HSBC can benefit from services and advice from a company with international experience, one delivered by people who are sensitive to community customs and needs.*

The campaign ran on TV, in print and online, sponsoring key global properties such as airports in major cities, Formula 1, and World Matchplay golf. Over the

'The world's local bank'

course of 2002, it appeared across the eighty-one countries and territories that HSBC served worldwide at that time. Subsequent campaign expressions extended the depth and breadth of the brand's equity by adding contextual layers to the same notion that HSBC is 'the world's local bank.' In keeping with the theme of global diversity, the bank employed thirty directors to assemble HSBC's award-winning and locally-slanted 'cultural collisions' TV ads. (Individual country teams were in charge of devising culturally relevant versions of the original core idea.) Since then? Well, the results speak for themselves. HSBC has steadily risen in the ranks of the world's most admired corporations. Along the way, it's won numerous accolades, including ranking 40th amongst Fortune magazine's most-admired companies in the world, Interbrand and BusinessWeek 29th most valuable brand, and in 2003, The Banker magazine's 'best global bank'. This year it was ranked No.1 in Brand Finance's Banking 500.

The group continues to grow steadily. HSBC has fully integrated its various acquisitions across the world – most recently in the U.S. and Mexico – into the HSBC Group, and today, each one carries its branding. As of 2010, HSBC is the world's largest banking and financial services group and, according to a composite measure by Forbes magazine, the world's 8th largest company.

HSBC has endured a lot of storms in the banking industry, thanks to its consistent performance against competitors, and its strong, well-defined brand. Customers across the world trust HSBC – and over the long term, too. Which again reminds us: strong brands give confidence to customers, help unify and develop a significant sense of pride in its employees, and provide value to investors. And by reinforcing its position as 'the world's local bank,' HSBC has done just that.

Purposeful Positioning

The Body Shop. Starbucks. Sony. Whole Foods. Unilever. P&G. J&J. Each of these companies has a strong, purposeful origin. Each had founders interested in causes greater than just lining their pockets. Today, many of these companies are still going strong, and in some cases (and this may not be a coincidence), getting even stronger.

Brands and companies with a cause never engage with us (or anyone, for that matter) about *why* they're purposeful. They just are – end of discussion. That same purpose is a powerful draw for employees. And no one questions it.

These companies have also found that pursuing a purposeful positioning strategy makes good business sense.

Is purposeful positioning the same as Cause Marketing? No. Is it the same as throwing support behind the Chairman's wife's favorite charity with a penny contribution for every product sold? No. Our definition of purposeful positioning is simple. That a brand actively, fundamentally stands for something, a belief, and pursues a strategy that leverages that brand's reach and impact, and enables the brand and its users to make a positive societal difference.

David Gershon, Founder and CEO of the Empowerment Institute, '*Companies need to be part of the solutions to society's problems. The challenges faced by society need all hands on deck and are too big to be left to the exclusive domain of governments and NGOs.*'

Sounds like a good idea for all brands, right? After all, in boom times, pretty much everyone likes to spread his or her success. But our work with many 'purposeful' brands finds that the rubber only really hits the road during rocky economic times.

In the spring of 2009, we hosted a 'Purposeful Positioning' Roundtable. Among the attendees were brand leaders from many of the most purposeful brands out there, including Ben & Jerry's, Dove, Levi's and Starbucks, plus a handful of less renowned companies whose mission statements extend beyond money-making.

What quickly becomes clear when you talk with the leaders of these organizations is that their purpose infiltrates every layer of the organization. It's a 'raison d'être' that can't be switched on or off – even during tough financial eras. It doesn't depend on a CEO saying, 'I don't think we can afford to do that this year.' It's simply what the brand or company does every day.

Note that many of these purposeful brand organizations lack a standalone Corporate Social Responsibility department. Why? Because social responsibility comes with the job description. It's the responsibility of the CEO, the global brand leader, the sales manager in Panama, and the guy who picks up the phone at 3AM in Brussels. Purpose and business are tethered at the ankles.

But how can a purposeful brand possibly make business sense? Doesn't doing things purposefully cost money? Is it sustainable over the long term?

Compared to just two decades ago, today's market looks – and is – strikingly different. The average Western consumer is exposed to roughly 3,000 brand messages a day. How can confused, glazed-eyed consumers claw through the clutter? How can traditional market leaders regain their leadership and create new areas of competitive advantage?

To stand out again, brands must *do* more, must *be* more.

Join Together: A Global Brand Opportunity

We believe that today's marketing leaders – particularly *global* brand marketers – can build competitive advantage by crafting more purposeful positioning. Today's consumers welcome those brands that take on a more active, purposeful role. In an era when consumer confidence in traditional 'trusted' sources of authority (the Church, the Government) is at its nadir, and new, mostly global NGOs are more prominent than ever before, consumers accept and even *expect* a brand to adopt a more active role.

And we're not talking about sustainability or ensuring your offshore plants turn away underage minors. These 'standards' have quickly become table stakes for doing business today. We're talking about a brand that boldly plants a stake in the ground – that stands for the purpose in which it believes, one that's good for the world and its citizenry.

Says Peter Vaughn of American Express, *'To me, 'purposeful positioning' means that you understand the difference you're going to make in a consumer's life. I think it's important that every single company has a role to play in making the world a better place to live.'* Yet he cautions that *'the way a company does that needs to be consistent with the core values of the brand.'*

So what better entities to take up and support important global challenges than global brands? Retail or discount brands can manage this only stumblingly. In other words, we believe that purposeful positioning represents a huge opportunity to create competitive advantage relative to the other market players. Employees win big, too. Many of the CMOs we spoke with mentioned that employee engagement is a significant challenge. But 'purposeful' brands boast less employee attrition than their competitors. (To wit, Starbucks' employee turnover rate is less than half that of Dunkin' Donuts.)

Higher Ground

What about on an individual level? We have also found that working for a purposeful organization creates more meaningful careers. Jonathan Moore of Sara Lee recalls working on brands, *'Some with what I would call a real purpose, and some with no bigger goals than making lots of money. I can tell you - the difference is stunning. Why would I spend my blood, sweat and tears on just making money?'*

Aline Santos of DIG says with quiet satisfaction, *'Since we connected the DIG brand positioning to the ultimate purpose of Child Development, I have seen a remarkable improvement in internal and external loyalty to the brand. Standing for something meaningful makes all the difference.'*

Still, the challenge remains. Purposeful positioning needs to 'fit' with the brand, and in some cases, with a company's entire portfolio of brands.

Phil Mirvis of the BU Centre for Social Responsibility says, 'Branding starts from the inside out. 'What kind of a company are you? What is your philosophy and approach on whatever it is you're producing?' These questions are prerequisites to purposeful positioning. When I hear an executive say, 'Well, we've got two or three green products, and then a couple related to causes, and then a bunch of other stuff – that's an executive who's thinking only about products and market niches. Segments matter of course but so does knowing who you are as an organization and what you stand for. Take Unilever. Dove's inner beauty campaign says, 'We are a company that cares about women. Women come in all shapes and sizes, and all can radiate beauty.' Hurray for Unilever combating the media's 'skinny model' imagery. But Unilever also offers Axe deodorant and soap targeted to young men. Their message to young men: 'Use this and you'll get a sexy, skinny model – in bed!' You begin to wonder: Who's the company behind these two different messages? Is it schizophrenic or tricky to talk out of both sides of its mouth?'

All our interviews with CMOs found that a focus on 'people, planet & profit' has become imperative both from consumer and internal motivation perspectives. Younger employees are even taking jobs with companies that may not pay as well as others, but are devoted to making a difference.

Walking In Your Footsteps

That said, nearly nowhere are consumers willing to pay extra for the privilege of virtuous intent. Purposeful positioning is competitive advantage assuming that all other things are equal – especially in developing economies where price matters most. As our colleague Helen Duce says: 'It may take years but over time consumers will decide that the 'best' brands are those that strive to make a difference in the world, and that behind every great brand is a great person and an inspired organization.'

But first, global marketers should build up credibility. Educated consumers will then (potentially) ladder up to a greater appreciation of a brand's purpose. In time, they'll be willing to pay more. Inevitably, the brand will benefit. Think of the countless coffee-growing co-operatives in many third world countries, where companies like Starbucks willingly increase their

'We're continuously focusing on the needs of human beings: what are their physical needs, what are their social needs, what are their spiritual needs, and asking ourselves, *where can we appeal to those needs* with a brand proposition that resonates with that?'

TEX GUNNING - BOARD MEMBER, AKZONOBEL RESPONSIBLE FOR DECORATIVE PAINTS cost price in order to stake a claim to responsible farming. Now observe how the brand has benefited in *everyone's* eyes.

Thus, market or category leaders have a choice to make. They can elect to lead by example as Starbucks does, or they can use their size and leadership position to alter an entire category. Mars, for example, works as a category leader to evolve the *whole* cocoa market to a higher platform of responsible buying, thereby ensuring that no one undercuts their price. Right now at least, Mars willingly sacrifices the opportunity to create competitive advantage.

Suffice to say that purposeful positioning is the way forward. Greg Welch of Spencer Stuart says he *'can't imagine unveiling a new brand today that isn't transparent, that doesn't mean something other than just product, technology or price.'*

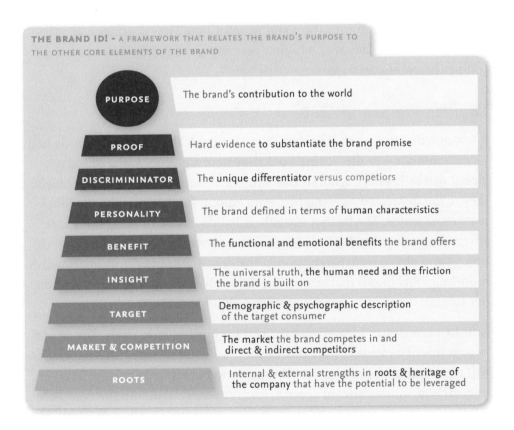

THE BRAND ID! - A FRAMEWORK THAT RELATES THE BRAND'S PURPOSE TO THE OTHER CORE ELEMENTS OF THE BRAND

PURPOSE	The brand's contribution to the world
PROOF	Hard evidence to substantiate the brand promise
DISCRIMININATOR	The unique differentiator versus competiors
PERSONALITY	The brand defined in terms of human characteristics
BENEFIT	The functional and emotional benefits the brand offers
INSIGHT	The universal truth, the human need and the friction the brand is built on
TARGET	Demographic & psychographic description of the target consumer
MARKET & COMPETITION	The market the brand competes in and direct & indirect competitors
ROOTS	Internal & external strengths in roots & heritage of the company that have the potential to be leveraged

Total Brand Experience

The third and final characteristic common among the most successful brands we work with and study is an approach to developing innovative solutions, communication and activation that we dub *Total Brand Experience*.

This means stepping away from the old-fashioned, product-driven, manufactured, then-sell-it mindset. Instead, brands are well-advised to understand, then leverage every single consumer touchpoint. Consider Disney, Marriott and many other service and hospitality organizations. Typically, they take a head-to-toe holistic approach to what role their brand plays in consumers' lives. They then use every touchpoint to drive a consistently branded and appreciated experience.

Marketers who understand the *Total Brand Experience* cast their minds across product, communication and promotions. They don't look at market share. Instead, they seek a higher percentage of the true metric for 21st century brand success: *share of experience.*

Divided We Stand Out

A few decades ago, when Ries and Trout famously declared that brands had to 'differentiate – or die,' it turns out they were right. Yet some of today's global marketers have ignored this simple, obvious principle. Why? Maybe they're too distracted fighting turf wars among local, regional and global marketing teams. Maybe they have their hands full calculating the 'exact' advertising campaign ROIs. Doesn't matter. Point is, as sophisticated technology and global transparency open the door for brand duplication within months, global brand marketers find themselves struggling day in and day out to uncover what's special, or unique, about a product.

But the expenses and lead times for real innovation have risen. The chances to reinvent a category have diminished. How many more shaving blades will we be using in 2020? 12? Adding value today expands from product only, to non-innovation led growth, from content...and into the complete experience a brand can offer consumers. By expanding into full-experience solutions, global brands can build both global consistency (by adopting a single global campaign platform), and competitive relevance (by differentiating at a local level within the framework).

We dub this the opportunity to create more complete consumer experiences while leveraging context. This struggle to maintain equilibrium between global leverage and local relevance is one that keeps global marketers dancing as fast as they can. Karin Koonings of Starbucks found that while, *'our core coffee offerings could remain quite consistent globally, we needed to recognize local difference especially in the complementary assortment like food and cold drinks.'*

The Holy Grail? Finding an innovation that brings entirely new solutions to market. Apple has an uncanny knack for this. Nestle scored with Nespresso. (Nespresso has helped the P&L health of Nestle in just a few short years.) Oh, and Apple just overtook Microsoft as the world's largest technology company. No mean feat.

Thinking Complete Solutions

Properly managed global brands can build markets, create an impact beyond their geography and reestablish new standards within a market and even an industry.

How? By thinking big.

Egbert van Acht, CMO, Philips Consumer Lifestyle says that his employees have worked hard to avoid splintering resources. Internal research confirms that Philips has *'developed a culture where marginal and incremental organization is frowned upon, and it's only cool to do big, new things.'*

Van Acht says that, *'When we first adopted our new brand promise and aligned our businesses around our brand promise, there was some internal resistance. But we worked hard to overcome that, by having Sense and Simplicity permeate all customer touchpoints as well as internal processes. Today, that sense of brand ownership is shared by everybody: not just the guy who runs marketing;*

but also the supply chain head; the leader of R&D; the guy who runs finance; everybody. It is now so deep and so ingrained, people don't want it to go away.'

Many brands have recognized the value of multiple touchpoints that felicitously serve to communicate and deliver to consumers a brand's promise. Again, consider Apple. Their retail stores, call centers and website are all fully integrated. Each supports the Apple promise that things should be simple or, in the company's words, 'different'.

These then are what we believe are the three pillars, or components, of today's winning global brands. Don't mistake the *'what'* and the *'how'* of global brands as separate entities. They're not. The Yin of *'what'* and the Yang of *'how'* work strongly to re-enforce each other. And an inspired, well-connected organization focused on ambitious business and brand objectives, with clear roles, responsibilities, good marketing capability processes and stimulated team members, will always come up with superior insights, positioning and execution.

How global marketing leaders manage these assets to yield true marketing effectiveness is the subject of the chapters ahead.

COCA-COLA: LIVING POSITIVELY

Established in 1886, Coke is arguably the world's most famous and successful global brand. It's also one of the world's largest beverage companies, with almost 500 brands and 3,000 beverage products sold in over 200 countries, and almost 100,000 employees scattered worldwide. Its global brands include Coca-Cola, Fanta, Vitamin Water, PowerAde, Dasani and Minute Maid juices.

How best to describe a consistent global icon such as Coca-Cola? Nearly everyone in the world has grown up appreciating its famous polar bears, Santa Claus, and more recently *The Coke Side of Life* and *Open Happiness* imagery. That said, marketing academics and practitioners have studied those periods when the company has swayed between local and global brand direction.

Global marketing skeptics cite Coke's alternating leadership as 'proof' trends towards more global marketing may be nothing more than a sign of the times. But discussions with Coca-Cola executives paint a different picture.

'I don't think there can be much arguing about the fact that the world has become a more global market place over the last decade,' says Marc Mathieu, former head of global brands at Coca-Cola. *'And I certainly do not think for a moment that the development towards full global transparency and consumer accountability will in any way reverse back to how things were in the past. All marketing leaders need to now accept that we are now living in a fully connected world and that we need to take our responsibilities as leaders, but also as brands with the assumption that we are playing on a global stage, there for everyone to see.'*

New Coke brand campaigns or major marketing developments are always the subjects of massive global media attention. The launch of The Coke Side of Life generated millions of dollars of free publicity in trade and consumer press, as did the 2009 launch of the follow-up campaign, Open Happiness.

Less publicized, yet perhaps even more critical to Coke in the long run, was the company's internal (and now external) roll out of Coke's Live Positively campaign. Live Positively has the potential to be far bigger and more transformational than any single brand campaign to date, especially given Coca-Cola's worldwide influence. Growing concerns about obesity and the environment have placed the company in the hot seat for its sugary drinks and water use, as well as the ecological impact of its packaging. On the other hand, people also recognize Coke's stellar, longstanding work with NGOs and governmental agencies.

The company knows that in today's flat world, a proactive approach is the only option. The world will perceive Coke as a leader (or a follower) based on how it interacts with the world inside and outside the company. Nor can Coke delegate this responsibility to a CSR officer, or anyone else, for that matter. As Muhtar Kent, the chief executive officer of Coca-Cola, said in a recent Fortune interview when a reporter asked him who was in charge of the CSR initiatives, *'I have not appointed another one and never will. That's me.'*

The story behind the development and roll out of Live Positively deserves close attention. In early 2007 as Coke's Leadership Team was working on the company's strategic plan, it realized the company wasn't succinctly articulating the brand's defined 'purpose.'

Mathieu and his colleagues felt there was an opportunity to address this and take the company's business planning process to the next level: *'We had defined our business objective as becoming the world's beverage leader and set out very clear business goals and financial targets, but we felt there was an opportunity to leverage the overall 'purpose' to bring everything together. It just felt like we had a chance to go beyond the business goals alone to express why we, each and every one of us, was excited and proud to be part of Coke, why we were all working so hard for this wonderful company.'*

Coke's global leadership team reviewed the company's core business activities and performance. They connected with their local business counterparts, bottlers, and retail partners. They delved deep to understand priorities and needs. At which point, Mathieu and his colleagues discovered that there was a lot more going on behind the scenes than just the pursuit of hard business goals. Across Coca-Cola, across all brands and continents, were countless initiatives that, from a money-making perspective, quite simply did not 'fit.'

Among them were projects supporting local and regional education initiatives, sports, and science. Some involved collaborations with water technology scientists; others involved local sports councils. Coke funded many, and 'paid' for others by sharing its knowhow. Every initiative was focused on making a positive difference in the world around Coke. None was about making money. And all the stakeholders spoken to saw these projects as not only important, but essential to what made Coca-Cola the company it was.

Along with a small multidisciplinary team, Coke asked Mathieu to map and capture the spirit of these various initiatives. Could he develop an overarching ambition and framework that would better connect this work to Coke's overall

Making a positive difference in the world around Coke

business strategy? They were looking to help better communicate and enable progress in this area, and of course to ensure that colleagues and partners everywhere would understand the importance of these projects, be inspired to do more and feel guided. And of course to ensure that everyone acted consistently with what ultimately became the company's purpose.

The team immediately struck a company-wide nerve. HR came up with suggestions on how to align hiring, retention, and development with the company purpose. Key suppliers in the Supply Chain threw in their two cents on how to bring the purpose to life. Most importantly? Every single colleague Mathieu and his team spoke to was over the moon that Coca-Cola was now making this work important and integral to its long-term future and vision.

It also turned out that many colleagues in charge of purposeful initiatives for Coke knew that with corporate support, they could be doing even more.

CEO Kent recognizes this: *'When we started this journey, we were doing things, but we weren't getting traction. So we analyzed why we were not more successful. We came to the conclusion that our efforts weren't embedded in the business plan properly. It didn't have the right metrics around it. It was just a warm and fuzzy. We also didn't have proper alignment with our bottling partners. The first prerequisite of being successful here is that you work as a global system. Second, it's got to be embedded in the business plan. Third, you've got to have the right metrics around it; it's got to be measurable. And then it's got to be beneficial from a financial perspective.'*

Ultimately Mathieu and the team developed what is now broadly recognized as the Coca-Cola purpose; *Live Positively*. This purpose defines a long-term vision for Coke's business and a 'Roadmap' for winning together with the company's bottling and retail partners.

Mathieu: *'The response internally, and now externally, to Live Positively has been tremendous. We clearly struck a chord that resonated with the formulation of a holistic business purpose that went across brands and geographies. Many new initiatives that drive the purpose, and therefore our business growth, have been started since we started communicating the purpose and challenging ourselves how we could do more. It's been a tremendously exciting and rewarding journey to see doing business and doing the right thing coming together.'*

Drivers Of Global Marketing *Effectiveness*

Unlocking The Value Of Global
Marketing Organizations

Group

KHALIL YOUNES – SVP GROUP SALES, MARKETING &
INNOVATION, CARLSBERG BREWERIES A/S

A personification of the global citizen of the future, Khalil Younes always knew his career would span continents. Half-Lebanese, half-French, educated in France, with an undergraduate degree in accounting, Khalil began his career during his civil service with a two-year stint as a New York-based Trade Attaché for the French Embassy. The job description included interviewing advertising agency owners about the opportunities for French agencies in the U.S. (Not a bad alternative to digging trenches in the countryside.)

In 1989, Khalil's marketing career took off when he landed a job as brand assistant working on Dash 3 detergent for P&G in Paris.

After a few years at the famous P&G marketing boot camp (with a Harvard MBA thrown in along the way), Khalil was lured to Atlanta by Coca-Cola, where he soon became, among other things, Global Brand Manager for Cherry Coke.

From 1996 on, as local and regional Marketing Director across various Eastern European markets, Khalil worked out of Hungary, Istanbul and Vienna, developing a reputation for getting both strategy and execution right.

'I'm someone who learns by doing. So what I've tried to do is create building blocks in my career by putting myself outside of my comfort zone, seeking new work experiences that would stretch me beyond my previous roles. I believe that's one of the best ways to build marketing capability, developing one or two new competencies in each and every role you move into.'

In 2001, Khalil took his first general management role, again in Hungary, this time as President responsible for all aspects of the business. During difficult business circumstances, his eventual success earned him enormous respect and an elevated profile back at the mothership in Atlanta.

Two years later, Coke asked Khalil to return to Atlanta to turn around the flagging Fanta orange drink business – a brand suffering from years of decline, and a near-complete absence of strategic direction from the center. When Khalil came aboard, the brand was still drifting here and there across the globe. Khalil's instructions were unambiguous:

Bring direction, cut duplication and grow the brand.

Less than a year later, Fanta's global re-launch was piloted and rolled out quickly in several countries. It was a textbook example of ensuring that local marketing directors could fully support a mix that had been developed elsewhere.

The success of the Fanta re-launch in market, the speed of the roll out, and the significant savings resulting from pruning unnecessary complexities – all these elements led to Khalil's promotion to Head of Marketing for the enormous, Coke-owned global juice business that includes all the Minute Maid brands.

In 2009, Khalil moved back across the Atlantic to become the new CMO of Carlsberg Beer in Copenhagen. With responsibility for many beer brands including Carlsberg, Kronenbourg and Tuborg, and adhering to his Strategy into Action principles, Khalil took only a few months to reach out to key stakeholders, listen, and then develop the brand's strategy. Today, Khalil is again working closely with local markets everywhere to explain and implement the global plan that will help local growth. Why change a winning formula?

NO LACK OF GREAT GLOBAL MARKETING
STRATEGIES

CONNECT

INSPIRE

BUILD

Universal Truth
Purposeful Positioning
Total Experience

ORGANIZE

FOCUS

There's not much point in asking Khalil Younes how he defines success. In every conversation, his philosophy and business approach come through clearly. As he describes various marketing challenges he's resolved throughout his career, he exudes a 'glass half full' mindset, and an approach that could be easily broken down to 25 percent strategy and 75 percent action. For Khalil, it's all about connecting to key markets, swiftly developing strategic insights, inspiring the troops with a strong vision and then focusing on execution. That's all there is to it.

The best market research? Results. After all, the most sophisticated strategic plan in the world isn't worth the paper it's written on if a marketer can't pull it off. Which happens to be the foundation of Larry Bossidy's business bestseller, *Execution: The Discipline of Getting Things Done*, written with management guru Ram Charan.

Bossidy happens to know a thing or two. During his tenure, the former chairman and CEO of Honeywell International strung together 31 consecutive quarters of earnings-per-share growth of 13 percent or greater. Bossidy believes, *'Many people regard execution as detail work that's beneath the dignity of a business leader. That's wrong. It's a leader's most important job.'*

Honeywell's former CEO often comes to mind when we discuss execution with great global marketing leaders, as most feel the same way. As Folkert Kamphuis of Novartis points out, *'I have seen global marketers that develop great strategy but never succeed in getting the plans adopted. It's about more than just great strategy in global marketing.'*

Especially in a job like global CMO. By definition, the position is slightly removed from the daily hustle and bustle of a 'real' market. Its risks include others' perception that the CMO is out of touch, and/or developing unrealistic plans. (Give us a dollar for every unused or ignored global marketing strategy we've 'found' in the dusty top drawer of a long-departed CMO, and we could retire today.)

It's not even that these strategies were bad, or poorly conceived. It's that they were *only* that: strategies scribbled on random pieces of paper. We started our company on the back of a simple insight: That development of strategy is often less of a challenge to global marketing leaders. More so: *How* to ensure that a global brand can effectively implement that strategy? *How* do global leaders ensure that as the strategy develops, and the team finds consensus, they build the support and capability to effectively implement the strategy?

Philip Gladman of Diageo agrees with the distinction: *'I think you've got to be a black belt in strategy, and you've got to be a big black belt in turning that strategy into brilliant marketing execution.'*

Adds Jennifer Davidson of Molson Coors, *'Once you've finally created a global positioning, you may think you've got it solved. Nailing your brand strategy doesn't mean the job is done. It's only the beginning. Now comes the execution.'*

But here's the problem. Even though some leaders make it a point to reinforce the importance of combining effective strategy with embedding the plan, they're the exception, not the rule. Our *Leading Global Brands* study and consulting experience lead us to conclude that few global marketers are very comfortable with merging this Yin and Yang of global marketing.

Before we start a new project, we first conduct an internal temperature check, followed by a benchmarking against best-in-class global marketing leadership practices (we know, that's a lot of words). More simply, we call this the *PulseCheck*. We've found this consulting tool to be incredibly useful in gauging where CMOs or Global Brand Heads should focus their time and resources if they want to grow their businesses.

Over the years, our experience has led us to conclude that global marketing heads are seemingly at ease with developing the foundational pillars of marketing: An insight based on a universal truth; a brand vision that's purposeful and differentiated; and the creation of total experience solutions with big ideas. Most CMOs have got the vision, mission, brand identity, equity, insight, and strategy nailed down. In other words, the strategic *WHAT* is just fine.

But…what board colleagues often complain about, and honest global marketers tell us keeps them up at night, is this: they don't know *HOW* to best *implement* that strategy. They worry about *how* to cluster countries for relevant leverage; *how* to instill local ownership of global initiatives; *how* to bundle resources to innovate in ways that are bigger, bolder, and better; and *how* to get people focused externally instead of operating in silos and jockeying for budgets and influence. The new global marketing challenge is ambidextrous: How to increase global leverage and local relevance *at the same time.* Our colleague Robert Jan d'Hond often reminds us that the two go hand in hand: *'The more we can improve the skills and competencies of the marketing leadership teams in the 'how', the more consistently we will improve the quality of the 'what'.'*

GLOBAL OR LOCAL?

Many companies that struggle are stuck in what we consider a false choice between global leverage – that is the benefits of scale – and local relevance and consumer intimacy. The result is often a volley of endless debates that contrast the pros and cons of centralization versus decentralization, or marketing efficiency versus marketing effectiveness. In our opinion, this thinking is far too black and white. No CEO has the luxury of a simple choice between profit and growth. From where we sit, leveraging scale, otherwise known as the *efficiency equation,* just isn't enough.

Matter of fact, generating economies of scale may feel like the easy part. Given our recent economic challenges, most management teams have become quite proficient at this (well, they have no choice, really). Generating economies of scale is what the big management consultancies will storm in and tell you to do. But from a marketer's perspective, pruning decision-making levels, combining jobs at regional levels, and clustering markets typically cause more headaches than they solve. Does it make sense to cluster markets based on dubious criteria, such as proximity to warehouses?

No. What's much harder is to increase the *effectiveness quotient*. Global marketing success depends on a combined approach, one that addresses efficiency principles as well as long-term marketing effectiveness. More than once, we've witnessed the reversal of efficiency improvements. Why? Very simple. The new global marketing organization didn't take the trouble to develop effective strategy, structure and capability.

From our perspective, the landscape is clear. For the last ten years, the question is no longer (and will never be again) about trading off efficiency against effectiveness. It's no longer about whether or not to embrace a global marketing approach. The only question that matters is *how to go global effectively.*

'The drivers are incredibly useful as a construct. Our team realized that we needed to *completely change the way we work* with our markets.'

PHILIP GLADMAN – SVP GLOBAL MARKETING, SMIRNOFF

Unlocking The Value Of Global Marketing

Successfully leading an organization with global brands into the future requires a new set of insights and competencies from the top marketers, from leadership to organizational leadership skills. Just ask Unilever, Sony and Molson Coors.

Global marketing chiefs frequently struggle with how to generate – or as we call it, 'unlock' – more value from global marketing organizations and their global brands. It isn't easy. Success requires insights, skills and competencies that many marketing leaders simply have not been trained in, or exposed to. Not to worry – it's possible to get it right.

We like to frame this challenge as *building the ultimate global marketing machine.* We find that *winning* global marketing leaders typically focus on five key drivers of global marketing success. These drivers offer leaders guidance on *HOW* best to lead the global marketing process. Each one defines an important area that marketers must focus on before, during and after they develop and deploy their strategies. Each one enables marketing leaders to align an organization, and execute with discipline and consistency.

What are they? The ability to *Connect*; to *Inspire*; to *Focus*; to *Organize*; and to *Build*.

Let's briefly examine each one in turn here (we'll be covering them in greater detail in the chapters ahead).

CONNECT: *Fostering Interdependency*

Connect is about building and maintaining interdependent mindsets and behaviors in the organization. It's about the level of trust among disparate marketing parties, whether it's between local and global or regional; between category and brand; or between marketing and sales and/or research and development.

We're not evolutionary psychologists, but perhaps humans are born with an innate desire to do things 'their way'. The *Not Invented Here* principle is certainly relevant for global marketing. We've seen very few marketing organizations where local marketers automatically accepted strategic and executional guidance from HQ.

Succeeding globally requires ensuring that all players share a common understanding of market realities at both local and global levels. Key local marketing team members need to know that their market's success directs the global team's work. From the perspective of global teams, the prevailing mindset among local marketers should be to seek out similarities, rather than differences.

INSPIRE: *Igniting The Organization*

Behind every successful global brand is the nugget of a universal insight that attracts consumers. It also *inspires* everyone who works with the brand. Effective global brand leaders instinctively understand how important it is not just to inspire consumers, but to fire up an internal passion for the brand. These brand champions go out of their way to nurture excitement, ensuring that colleagues and employees in all relevant parts of the business not only *personally* take pride in the brand's purpose, but work hard to deliver the brand promise. Which, in turn, powers the brand's growth and success.

The capacity to inspire others isn't just some soft skill that's 'nice to have.' Leaders cast a long shadow. Peers and colleagues observe, even scrutinize, their leader's every move. Former U.S. President Ronald Reagan famously said a leader is always 'on camera,' and internal stakeholders, and even customers, invariably take their cues from the alpha leader.

Greg Welch of Spencer Stuart confirms the importance of inspirational leadership: '*It's not uncommon for many of these CMOs to have three to four thousand people in their teams; so the bulk of their time is actually in leading. I see the very best CMOs spending their time engaging their teams; letting the horses run but in a consistent direction.*'

FOCUS: *Aligning Priorities And Targets*

Let's assume you've identified, and connected, with your brand stakeholders across the company. You've inspired them to bend and stretch beyond their beliefs. Now you need to *focus* the team on an aligned strategy that gets them towards the vision, making sure that all present know the location of the goalposts. Focus is about creating clarity. *Focus* is about setting exact goals for the year ahead. *Focus* is about deciding how targets interconnect. *Focus* is about aligning definitions of metrics, e.g., which ones matter and which don't. Without *focus*, you may find yourself with a highly motivated, but ultimately scattered marketing machine.

Critical to the success of a global brand is a vigilant *focus* on, and commitment to, an agreed-upon set of global brand priorities. Many global brands struggle with unaligned strategies across regions and businesses, resulting in unspoken or explicit friction, not to mention wasted resources. Global brand leaders must be intrepid enough to step back, look forward, and make the hard choices about what's important and what's not. That way, the organization can attain the speed, scale and success of which it's capable.

ORGANIZE: *Clarifying Roles And Responsibilities*

Caution, pitfall straight ahead! Make absolutely sure that early on you *organize* roles and responsibilities. Few things are more crucial than defining the structure, operating model and exact roles for all key marketing decisions. Just as crucial is diligently enforcing the new operating model and required behaviors. If and when leaders tolerate behaviors inconsistent with the model, the counterproductive results can lead to delays and frustrations.

As companies globalize, they often reorganize to reflect a more central approach. Our *Leading Global Brands* study shows that for the vast majority of organizations out there, brands are led much more centrally today than they were 3 years ago. Almost every global brand now has a dedicated global brand team. But as these companies reorganize to reflect the new centralized approach, all structures, roles, processes and operating models need to be adapted. Sad to say, companies usually address this problem only when things have gone repeatedly wrong.

Our colleague Stef Gans: *'Why is the average tenure of a CMO in a given company only 17 months? I think a big part of this is that most companies are not organized around this kind of holistic, integrated view of what it takes to be best-in-class in marketing.'*

BUILD: *Developing And Leveraging Marketing Capability*

Companies can only leverage global marketing growth and efficiencies if all global markets speak a single marketing language, and *build* swiftly on one another's successes and mistakes. How? By cultivating what we call a community of marketing excellence within the company that enables marketers not only to trade success and failure, but to swiftly adapt and apply whatever lessons they've learned.

James Cali of Cadbury Schweppes contrasts standards past and present: *'In the old world it used to be like, hey, let's just do our best effort to collaborate and share ideas and stuff. But it wasn't really anyone's full-time job to drive it, so it didn't consistently happen, even with the best intent. That's just not acceptable if you want to win in today's global marketplace.'*

And Then There Were Five

These drivers of global marketing effectiveness – *Connect, Inspire, Focus, Organize,* and *Build* – apply across all borders, cultures, and industry sectors.

Philip Gladman of Diageo, who has used the five drivers approach in his Smirnoff business, is now a firm proponent of the model: *'It's changed the way we communicate, changed the way we talk, changed the way we present stuff, changed the questions we ask, changed the way we ask the questions, changed the way we develop our work.'*

Of course, not every company or brand can – or should – prioritize all five drivers at any one time. It's important to maintain a proper sequence. There's no need to detail operating models when no one in the organization knows how crises will be handled, as this would feel like rearranging the chairs on the deck of the Titanic. But we do believe that every company must understand the meaning of each of these drivers; how best to influence them; and how a leader equipped with all five levers can arm you with the tools you need to build what we call *The Ultimate Marketing Machine*.

Stephen Quinn, of Walmart underscores the importance of an approach that combines WHAT thinking with HOW thinking: '*I think that the most successful global marketers probably naturally think about both what the global brand vision needs to be and how the organization will be able to deliver the brand most effectively globally.*'

In the following chapters, we'll explore each of these five drivers in greater depth. The *Dirt is Good* case study demonstrates how powerful they can be in action.

UNLOCKING OMO'S GLOBAL BRAND POTENTIAL

FMCG giant Unilever produces and markets the US$ 2 billion-plus laundry brand known to consumers around the world as OMO, Persil, Skip, ALA, and a few other names. Under the leadership of Keith Weed, now Unilever's CMO, the OMO franchise has evolved radically over the last 5 years.

The brand has gone from a loose confederation of brands with over 25 wildly assorted positions, names, and packaging designs, to a strong global brand bearing a single global proposition: 'Dirt is Good' (DIG). With a new winning brand development strategy and world-class marketing mix, OMO's consolidation under the DIG umbrella exemplifies the process and benefits of creating global marketing alignment.

When Aline Santos, Global Brand Vice-President and leader of the DIG Global Brand Team, took on her role, the 'Dirt is Good' umbrella was already in place. It was hugely successful in a few markets...but there was no clear brand vision or agreement around its global roll out. *'Once DIG's strategic role in the Unilever laundry portfolio was set,'* Santos recalls, *'we quickly agreed that the 'Dirt is Good' brand proposition was what we needed to cut across all markets with relevance and resonance. Our job was to inspire the teams, building alignment and consistency and speeding up the roll out.'*

CONNECTING TO DISCOVER SIMILARITIES

DIG's significant global differences meant there was a great need to connect across the brand community. An internal survey was used to reach out to all brand stakeholders and identify key areas of opportunity for growth, as well as benchmark DIG's brand effectiveness against other world-class global brands. Aline Santos and her global marketing team knew it was important to promote and foster a culture of 'looking for similarities' across the brand community if more intense global collaboration was to succeed.

INSPIRING WITH PURPOSEFUL POSITIONING

Winning global brands inspire their consumers and stakeholders with a vision that defines success in terms of both business and purpose. Stakeholders inspired by a brand's purposeful vision and positioning often surprise brand leaders with ideas and actions that go far beyond the call of duty. Aline Santos: *'A brand with a social mission is always more appealing to consumers as well as to the organization.'* The Fabric-Cleaning category had touted technical brand attributes in ad pitches for years. Over time, these campaigns had lost their power to inspire consumers and internal stakeholders. For DIG, whose technical claims were relatively inconsistent across geographies, it also served to amplify the brand differences across the world. Aline Santos: *'When you have so many differences across all aspects of the brand, the best way to resolve this is to focus on the future, giving time to people to align. If you recognize the cultural differences and realities and then look forward everything is possible, and everyone has the opportunity and time to align.'*

The DIG Global Brand Team worked with the single, inspirational and purposeful positioning: *Unleashing Human Potential.* The brand idea was based on the belief that when kids are developing and learning they will sometimes get dirty – and some parents worry about this. DIG can free mothers from the worry by taking care of the dirt. In other words; the dirt goes, but the learning stays.

Aline Santos: *'DIG is committed to encouraging parents to leave their children free to get dirty and develop. Child Development is the ultimate benefit we want to offer as a brand.'*

To win that crucial internal inspiration and ensure broad understanding and complete company alignment around the global positioning for DIG, the Global Brand Team staged the brand's first-ever global brand immersion summit in early 2007 in South Africa, a significant DIG market.

To bring alive the power of the new positioning, the event even featured an afternoon of restoring an outdoor school playground and sports facility for a suburban Cape Town school. This built tremendous inspiration for the brand vision, and the teamwork ignited urgency around the need for a much closer global collaboration. Of course the event also created an incredible amount of positive rumor around the brand internally.

Since the South Africa conference, the brand has received awards for projects in many countries, including the building of more than 50 new public playgrounds across overcrowded Asian cities – even down to influencing the academic curriculum in Vietnam so that kids now have the right to recess and play.

FOCUSED ON DEVELOPING ONE STRATEGY
Agreement on the first fully aligned DIG global brand strategy was made possible by first explicitly recognizing the varying development stages of the brand across markets. Discussions between the global and local marketing teams became focused on the differing roadmaps required to get to the agreed destination instead of what the vision itself should be. The resulting Dirt is Good vision and

strategy document went on to guide DIG's priorities across all key marketing mix elements at local, regional and global levels.

With the new DIG strategy agreed upon, the global team worked to develop and implement a comprehensive internal engagement plan to win inspiration. The goal was to ensure that all key brand stakeholders quickly felt connected to the brand and the plan, and perhaps, most importantly, understood what was expected of them.

Free mothers from the worry by taking care of the dirt.

BUILDING CAPABILITY FOR SUPERIOR DELIVERY

The success of DIG's first brand stewardship workshop in South Africa helped the DIG Global Brand Team recognize the internal thirst for strategic brand direction and for tools that could help translate the global brand vision into concrete local marketing activities. Central to building DIG's global marketing capability was the creation of the *Dirty Club,* DIG's new global community to support brand stakeholders across the world.

Since its launch in 2007 the *Dirty Club* has employed podcasts, videos and email bulletins to communicate strategy and demonstrate its implementation. The brand's intranet site serves as a one-stop online resource for all brand vision and strategy documents, links to all advertising, and many examples of winning activation programs from around the world. The portal also offers tools and templates for brand planning and market implementation, as well as a DIG phone and email directory to promote global interaction and collaboration.

A second global brand conference was held in 2008, this time hosted in Turkey, another key DIG market. The event was used to further deploy the strategy, force discussions on tactical implications at all levels, and to celebrate the DIG team's successful results on the implementation of the new DIG strategy. Aline Santos: *'The gathering of hundreds of DIG people from all the corners of the world in Turkey was critical to forging the key brand strategies, share new learning, and more importantly connecting to inspire even more success.'*

RESULTS EXCEED EXPECTATIONS
By the end of 2009, DIG's double-digit growth and market share gains in key markets had contributed positively to Unilever's overall performance and made DIG one of Unilever's largest global brands. Motivation to work on the brand is now markedly higher; and DIG's more effective marketing activities have led to recognition and results around the world.

Significantly, DIG's activation programs have generated a huge amount of positive brand publicity, media coverage, and consumer response in many countries. The more global focus and ways of working of the DIG Global brand leaders have led to faster roll out for global programs, and more consistent marketing of the DIG brand around the world.

Today, DIG communications may still differ from market to market – but if this is the case, it is a conscious choice made to reflect differences in market, category or brand development stages, and not just because someone somewhere decided to reinvent the wheel. And the results of a second internal survey showed an enormous rise in internal alignment. There is now almost full understanding of the brand's global vision and strategic objectives and motivation to work on the DIG global brand has increased significantly.

Aline Santos: *'Our job as the Global Brand Team has been to take a great positioning and make it brilliant, give it focus, make it 'real' in all elements of the mix, and win the organization's full support for implementation. By accelerating the global roll out and striving for consistency, we can now truly benefit from our global scale. It's been a tough, but very rewarding journey.'*

The Science Of Getting Connected

And The Art Of Staying That Way

KARIN KOONINGS - HEAD OF INTERNATIONAL BRAND
MARKETING, STARBUCKS COFFEE INTERNATIONAL (2004 - 2008)

Imagine a feared, scolding global brand leader who flies in from HQ to tell a local marketing team how to run their market *just so…*

Sorry, that's just not how Karin Koonings operates.

Which is no doubt why Karin was such a hit in her role as head of international brand marketing at Starbucks Coffee international. When the domestic business began unraveling in 2007 and 2008, 'her' international business was as strong then as it continues to be today. A coincidence? We don't think so.

A Canadian with proud Dutch roots (and conversant in four languages), Karin holds an MBA from The University of Toronto's Rotman School of Business. She also studied marketing, branding, and international relations in Canada, the U.S., and Europe.

An accomplished global marketer by any measure, Karin's rise to the top – like so many of her global peers' – started with 'boot camp' at one of the big global marketing companies. Today, her career spans over 20 years working for both Fortune 500 companies and start-ups.

Karin began her marketing career in Unilever's Cheseborough-Ponds division. While working at Labatt Breweries, she moved onto another global brand, Carlsberg. It wasn't until 1996 that Karin became one of Starbucks's first Canadian marketers, where she carried out any number of progressive marketing assignments, all of which contributed to the swift growth and establishment of Starbucks as a leading global brand.

Once promoted to the role of the company's first Vice President Brand & Marketing for Starbucks International, Karin oversaw a marketing team that represented 43 countries. Among her responsibilities: Driving business results through marketing programs, and building a consistent brand voice and experience across the globe.

Karin's story reads like many of the new global marketing pioneers featured in these pages: '*I think the biggest challenge I had coming into the role was that there was no blueprint; I was literally starting from scratch.*'

In the course of leading the international team, Karin spearheaded the creation of Starbucks International's *Learning Journey* – an internal training program devoted to inspiring brand leadership and building marketing skills and capability across the international business. (Learning Journey focuses both on clarifying business priorities and sharing best practices among similar markets.)

Coming in from a field position in North America, it was natural for Karin to start her global role by focusing first on improving connections between the international brand team and its varied markets and cultures.

Her work proved to be more challenging than was the norm. Starbucks works with many joint ventures, whose business cultures vary across the globe. Quite a few international Starbucks partners weren't, in fact, Starbucks employees.

'Don't forget you're working across many different continents with people who not only have, culturally, different approaches to their work style and how they view their job, but who are sometimes also driven by competing agendas.'

Karin liked to remind her colleagues that Starbucks was in the People-Business-Serving-Coffee – not the other way around. Which is why she believed that personal human connection, not just in stores but among fellow marketing colleagues (or 'partners,' in Starbucks lingo), was integral to the brand's success.

In her international role, Karin spearheaded a massive expansion of Starbucks's worldwide network, helping ensure that the company maintained brand consistency everywhere. Starbucks also strengthened local community relationships, too. Among the programs Karin oversaw were some that focused specifically on community-level outreach efforts. One globally structured program, for instance, helped local companies connect successfully with their neighborhoods and surrounding communities, sometimes at store level.

True to her convictions and after many years of international travel – with itineraries that would make the UN Secretary General feel like a local yokel – Koonings left Starbucks to focus on building iconic and purposeful brands closer to home in the North West, and spend more time with her own family and local community.

STAGES OF CONNECTION

'I never realized what a lonely role this job would be,' is a phrase we hear regularly from the global marketing leaders with whom we work.

And truly, despite the wonders of video conferencing, every global marketing role we know of consists of long stretches of sitting alone in airplanes, restaurants and hotel lobbies. Unless you're into amassing air miles like George Clooney's character, Ryan Bingham, in 'Up in the Air' - *'Let's just say I have set myself a number and I haven't hit it yet'* – travel quickly becomes one of the most difficult aspects of being a global marketer. (Someone recently reminded us that relationships, in general, are still wine-enabled, not Web-enabled.) But while the marketing role may be physically taxing, most global marketers know that we're talking about a different kind of lonely.

How Karin Koonings influenced her Starbucks International team to better connect, and become more outside in-focused, is one of the topics we'll explore in this chapter.

Connecting with internal stakeholders is especially important in complex, matrix organizations. There, leaders won't succeed unless they can achieve their goals by working with, and often through, others. Soren Lund of LEGO candidly concedes that, *'Early on in my career I had to learn the lesson the hard way. Perhaps I thought that having the right answer was all that was required. It took me a while to realize that building relationships, listening better and interacting effectively with all the local leaders was perhaps even more important.'*

Marketers promoted to a global leadership role suddenly find themselves sitting in a sterile desk, often in HQ. They're no longer surrounded by the traditional market success trophies of their previous local marketing role. No more promotion signs adorn the wall. No more sales colleagues stop by to tempt them into going golfing with lead buyers. No more junior market-ers haltingly request help with their first-ever advertising briefs.

At HQ, marketers are more likely to find themselves surrounded by people who don't 'get' marketing and find it tedious, not to mention expensive and inexact. These colleagues from Accounting, Compliance, HR, Legal, and perhaps Supply Chain trade very different war stories at lunch.

If these new colleagues are lured into a conversation about marketing, a couple of things fast become apparent. Firstly that they puzzle over why 'your' brand isn't completely global in its approach; and secondly that they wonder why marketers 'waste' so much money by 'redoing' advertising and innovation. Why not just harmonize the whole deal? Apple does it – why can't you?

As global leaders conduct their first round of market visits, even more pain-ful is the realization that the people with whom they used to have the most fun – their 'marketing buddies' – overnight seem to treat them differently. Or is it just their imagination playing tricks on them?

True, we've exaggerated most of the above to make a point. Yet we've never worked with a single global marketer who didn't reflect on the isolation of the global marketing role. Still, much can be done to counter these com-mon relationship divides.

Folkert Kamphuis of Novartis puts it this way: *'To me personally it's very important to have a connection with my key markets. If they do not know that we at the global level are obsessed with their success, we run the risk of losing their support and without that there is no global business.'*

Question: What do organizations that sustain high performance over time have in common? Answer: They've learned how to mobilize their informal organizations while maintaining and adding formal structures, keeping all elements in sync with one another.

The winning global marketing leaders we've studied instinctively under-stand the power of the informal organization. They demonstrate servant leadership. (We'll be exploring this concept in greater depth later on in this chapter). Not least, they employ a slew of interpersonal skills to fine-tune their global marketing machines.

Degrees Of Separation

A popular (though unproven) social theory maintains that anyone on the planet can connect to any other person via a chain of no more than five intermediary acquaintances. The 'Six Degrees of Separation' between you, us and everyone else in the world is a mind-bending notion, particularly in an information era when our world gets smaller every day.

Let's apply this theory to organizational behavior. You'd assume it would be a total cinch to connect everyone. Considering that the largest multi-national corporations maintain organizational charts and intranet directories, surely adults can handily find one another and work better together – right?

But reality paints a different picture. There's a big difference between making the acquaintance of a room full of new colleagues…and trusting that they share your agenda and can deliver on *their* commitments so you can achieve yours. Our work with global marketing organizations across industries and geographies has uncovered case after case of dysfunctional teamwork, sub-optimal collaboration and a lack of shared purpose and trust… without which there can be no high performance or satisfaction.

Come to think of it, maybe these examples aren't terribly surprising. The tempo at which business has evolved (and continues to evolve) poses formidable challenges to natural interpersonal communication.

For one thing, people remain at their jobs for a shorter period of time. They move on (or are politely or impolitely moved on). Job security is an old-fashioned ideal. Lifelong employment is all but extinct. Performance horizons have diminished from years to quarters. Cost pressures have clamped down on business travel, obliging scattered teams to work across time zones and connect via phone or video-conference.

In fact, as the old saying goes, the only constant nowadays is *change*. To compensate, organizations are churning out more complex structures. By way of illustration: In the course of our *Leading Global Brands* study, we came across marketers who have three solid-line reporting relationships with managers spread over two continents – and who've worked for years with assorted team members without ever having met them face-to-face.

Obviously, getting and staying connected is easier said than done. But we know for sure it's among the most critical drivers of effective global brand leadership.

3 STAGES

Maybe you've read Stephen Covey's *'7 Habits of Highly Effective People'*. We decided to borrow a concept from Covey. It felt relevant, seemed applicable, and since then it's served us well to help bring alive the local-global marketing relationships we encounter.

Here it goes:

Generally speaking, we find three differing stages of global local relationships. The first, which we call 'dependent,' is where global completely dominates what local marketers do. ('*Ahh, bliss…*' we can hear people muttering in the background). But please note: this is *not* where an effective global marketing operation wants to be! The second, which we dub 'independent,' is an energetic, contrarian relationship between local and global. The third, highly desirable, relationship we call 'interdependent.'

Let's dig a little deeper.

OVERLY *DEPENDENT* RELATIONSHIPS

Stephen Covey describes the dependent relationship as similar to the one between a parent and a baby or toddler. In this relationship phase, no one questions parental authority. Now and again, we come across these relationships in the global marketing world. Most often we find them in companies that are going global for the first time, venturing into new and uncharted markets, hiring their first local marketers and trying to work out how to excel at global marketing.

In the 1990s, these relationships were common in fast-developing countries, like those in Eastern Europe. More recently, we've witnessed them taking place between present-day global and local Asian marketing teams. Yet although the dependent relationship may be healthy and appropriate when it occurs between a parent and child (it may even sound appealing to some global marketers), most people want to move past this kind of relationship as fast as possible.

Which is another way of saying that local marketers who merely say 'Yes' are dangerous for companies. Why? They're failing to provide the necessary filters that will ensure a brand's local relevance. The downsides: wasted budgets due to the wrong advertising being run in the wrong market, and customers disgruntled by a company's apparent indifference. Success can't happen unless all global strategies parcel in a local reality filter (which begins with understanding local consumers and developing tailored market strategies that recognize local verities).

It's a good thing that very few markets stay in this phase for long.

PAINFULLY *INDEPENDENT* RELATIONSHIPS

We borrow again from Stephen Covey to take a look at the typical relationship between parents and their teenage children. Sure, teenagers respect their parents deep-down, yet at the same time they seem determined to prove Mom or Dad dead-wrong.

Sad to say, in the global marketing organizations we serve, we regularly come across similar relationships between local and regional, or between regional and global. Paradoxically, no matter which client we're working with, 'teenager countries' tend to be places that are mature from a market development standpoint, with experienced, well-educated marketers in charge.

'Independent' teenagers are those countries that, after reminding you of their share of global sales, then make a detailed case about how your global strategy won't work in their market. These marketers have the wherewithal to hire their own agencies – then 'suddenly' appear to have misunderstood earlier agreements by developing their own campaigns without anyone else knowing. On occasion, these countries have even duplicated research to show that various innovations developed and tested in their own markets will flounder.

Countries that often appear on this list include the U.K. and the U.S. (whenever global HQ is based outside the country), and to a lesser extent, France and Germany. Japan also makes frequent appearances on this roster (yet the thing is, almost every global team agrees that the Japanese market really *is* different).

One MD quipped that in the past there would be a fight with the French about whether or not their market was different. *'This has now been resolved. We now agree on the point that they are different, but we still treat them the same!'*

When the global team and a handful of big local countries find themselves stuck in the independent phase, we quite simply recommend they go back to square one, and start all over again. Quite simply, there's not enough trust (which isn't to say that this stalemate came out of nowhere).

Both local and global marketing leaders are responsible for evolving a relationship to the next level of development: the interdependent relationship.

BLISSFULLY *INTERDEPENDENT* RELATIONSHIPS

The most effective global marketing leaders we know – like Karin Koonings at Starbucks – understand that succeeding in global marketing is a two-way street. They're able to distinguish between their most important markets, and those that really need to go with the plan set out for their cluster of countries.

In Covey terms, interdependent marketing alliances are akin to the relationship between two adults who respect, enjoy and learn from each other. The markets that regularly make it onto this list are more or less consistent. Most global marketers claim their most fruitful relationships are with countries like Canada, Brazil, Turkey, the Netherlands and Portugal.

Why is this? We're not entirely sure (we must also confess that our quantitative Leading Global Brands database can't back up this theory, either). Our guess is that the marketers in these countries are likely to be highly educated, experienced, well-traveled and at ease working beyond national borders. Another theory: while these countries may be small, with the exception of Brazil, each one has a rich heritage of collaborating outside its borders.

An interdependent marketing relationship is one often characterized by learning going both ways. Local teams are typically open and hospitable to global and regional input, and also take the trouble to share their experience with others, including codifying the details of successful local programs. What global team can't benefit accordingly? If and when interdependent local countries push back, the global team takes it seriously – and the two of them eventually collaborate on a workable solution.

WHAT TO LOOK FOR

As we mentioned earlier, at the start of a project in any company, we recommend conducting an assessment to identify the biggest opportunities and challenges to address.

Among the first areas to begin probing is an organization's degree of connectivity. Commonly, its a good idea to reach out to the top 5 or so marketing directors around the world and ask them what the global team or CMO is focusing on nowadays. It doesn't take long to gain a sense of whether or not these leaders feel as though the others in the organization understand their market reality. Even more critically, does the organization recognize their priorities by adopting them as the *global* teams' priorities?

Where, and by whom, are the biggest contributions taking place? Locally? Regionally? Globally?

In addition, make it a point to ask the local marketers, all of whom are in the quantitative survey, if they feel global and regional marketers genuinely understand the needs and realities of their specific markets. If the answer is no, the challenge is obvious (and it begins with both parties sitting down and listening). Also probe to understand whether – and how well – the local team understands the brand's vision, mission, and global strategy.

As well, ask the organization's marketing stakeholders whether there's sufficient cross-regional and cross-discipline communication and collaboration to deliver against the stated brand and business objectives. Hard to believe, but in many companies, when a local marketer is asked how they can deliver feedback on a globally developed program, they have next to no idea!

Finally (and this may ultimately be a gut call), determine the overall level of trust among individuals, no matter where they're stationed.

What It Takes To Connect

Becoming a well-connected organization, creating genuine trust, and achieving sufficient interdependent relationships across the global marketing community, takes hard work. In our experience, it demands two very differing but equally important traits that all global brand marketers must adopt:

1   SERVANT LEADERSHIP MINDSET
2   LOOKING FOR SIMILARITIES MINDSET

By far the most important trait affecting the successful adoption of a new and more global marketing strategy or organization is the prevailing organizational mindset. Many of the companies we work with come from a past of highly successful and separate regional or national operating companies. Each was a kingdom, even an empire. Country heads were Chairmen or Chairwomen. A promotion to the head of a country's marketing or general management role was akin to ascending to the throne. As we look at what distinguishes the successful global marketing organization, the overall mindsets regarding global collaboration consistently turn out to be instrumental to winning.

Servant Leadership Mindset

In his 1970 essay, 'The Servant as Leader' Robert K. Greenleaf created the concept of the 'servant leadership movement.' According to one website, great servant leaders show unusual character, place others before themselves, are skillful communicators and compassionate collaborators, use foresight, and are systems thinkers as well as natural moral authorities.

As opposed to a leadership approach with a top-down hierarchical style, servant leadership emphasizes collaboration, trust, empathy and the ethical use of power. At core, these leaders are first and foremost servants.

They've made a conscious decision to lead in order to better serve others (as opposed to enhancing their own power). Their ultimate goal is to nurture the growth of individuals in the organization while increasing teamwork and personal involvement.

We feel strongly that all marketers in an organization should perceive the global brand leader and CMO as servant leaders. The role of these servants is clear. Since no such thing as a global market exists, the marketing heads in each of the key local markets need to know that the global team truly understands their competitive, consumer and retail realities – and that the global team is working nonstop to help the local team win under these market conditions. The top five markets, of course, represent 60 to 80 percent of sales. If you don't win those, you don't win, period! (These top five may well include one or two up-and-coming markets that show room for growth; needless to say, no global brand we know doesn't have China written in large on its 'key markets' list.)

That said, global marketing leaders and their teams need to understand that theirs is not at all a *'tell-me-what-to-do'* relationship. Once a global leader has taken the trouble to understand what key markets need, it's perfectly acceptable, and in fact *required*, to make a decision that doesn't quite deliver against any one of the specific briefs given at local level. Local heads understand that working in a global market requires give-and-take. Usually they'll understand, and buy into, any given global decision if global leaders not only listen to them, but invite them to participate in the strategic planning process.

Here's where the *leadership* part of the mindset comes into play. Our CEO Stef Gans likes to say that all employees deserve real leadership. A strategic framework is comforting. A CEO works to deliver shareholder value, and typically reports to a Board. A CMO helps contribute to the overall business objectives. A global brand leader has a brand whose portfolio role he or she has to fulfill. Great global marketing leaders listen, analyze, discuss...then decide. In our view, there should always be one person who 'owns' the vision for a market and for a brand.

'When we started reaching out to key stakeholders and asking them 'How can I help you to win in the market with OMO?' we immediately noticed a difference. *Just because we were asking* we were already making a difference. And the answers helped my team develop a much better global strategy.'

ALINE SANTOS - VP, OMO GLOBAL, UNILEVER

Therefore, if someone produces any significant work (whether it's in advertising, innovation or new packaging) that is pointedly 'off-brand,' we feel it's imperative that someone, somewhere, should be getting really steamed! If you lack that certain someone in your organization, frankly you're in trouble. Often this person is the company founder – Morita-san in Sony, Jobs at Apple, Walton at Walmart – but as time goes on, and companies grow and ripen, this role often falls to marketing.

Stephen Quinn, the CMO of Walmart, remembers what it took to get this notion accepted within the world's largest retailer. *'One of the keys to the success in our particular case was finding new expressions of what Sam Walton probably would have done, or did in fact say or do back in his era.'*

He also stresses the importance of picking your battles carefully: *'As a marketer that operates in a complex organization you need to be open and flexible. You have to be able to influence people. At first the other disciplines in this company were wondering why marketing wanted to be in all these meetings. Over time I think we earned some respect and now we are crafting what the brand wants to stand for. That motivates the marketers on the team, and me.'*

Servant leadership is just as much about setting the vision – and communicating that same vision clearly and efficiently. It's about making sure that everyone around the organization understands the basics, the brand mission and the things that are 'fixed' – e.g., not to be tweaked, altered, folded, spindled, mutilated, or changed by anyone. Our colleague Terry Rosenquist always tells us to glean lessons from P&G. If you are the product manager of Tide in Argentina and you detest the color orange, well, unfortunately there's no 1-800 number to call. If you disagree with Steve Jobs on how to launch the latest iPhone, well, *hasta la vista.* Learn to make do, or leave.

To sum up: Servant leadership is a mindset that requires relinquishing some of the traditional reins of power. It's less about direction and power than it is about good listening, strategic influencing, and empowering others in their roles around the global marketing organization. On leaders' parts, it requires a maturity that ultimately makes sound business sense. The alternative? A bunch of smart but unrealistic strategies that sit somewhere in a drawer at HQ.

Looking For Similarities Mindset

Typically we can tell (usually within five minutes) whether we've entered the premises of an organization where the overarching mindset is to seek similarities – or to ferret out differences. As a lens through which to look at the marketing world, this first impression colors all aspects of the marketing mix and organizational spectrum.

Is the glass half-full or half-empty? Are your brand's global consumers similar – or radically different? Naturally, there's no hard and fast answer or truth. It comes down to perspective, and mindset. And if your goal is to be an effective global marketing organization, only one mindset need apply.

We've all sat in on global marketing meetings where someone stands up and begins to explain how different his or her market is - how global trends are irrelevant to events taking place in *this* market, and how future global trends simply don't apply. We're not saying that some of this may not be true, but isn't it all about what you're aiming to achieve? If the goal is to beat competition by increasing global leverage, achieving economies of scale, faster roll outs and lower costs, then global alignment on objectives and ultimate vision is an absolute necessity. Otherwise, why are we even having this conversation?

In the end, it comes right down to making the case for working more globally – and determining who's aboard the 'going global' bus, and who's not. It's the responsibility of the CMO, or the head of global marketing, to shepherd the key players in the organization through a sound strategic case that makes this necessity clear. Whether it's about cost reduction; the changing nature of competition; the need to increase speed to market; the simplification of the supply chain; or the clustering of resources to fund real Innovation (or a bigger, better communication campaign), the CMO or the head of global marketing has to make a sound, well-defined case.

The very top of the company needs to visibly support the premise that working more globally is required in order to survive, or win. Why? Because the absence of alignment at board level allows naysayers to start playing the system. Once leaders have clearly communicated this new way of working more globally, they'll then have to map out the details; e.g. what's the strategy as it rolls down, and who does what precisely (more about this in later chapters). A well-connected global marketing head will swiftly spot the people who are resisting the premise, or scheming to show that 'more global' is the wrong strategy. Now's the time to act. Whether you see it as an act of ceremonial slaughter or one borne of pure necessity, we strongly advise you to stamp out resistance sooner rather than later.

It helps that others perceive the leader who embodies the new, more global strategy as someone who has truly tried to bring someone onboard. Nonetheless, a leader has to make a hard, swift choice. Is this person in or out? Any indecision will hamper and damage everything else later.

An organization that seeks similarities is a wondrous thing to behold. Imagine local teams informing global that they understand most of the components of the proposed mix, but feel the best bet would be to adapt two or three to better serve their local markets. (Conversations tend to start with 'How can we...?') The result? Global leaders better understand a key market – and local teams are able to leverage global insights.

Leading By Example

Occasionally, new leaders erroneously believe that asking questions somehow diminishes their ability to show future leadership (as if they're supposed to have all the answers already). We believe the opposite is true. Our advice? Lead by asking the right questions. Oblige your local teams to reflect on what's important. Our colleague Kimberly Orton always reminds her clients that asking questions now - and listening with an open mind - will give them the license to lead with decisions later.

Pieter Nota of Beiersdorf notes the basics of global team best practice: 'I always make sure that when I travel to the different markets, I get an opportunity to meet both marketing and sales teams. It's important to connect across both.'

On a strategic planning level, we believe it's fairly easy to create a shared sense of urgency around the need to work more globally in marketing. We've organized and facilitated countless global marketing strategy sessions where global and key local marketing heads kicked things off by comparing the outside in 5C marketing environment (Context, Consumers, Customers, Competitors, and Company). Often they find that on one hand the brand's biggest opportunities and challenges are consistent across geographies. At the same time, the competitive environment reveals that a more global approach is, in the end, the only viable strategic option.

You can achieve this goal if you adopt the view that in the Internet Age, the world is shrinking for consumers...so why shouldn't the people inside the organizations become just connected? You can progress from endless debates about Should-We-Go-Global? to mature discussions around possibilities, e.g., the extent to which local markets can both gain flexibility and respond to local events on the ground. Rob Malcolm of Diageo says that *'the more time I spend working on global brands and multiple markets, the more interesting I find the puzzle of how to solve for different consumer and cultural nuances and needs while operating on a global scale.'*

What Success Looks Like: Trust

Ultimately it all comes down to earning respect and trust. Says Lennard Hoornik of Sony Ericsson, *'The key point is that people trust each other, right? That my colleague at Sony Ericsson in Indonesia, for example, trusts that there will be a campaign relevant to him/her coming from marketing, and in a timely manner.'*

Later on, we'll talk more about the importance of aligning key performance metrics and important leader's personal performance targets. But it's also worth bringing up now. We often find that there's a major disconnect between the targets at global and local levels. Did we mention that this disconnect also fosters distrust? If an organization measures a global team exclusively on the delivery of innovations on time for launch (bypassing whether or not the launched products succeed in market or not), it can create an incentive to meet the timeline, at the expense of quality. (Now we know why local marketers are so wary of statements such as, 'Of course this will work in your market!') After the recent financial meltdown, the financial markets created so-called clawbacks systems, to recoup erroneously paid bonuses. But are there any similar precautions within marketing?

Global marketers have taken on additional shared targets with local colleagues and key local marketing heads. Target-sharing and transparency work wonders to foster trust between teams around the world.

Checking The Pulse

It's very important to regularly reach out across the total audience and get a temperature check on the health of the relationship, the connection.

Says Marianne Schoenauer of Unilever, 'I have this conversation twice a year with every SVP, where I actually show on the basis of statistics how engaged their teams are, how they are connected with the leadership, and how they respond to leadership messages, how they use online facilities in terms of learning, in terms of latest insights sharing, and tools that the category is developing. We have some clear measures that are discussed twice a year with the category leaders and their partners in order to adjust future plans. The metrics clearly indicate success or not in connecting the different brand stakeholders.'

Kicking things off by building open, connected, transparent connections across organizations is (by a long shot) the very best way we know.

STARBUCKS IS ABUZZ
ABOUT GLOBAL GROWTH

Starbucks is the largest coffeehouse company in the world, with over 17,000 stores in 49 countries, including more than 11,000 in the U.S. alone. From its launch in 1971 as a Seattle-based coffee bean roaster and retailer, the company has expanded at the speed of light. During the 1990s, Starbucks opened a new store every day, a pace that continued into the 21st century. How? By establishing a set of clear guiding principles (marketing, branding, and operational) that allow Starbucks's employees around the world to work together as one.

When Karin Koonings took on the role of Vice President of Marketing, Starbucks Coffee International, global marketing was hardly in place. At the time, Starbucks was a young, upcoming brand with a successful U.S.-based foundation. Going global meant opening new stores, focusing on delivering consistent product and service at store level; and establishing collaboration among various marketing teams around the world.

Although the company was expanding more quickly outside the U.S. than domestically, all marketing ideas and practices originated from the U.S. (the nerve center for all international operations). Moreover, the Seattle-based International team was all-American. This U.S.-out thinking didn't sit well with Karin. Instinctively she understood that Starbucks's future would be based on the common strength of international operations, and the very best ideas, whether they originated in the U.S. or elsewhere.

China, Brazil, Egypt, India, and Russia were the new meccas of growth and success – but only if Starbucks made the right connections. Relationships were important. What were each region's priorities? Karin immediately set about making things right at the Support Center.

'When I joined Starbucks Coffee International, I made it a priority to build a team that would connect with and provide substantive support to our international markets, while at the same time affording them the flexibility to engage their communities in ways that were locally relevant. We have made a lot of progress toward better understanding and delivering against our markets' needs.'

First things first: Karin decided to focus on improving relationships with the company's regional teams. The key? Listening to their needs and problems –

in person, face-to-face, no matter where it took her. Karin returned from her global travels buzzing with ideas. She launched international rotational assignments for all marketing and communications employees – and continued to maintain direct, almost weekly, personal contact with each of the five key regional colleagues.

Having reviewed and analyzed what regional and local marketers were telling her, Karin concluded that there were significant and important similarities across various regions. As the company expanded globally, she could boil down its challenges to half-a-dozen or so. Recalls Koonings, *'The more you can take the opinions and 'not invented here' out of the equation and get people to focus on tools, commonalities, and the things that are universally applicable, the more effective your marketing organization will be.'*

Significant and important similarities across various regions

Disparate time zones proved to be no match for Starbucks's re-launched international team's zeal and enthusiasm. Karin organized new, regular marketing and communications immersion sessions. Before long, the regional teams and the Support Center had established a much closer working relationship.

Now it was time to expand the focus of the international marketing team. Karin and her regional colleagues – now meeting on a quarterly basis to agree upon strategy – commissioned a global marketing effectiveness benchmarking exercise to identify what key global marketing opportunities and challenges they should address. What did key general managers need from their marketing colleagues to support the company's rapidly accelerating global expansion? What information, support, tools and training did global, regional and local marketers require in order to carry out their jobs faster and more effectively?

The benchmarking also contrasted Starbucks's core marketing practices to leading-edge global marketing programs - and identified areas where the company needed to focus during this phase of rapid expansion.

Karin was excited to see that the Brand Benchmark results revealed that the Starbucks brand generated a high level of inspiration *everywhere*. Not only that, but marketers worldwide recognized the opportunity of working together more closely globally.

Until that point, country marketers had functioned more or less independently. This was natural; they'd been left alone. In other cases, exploiting the absence of alignment between regional and global marketers, they'd seized the opportunity to do things their own way. Those days were over. Recalls Koonings:
'The global marketing benchmark brought the regional and central support teams closer. It was clear that countries saw us as one, it helped our teams become more outside–in focused.'

In short order, Karin and her regional colleagues set out to develop what would become Starbucks's first overall global marketing strategy. Comparing brand objectives and the competitive situation across regions – and agreeing on one list of prioritized strategic activities – provided a breakthrough.

Among the key areas of opportunity the benchmarking study revealed was that Starbucks should roll out certain core marketing skills quickly globally, such as new store launch management. The study also emphasized the need to align the execution of these programs across all markets.

In collaboration with regional marketing units, this finding led to the development of a single international training agenda. Here, the roles were clearly delegated. The Seattle-based team would create the training programs, while the regional heads would manage their execution. It was an approach that proved to be enormously effective.

Karin wasn't done yet. She and her team launched a brand-immersion program to help marketers worldwide understand and share manifestations of the Starbucks brand values. Starbucks also launched a newsletter designed to facilitate the communication of global marketing objectives and best practices. Local teams now had a convenient platform to share their best programs for the overall benefit of other markets.

BUILDING CONNECTIONS FOR GROWTH

Does Karin recognize the common 'loneliness' aspect of the global role? *'Absolutely...'* she says with a smile. *'I felt pretty much the same way for at least the first year of my job. I don't think there were many people in the company that fully understood the challenge. But I have to say that this feeling is far behind me now. Working more closely with colleagues responsible for global category (food, beverage, and product) management and innovation and, most importantly, my regional marketing colleagues have helped us all see and share the same goals.'*

'Together we have found that leveraging global programs is precisely what local markets want. It stops them from having to reinvent the wheel – which is costly and time consuming for them – and frees them up to focus on the things that help them create local programs that connect with their customers and communities. A balance of global leverage and local relevance has made everyone's life a lot easier, more productive and, frankly, more fun!'

The Magic Of Inspiration

Igniting The Organization

BRITISH AIRWAYS

KERRIS BRIGHT – CHIEF MARKETING OFFICER, BRITISH AIRWAYS

Kerris Bright, Chief Marketing Officer of British Airways is a global marketing leader whose motivating support team members can always count on – but only if they're prepared! If raw intellect mixed with real empathy is a key characteristic of effective global brand leaders, Kerris fits the bill.

Could it be because she received a degree in Biology, plus a PhD in Molecular Neuroscience from the University of Sussex? Ever intent on uncovering a novel angle en route to reaching a solution, and drilling down to expose an issue's root cause, Kerris is driven by a deep desire to learn, evolve and excel. Just ask her colleagues about the relentless way she challenges everyone around her (not to mention herself).

Like so many of the leaders we've profiled in this book, Kerris began her career in 1991 as a marketing graduate trainee with one of the big marketing companies, in Kerris's case: Unilever. After spending three years with Quest International, she migrated to the company's consumer healthcare division, where she held senior roles in Marketing and General Management.

Home-based in London, these days Kerris spends most of her working life thinking about flying as opposed to actually doing it. Interestingly, Kerris only first boarded a plane when she was in her early twenties. But she quickly got into the new habit – she was a BA Gold Card holder only a couple of years later, and hasn't stopped circling the globe since. Her motivation? *'I just love travelling and working in international businesses. Learning about different cultures and working with teams from across the globe really gives me a kick.'*

Before Kerris joined British Airways she was Chief Marketing Officer for AkzoNobel's global Decorative Paints business. It was a role she took on after ICI Paints (where she'd served as CMO) was taken over by AkzoNobel. Having joined ICI Paints in 2001 as U.K. Marketing Director, Kerris was responsible for the brand development and activation of many well-known DIY brands but most importantly - Dulux. At the time a famous, but somewhat jaded British paint brand that desperately needed to increase its relevancy to its consumers. Who said anything about a striking resemblance with the brand she has just sunk her teeth in to?. And that was her first great contribution: adding color to the Dulux brand.

As CMO of ICI Paints and AkzoNobel, Kerris built significant market success, recognition and respect for the transformation of the marketing organization. It took her just a few years, and a CEO approach to build a highly effective global marketing machine. Capability building was a focus point for her but she also introduced a global approach to market segmentation, brand portfolio strategy development and brand positioning: through these approaches the opportunity to build a global Dulux brand was identified.

Looking back on the transformation she now says *'The big motivation for me in leading AkzoNobel from a multi-local to a more global way of working was to unleash the potential that I could see in the organization to support the development of fewer, bigger, better ideas that could drive faster growth. And to create an organization that became a much more exciting place to work because teams could be part of a greater whole, working towards a bigger ambition and working and learning from others in different countries with different cultures.'*

Although the restructuring of AkzoNobel's marketing organization, processes and ways of working were probably Kerris's biggest accomplishment around the how of global marketing – she will most likely be remembered even more for the accomplishment on the *what*, that is the purpose of the Dulux brand and AkzoNobel Paint business.

Her legacy: Leaving behind a far more motivated, inspired marketing organization than the one she'd joined only five years earlier. For Kerris, the development and implementation of the now-famous 'Let's Color' campaign was a personal mission. By rolling up her sleeves and setting an example in locales ranging from the neighborhoods in Rio to the inner townships of France and cities in India, she showed that AkzoNobel's initiative wasn't just another marketing idea, or advertising campaign, but a living reflection of her personal and business beliefs.

As Kerris today says; *'Our greatest idea has been the development of a purposeful positioning for Dulux: the brand idea is based on a powerful universal truth about the magical power of paint and color to not only transform spaces but to impact our spirits and how we feel. We believe we sell tins of optimism, not just tins of paint – and can add color to people's lives'.*

TAPPING INTO LATENT RESOURCES

Brand inspiration? Obviously, Kerris Bright's work at AkzoNobel made a dramatic difference. Think about it: Inspired customers. Inspired consumers. Inspired employees. So what does it take to fire up a similar level of energy and enthusiasm?

Imagine the following scenario. One day, your Chief Financial Officer strolls into your office with a surprise for you: he's dug up an additional 25 percent of your pre-existing budget. So long as you're willing to put in a little extra work to tap into these funds, they're yours in six months. We don't know a lot of people who'd walk away from that deal.

Then again, we *do* know some people who would. We see it happen over and over again. Inspiration is the critical X-factor that can impel the human spirit to push beyond limiting beliefs – to strive to do more and be more. Why? It's very simple. Because things matter more.

From our perspective, inspiring an organization is among the most over-looked, underused drivers of effective global brand leadership. Sure, every-one likes to talk about the importance of motivating the members of the team. Yet the sad truth (or exciting opportunity, depending on how you look at it) is that few leaders bother to pluck this low-hanging fruit.

If global marketing leaders emphasize inspiration, we believe that there's roughly 25 percent of extra energy and ideas up for grabs. We call it *'shower time,'* or *'stuck in traffic time.'* It's when a 9-to-5 employee glances absently through a newspaper. It's when he or she is in a woodwork shop, riding a bike, pedaling on a Stairmaster, or volunteering for a local charity. That's when inspiration tends to strike (or, to paraphrase John Lennon, inspiration is what happens when you're making other plans).

So what if teams around the world applied merely a portion of inspiration behind their brands?

Recognizing The Opportunity

Time and again, we've found that successful global marketing organizations and brands inspire consumers, trade partners, and internal stakeholders with a vision that defines how a brand can thrive, and make a genuine difference in the world. Key stakeholders who are ignited by a brand's vision and strategy often achieve the seemingly impossible. They surprise (and elate) brand leaders with ideas and actions that go well beyond the call of duty.

Years ago, we were told the story of how Orange, the U.K. mobile operator, got its start. Its founders imagined and created Orange as a 'Robin Hood' challenger to two U.K. incumbents – British Telecom and Vodafone. (They knew it would take a lot to thrash these two massive players.) The Orange marketing team went to enormous pain to create a strong brand positioning. The team also rolled out employee engagement programs to ensure that every staff member knew precisely what *kind* of challenger the company aspired to be. Could Orange translate that mindset and those behaviors to their own line of business within the company?

A week or so later, a financial manager conversant with the brand program walked up to Orange's marketing manager. Granted, we weren't there, but evidently, the conversation went something like this:

'You know that presentation you gave about how we were going to be like a Robin Hood in the mobile phone market?'

'Yes – what about it?'

'Well, I have been thinking some more about it. And I actually discussed it with my wife last night...and she also agrees, we need someone to shake things up, both the other players clearly have too much power – they don't seem to care about the consumer at all. Last month my wife got a 40 pound bill, and she hardly used her phone that month.'

By now, we can imagine that the marketing manager was secretly thinking, *Why Don't You Go Back to Your 3rd Floor Cubicle and Leave Me Alone?* Yet he was taken aback by what the financial manager said next: *'And my wife's story got me thinking. And something is troubling me. Let me ask you: Why is it, if we want to be the challenger brand in the category that we overcharge about 35 percent of all of our consumers every month?'*

Turns out this was (and often still is) common practice. Many consumers go into a shop, buy a phone, and find themselves stuck with a monthly rate plan that's wrong for their needs. The phone company knows this very well – after all, they monitor consumers' call behaviors – but why bother addressing a faulty service plan if it boosts their profits?

That deceptively simple lunchtime conversation was pivotal. From then on, Orange changed the way it calculated consumers' bills. Thanks to a boost of accompanying publicity that also drove share gain, Orange became the first U.K. mobile phone company that adapted consumers' monthly rate plans based on their actual call behaviors.

For us, the Orange story shows what every marketer should be fighting hard to unleash: the power of inspired colleagues. Only when everyone who matters within the organizations 'gets' what the brand stands for, and is inspired to bring it alive in every way possible, can a brand really showcase its magic.

In short, winning global marketing leaders inspire their organizations. Believe it!

What To Look For

When we engage with a new client for the first time, almost immediately we begin looking for team inspiration. Yes, inspiration begins at the top – but generally, winning leaders are invigorated about what they want their organization to stand for, and what road they'll take to get there.

We'll go so far as to say that inspiration begins at reception. Are employees fired up about their company, or are they simply tiredly manning a desk? When he once asked a janitor at NASA about his role in the company, Stephen Covey once famously described the man's response: *'I help send people to the moon.'*

As part of an assessment, we recommend probing: How well does everyone in the organization understand a brand's vision? Are they proud to work there? Do they believe the brand makes a positive difference in consumers' lives? Do they recognize how they can make a difference?

Inspiration can unlock energy and effort in limitless ways. Imagine, for example, employees who are so proud of their work they discuss it with their friends and family members – and continuously mull over how they can deliver value. Imagine team members who hold one another accountable to higher standards because they believe that only the best will do. Imagine a collective energy that literally inspires new ways of collaboration, not to mention entirely new perspectives.

That's the part about inspiration we like and admire most. You never know how, and in what form, it'll show up. Which is – not to be corny here –inspiring by itself.

Making It Personal

Inspiration is personal. Which is why great global marketing leaders make it their business to make it personal – over and over again. Starting at the top to gain company-wide endorsement, leaders must first ensure that the organization expresses a brand vision in such a way that colleagues not only connect with the brand but personalize it.

Effective global marketing leaders understand this instinctively. They make time for it. They'll fight to make it happen. At the peak of the 2009 financial crisis, almost no one was willing to spend money on global conferences. Most companies had deemed expenses wasteful.

But Dirt is Good's Aline Santos – who was only in her second year of building a single global brand out of countless smaller regional and national brands - thought differently. This, even though the word on the street inside Unilever was that the CFO had personally insisted that her conference should not go ahead.

But Aline made it personal. She went straight to CEO Patrick Cescau to make her argument. The crux of her reasoning? We're being penny-wise and pound-foolish. How could people from all over the world possibly work as one team when they'd never met even once? Saving three hundred thousand dollars in travel, when this particular multi-billion-dollar brand was poised to grow by hundreds of millions of dollars that year, simply wasn't smart economizing. Aline was persuasive, the event proceeded, and today 'Dirt is Good' is among Unilever's fastest-growing brands.

But how many Aline Santoses are there in the world?

Personal inspiration begins with the knowledge of what you're trying to achieve. The best global brand leaders know that inspiration begins with a universal insight and a real purpose that can both attract consumers and ignite the passion of employees who work with the brand.

Real Purpose Inspires

Time and again, we come back to the same conclusion: *Purpose Inspires.* Another one of our clients sells a smoking cessation product. The team knows the product saves lives. They've created wall charts around the office on which they showcase and celebrate the number of lives they've extended within a quarter. By correlating their sales to the actual lives they've saved, they can see clearly how their work makes a real difference across the world.

If inspiration has such a game-changing impact, one can't help wondering: why don't more companies uncover their own 'proudest moment'?
The reasons are familiar. Lack of time. Lack of management will. Lack of corporate focus. Lack of leadership alignment. Above all, organizations tend to underestimate the amount of 'up-for-grabs' energy and ideas they have at their disposal. Sure, pride and inspiration matter, but are they really worth all that extra work and effort?

The fact is, when it comes to inspiration, pride and purpose, a company often neglects to give them the resources they need, and often ask a global team's most junior members to lead the charge (most of the time not very well, either). The result? Internal stakeholders become just as skeptical about brand messages as their external counterparts.

But mark our words: as economies advance, developed markets are seeing a natural, general shift towards service-based businesses. As well, brands are more and more becoming 'experience' brands that deliver value in ways that transcend their functional benefits. Which means that alignment and excellence in the company's execution become even more important.

Today, though, organizations can no longer control consumers' brand experiences or perceptions. The brand experience is far more variable and people-based. Companies are increasingly segmenting their markets by consumer experiences and values, rather than by sizes or sectors. The emergence of service-led companies, multiple channels to market and globalization all serve to make managing the brand experience more subtle, value-focused, and harder to achieve consistently.

Doing What It Takes

So what does it take to inspire well? What's the key to unlocking this latent energy from within the organization? The bottom line is this: *Think of your internal audience as potentially your most valuable customers anywhere. These days, many companies segment their client base into several categories. Typically there's a Most Valuable category. Well, that's who your team members are – and then some!*

As global marketing leaders strive to inform, equip and inspire their teams to create a better future, they'll find themselves drawing on some of today's tried-and-tested principles.

For one thing, leveraging one's own experience is key in building credibility. Jennifer Davidson of Molson Coors believes that, *'It's important that you have the respect of the team from the get-go. And one of the key drivers for that is that you need to have walked in their shoes. In my case, I've managed the brand in Canada. Plus I had a lot of other experience in the beer business.'*

If experience is the foundational factor, charisma and communication skills are the icing on the cake. Creating and sustaining a sense of momentum helps, too.

One way to pursue and preserve momentum is to focus relentlessly on adding value with each and every interaction among global, regional and

'I think that the Marketing Leader of the future is the man or woman who leads and inspires *with purpose.*

Who builds brands to be *purposeful.*

Who recognizes that the brand's success will be about *more than just sales.*

This will become more and more crucial!'

MARC MATHIEU, SVP GLOBAL BRAND MARKETING, THE COCA-COLA COMPANY (2003 - 2008) local teams. Establishing clear agreements between global and local teams on what's fixed and what's (potentially) loose, is another source of inspiration in and of itself – in much the same way that creative teams appreciate the possibilities provided by a tight brief.

Too often global marketing leaders forget that simply being part of a huge global marketing team can inspire their colleagues. Seeing and hearing stories about the brand you're working on from colleagues on the other side of the globe often works wonders, too. (Swapping experience never hurts, either.)

That said, we can't ignore the plain truth that among the biggest inspirations is...*success!* This may feel like the-chicken-or-the-egg conundrum, but it's one that also prevents many leaders from celebrating early wins. Imagine structuring the biggest, seemingly unachievable challenges in achievable steps, where leaders can measure and commemorate progress. It's all about thinking big, and defining the steps, the timing and the key performance indicators...then celebrating every single successful step of the way.

Finally, it must be said that some categories are quite simply more inspiring than others and that some brands have more 'badge value' than others.

Soren Lund of LEGO for one, counts his blessings: *'I think that LEGO, because it connects so strongly with something innate in human beings and specifically with kids, enables us to have some of the most inspired employees around. Everyone in the company is motivated to get it right, and it's infectious.'*

Granted, Soren has a leg up on many other categories, but having said that, we've seen inspired consumers and colleagues working in such categories as paint, car stereos, washing powder and margarine. So there!

When all these factors come together – prior experience; respect for other people's time and capabilities; communication and real collaboration; the strategic framework that a suitably tight brief accords – something good happens. People are energized. Motivation soars. Passion flows. Commitment is given – and honored.

Having said all this, we do have some practical tips from experience.

Not All Employees Are Made Equal

Employees of every stripe stroll down the hallways of companies daily. Each brings his or her own perspective of the company's brand. Each differs in his or her willingness to do something that champions that brand.

We generally create clusters around three main groups:

Brand Builders are people who spend a significant amount of their time on the brand. As we see it, via their actions, they can make or break a brand. Thus, they need to understand thoroughly the context, vision and strategy of the brand – as well as how what they do plays a role in the value created for the end-consumer. This group generally includes all marketing, communication and product development teams.

Brand Champions are people who deal with the brand in the context of the overall business. They can hurt or support that same brand by giving it, or depriving it, of time or resources. Typically included in this group? Senior members of the company, such as the board; the heads of other departments (such as R&D and Creative); and sales force members who need to sell-in the brand to customers. These stakeholders may require less information and detail about the brand, but at the same time, it's crucial for them to have an overall favorable – and supportive – view of the brand's accomplishments and goals.

Brand Supporters are comprised of all other team members whose support the brand needs in order to achieve its long-term ambitions. This group typically includes all company support staff, as well as retail partners.

Once you've clustered your internal target audiences, your next goal is to map where you need them to be in terms of *awareness, mindsets,* and *behaviors.* This requires rigorous analysis. It starts by identifying the key opportunity gaps (versus the current reality) within the agreed-upon company, or brand strategy. To assess contemporary reality, you may need to carry out an assessment to understand what stakeholders think, know and do with your brand on a daily basis.

Then when you've defined the top-10 internal communication challenges, begin mulling over the channels available to you inside the company. (We say *inside*, but in the past, we've gone so far to suggest that a CEO or CMO conduct an interview with an external publication to grab the attention of key company stakeholders. Reading an article about a CEO's new mission can be far more compelling than hearing yet another annual Chairman's presentation.)

As far as internal channels are concerned, here are some worth considering:

GLOBAL BRAND SESSIONS

A global brand session is the term we use for bringing together the top leaders and managers of a global brand for a few days of immersion and strategy clarification. These sessions typically bring together marketers and their colleagues in development and other key disciplines to focus on where the brand wants to go, how the brand fits in the overall company strategy, what the key strategic thrusts are for the year or two ahead and what is expected from everyone in the room moving forward. When developed well, these sessions can be hotbeds of idea and experience exchange and highly motivating for the different brand players that usually sit alone in their own country.

This is perhaps the most costly, but also the most effective 'channel' in our experience because they can be real 'change' events. What better way to inspire a large group of marketers and their colleagues to engage with the brand and think through and commit to how they themselves can best contribute? The Orange and DIG examples demonstrate how effective these events can be. When managed well, global brand sessions can become true brand experiences for key stakeholders.

We consider brand sessions to be an opportunity to take stakeholders by the hand, and make the brand's purpose relevant in overall business, consumer category and personal terms. We believe that global marketing leaders should design an event where every stakeholder leaves the conference ignited with a passion to make a brand purpose a reality - *plus* a clearly defined plan to make it happen. Oh and also, *by when* are they committed to doing what?

In our experience, there are four key components that comprise a winning global brand session:

Inspire is about painting a clear, tangible picture of the vision – a newly defined shared destiny.

How? By propelling the audience into the future by demonstrating what the world could – and should! – look like five years from now. (Great leaders can paint a picture that everybody can see, hear, feel, touch, and taste.) How has the brand affected the lives of its consumers? What about its employees? How do people discuss the brand? What problems has the brand solved?

Naturally, Moodfilms, BrandBooks and other materials can help to bring this vision to life. Why not use them?

Clarify is perhaps the most underestimated element of persuading colleagues to get aboard a new purpose or positioning. Otherwise, how can you be sure that everybody precisely understands your brand? Words mean different things to different people in one country, let alone several, let alone in different languages too. Clarity is the lens through which everybody can and must determine what to stop doing...and what to step up. And remember: while some might sum up the positioning of a brand like Volvo as 'the safest,' most effective positioning models have multiple components. (Our Inspire section emphasizes bringing each component fittingly to life.)

Apply is all about helping individuals in their own markets determine the implications of new brand positioning – whether it's in terms of pricing, product, online presence or through-the-line activation. See any gaps between current activities and where the brand wants to go? Bridge them. Also, within the marketing mix, what opportunities does this new vision create? How should you use them?

We have found it very powerful to display examples of each element of the marketing mix (like packaging and product) and also examples of how the brand touches the consumer per touchpoint (like store and website) – in a set of stations that everyone has to pass through to provoke a discussion on the (lack of) consistency across touchpoints. This is often a thrilling and immersive experience. For everyone. Non-marketers, too.

Commit is when all these elements come together. Earlier, we mentioned that a powerful brand session is neither easy nor cheap to develop and deliver. The positive side? It sends a signal to local leadership that you're not taking this brand session lightly. Although you wouldn't want a local chairman or general manager to sit in all day, you do want him or her to remain open. More to the point, you want local teams to present him or her with the key components of Inspire; the main guidelines and examples of Clarify; and the results of your re-prioritized marketing plan based on Apply. And now it's time to commit!

A local chairman's sign-off is the strongest way for others to perceive a positioning document as real and meaningful in a local market – even if someone put it together in a far-away HQ.

Lest we forget, GLOBAL BRAND NEWSLETTERS can help build internal engagement too. Managed carefully, few things are more effective than a monthly and/or bi-monthly one-pager that restates and revitalizes a brand's vision and strategy, with examples taken from inside and out-side the company. A newsletter not only allows a CMO or Global Brand Leader to address pertinent topics, it reports progress against previously stated goals. *Communicate, communicate, and repeat again!* is our credo! One recommendation? Keep it short and stick to the same targets, key performance indicators and deadlines. (And yes, people really *do* print them out and read them.)

Other important channels? Great BRAND BOOKS; videos that bring the brand alive for every individual stakeholder; quarterly webcasts and online meetings that permit two-way dialogues. Each channel has its pros and cons. Choose whichever one allows you to evolve in awareness, mindsets and behaviors.

Global Marketing or BRAND PLANNING PROCESSES are worth special mention. We've found them to be among the most effective ways to embed new behaviors into a team's daily routine. Almost every discipline, geography and stakeholder has some form of annual planning system that aligns resources with stated objectives. Embedding yourself, and trying to influence stakeholders' planning processes, is always hugely successful. Convince the target group to consider brand objectives along with their own objectives, and you've won 90 percent of the battle. The key isn't just balancing local and global, but long-term and short-term objectives. (We'll look more at this in our chapter devoted to Focus.)

Global Brand Engagement Learning

As you set out to engage the organization, here are a few pointers worth sharing for planning purposes. Overall, though, we'll say this: *Do everything, including the planning and evaluation, as diligently and thoroughly as you would for an external communication campaign!*

For some reason, many global marketing leaders make the mistake of thinking that an internal audience requires less work than an external one. In fact, the opposite is true. As described above, 'doing everything' motivates internal teams. 'Not doing everything' can often backfire.

Many brands pay next to no attention to internal engagement. It's somebody else's job, right? Maybe the CEO's, maybe HR's. Maybe the national country head's? Our advice: Assume these people need help. Give them the support they may need to help you do your job. We often create cascade packs, leadership conference decks, or 'presentations in a box.' Make it easy for other leaders of the company to support your cause, and they will. (It saves them preparing their own materials.)

Another key lesson that some leaders have to learn the hard way: *Respect the past in order to be able to change the future.* As we noted earlier, today, change is the only constant. Tell people that things need to change, and they'll most likely take your words with a pinch of salt.

Recently we spotted a new banner suspended atop a gas station near our New York City offices. It read: *'Under NEW and BETTER Management.'* The sign made us smile. At the same time, we wondered: if customers perceive that message as disrespectful to the past, they may just continue driving on. Respecting the hard work of the past always pays dividends.

Inspiration Without Perspiration?

Let's be clear: Inspiration doesn't just happen – *bam!* – like that. As many of the global brand leaders we interviewed for this book will attest to, you work very hard…then maybe, *just maybe!* you get lucky. Whenever we stumble upon an inspired workforce, we're pretty positive that someone, somewhere shed if not blood, then liters upon liters of sweat and tears.

Peter Vaughn of American Express applies the lessons of this chapter to himself as an individual: '*When deciding to take on a role like this, I think you need to be inspired by what you're doing because it's a tough job. The complexity of managing a global brand can be incredibly frustrating at times. Without inspiration and enthusiasm behind you, it's going to be difficult to be successful. So find your inspiration in the brand and use that inspiration to deliver the kind of robust and exciting marketing and customer experiences that will truly stand out. Make it personal. The really, really effective global brand marketers in any organization are those who are inspired. If you believe wholeheartedly in the mission of a brand – the universal truth of the brand – you can inspire your employee population and partners to get behind it, and you can inspire your consumers behind it, you will absolutely be effective and probably be the most successful brand in the category.*'

We couldn't have said it any better ourselves.

LET'S COLOR - DULUX INSPIRES
WITH PURPOSE AND PASSION

Part of AkzoNobel, Dulux is one of the world's leading domestic paint brands.

In 2006, AkzoNobel was still operating a heavily decentralized business structured around local markets. The business owned dozens of professional and consumer brands. Each market was in charge of developing its own marketing mix, and was mandated to pursue its own brand and business goals. In short, the control of these brands resided at local levels.

No surprise then, that results around the world turned out to be mixed. The Dulux brand soared in some markets and floundered in others. Which isn't to say there weren't pockets of good practice (not to mention inspired ideas) around the world. But no one shared these best practices, or was generating those few, big powerful ideas that could shift business performance and create lasting consumer loyalty.

As AkzoNobel started to globalize, the paints business followed suit. To lead the change, the company decided to appoint its first-ever global chief marketing officer, Kerris Bright. Kerris' brief and ambition were unambiguous: *'To unleash the potential… in the organization to support the development of fewer, bigger, better ideas that could drive faster growth. And to create an organization that is a much more exciting place to work because teams could be part of a greater whole, working towards a bigger ambition and working and learning from others in different countries with different cultures.'*

FOCUS ON THE CORE BRANDS

The company's global strategic planning emphasized its focus on fewer, more global brands – a striking detour from the previous policy of creating more than 40 brands with varying strategies. For the first time ever, leaders from all key markets agreed upon this simple yet profound strategic change. The number one global priority brand had to be Dulux, period. Accordingly, Kerris asked one of her leading global marketers to set the example for building the company's first truly globally run brand.

Meet Laila Skipper Nordby, global brand director of Dulux, one of those rare people who instantly fills a room with her upbeat energy, who thinks and acts positively, and whose unforgettable laugh immediately cheers up everyone around her.

When Laila took on the Dulux global brand leadership role in the second half of 2008, she took pains to listen and learn. Reaching out to key stakeholders around the globe, she focused on building credibility by first capturing the relevant facts; understanding the fundamentals of the business; and asking key leaders to name their biggest opportunities and challenges.

CONNECTING AROUND A GLOBAL NEED-STATE

At the same time, Laila and her team ensured that they built a much better understanding of category-specific consumer needs. They did this by using existing and commissioned research from across key markets to identify the most important human truths behind the success of Dulux. The results, it turned out, were remarkably consistent.

Even with the significant differences in culture, decorating styles and aesthetic tastes, the research uncovered significant commonalities. More importantly, the study also revealed a powerful common consumer insight and brand opportunity:

'Our home and surroundings have a powerful influence on how we think, feel, and live; we feel good when they reflect who we are and who we want to be – and by changing them we can even become who we want to be'.

This insight resonates in China; definitely has the 'nod-factor' in the U.K.; hits home in Brazil; and is recognized as true in India.

In short, it's an insight built on a universal truth. Building on this global truth, a new brand ambition was drafted: to add color to people's lives by selling tins of optimism, not just tins of paint. Laila and her team immediately intuited they were onto something big, one that also had genuine global potential. Yet Kerris and Laila both realized that if they wanted the business, and specifically the Dulux brand, to truly evolve to a global brand, they would need increased support from the very top of the company.

That support arrived with the appointment of Tex Gunning as the decorative coatings division new CEO. The charismatic, über-determined Unilever veteran made it clear from the get-go that his personal mission was to infuse the business with purpose based on the philosophy of the triple bottom line: People, Planet, and Profit.

Tex immediately challenged his marketers to ponder their brand's purpose: *'As global marketing leaders, we need to think about universal needs, about the bigger values of hope and dreams ... you know, the drivers of our lives. We need to ask ourselves, what can I do to ignite people's spirit?'*

When presented with the new Dulux brand thinking Tex at once saw that the repositioned Dulux brand had the potential to make an enormous difference in consumers' lives. What's more, he wanted to make it happen quickly.

This was just the break the Dulux global team needed. With the stars now clearly aligned, AzkoNobel set the agenda for a new era of Dulux global brand growth collaboration. To say the least, Laila was prepared. She'd already identified the people she knew she'd need on the bus to get the job done. In fact, she had already posted invitations for the first-ever Dulux global brand team meeting – later to be remembered as a decisive event.

Together for the first time in a room in the Lloyds Hotel in Amsterdam, to focus on their shared brand future, sat Laila and the marketing directors from Brazil, U.K., China, Canada, Central Europe, and Asia. Over the course of two days of candid, direct discussions, the directors agreed on the foundations for effective global brand leadership. The new Dulux Global Brand Team (GBT) resolved to focus not only on their top-five priorities, but also how they were going to work together and hold one another accountable.

Recognizing the importance of the brand summit, CMO Bright came to open the meeting to inspire and empower the team, rejoining the meeting only at the very end when Laila and her team presented the plan. Kerris was there to challenge, help sharpen some points...and then she signed off.

From then on, the Dulux GBT was on a roll. The team organized a global agency pitch, with Euro RSCG coming out on top. Why? Because the agency's creative proposals and personal passion touched the clients' hearts. As Russ Lidstone, CEO of Euro RSCG London put it, 'it was the best brief ever, and it just read one line: add color to people's lives.' A winning combination was born.

THE KICK INSIDE: INSPIRING INTERNAL MOMENTUM
To spread the gospel and bring in the complete leadership of the company, CMO Bright decided to organize a working session around the organization's new purpose. Kicking off a program that linked the company's purpose with its business objectives, and even assembling a homemade video that demonstrated the potential of 'Adding color to people's lives,' she fueled internal passion and alignment, along the way giving Laila all the air time she could possibly desire. An 'adding color to the AkzoNobel offices' program helped revitalize the purpose in the one place where AkzoNobel employees spent most of their daylight hours: the office.

As for Laila, she more than did her part. She did not send around a standard brand book, or organise a big-bang show & tell event near HQ, neither did she send a gimmicky USB stick with a PowerPoint presentation of the new Dulux positioning, instead Laila went on tour.

In a series of *Brand Sessions* around the world, Laila and the GBT took all key markets through a comprehensive workshop program. It included the 4 key components the GBT had identified as essential to inspire those colleagues whose job it was to deliver the brand promise to consumers.

Adding color to people's lives

A convincing Brand Manifesto and a world-class Brand Film inspired attendees by bringing alive the new positioning. (Even industry veterans later admitted they had the goose bumps.) To further clarify the positioning, structured exercises leveraging brand and consumer copy and visuals helped to define what was 'on' and 'off' brand. These led to an interactive exercise, where the team asked attendees to review the current marketing mix and identify opportunity gaps with the new brand vision and purpose. By the end, everyone was in agreement. But Laila refused to leave before local leadership committed to take the first steps toward integrating the agreed key actions into existing brand marketing plans.

To bring the brand's purpose alive outside the company, the global brand team initiated the 'Let's Color the World Program' to help transform and revitalize rundown neighborhoods in major cities across the globe. To date, Dulux teams have worked with local communities from Shanghai to Istanbul; Paris to Sao Paulo, rolling up their sleeves to paint streets, houses, schools and squares.

The rest, as they say, is history. The response from consumers, municipalities and corporations has been unflaggingly enthusiastic. A Chilean architect wrote to ask about collaboration possibilities during the reconstruction efforts in his country following the 2010 earthquake. An Eastern European photographer and university professor wrote to ask how she could roll out similar initiatives in Hungary. Social networks such as YouTube, Facebook, Twitter, and Flickr have all worked to fuel engagement with the Let's Color project, locking consumers and other groups into two-way dialogue with the brand. In short, AzkoNobel has never witnessed such across-the-globe brand loyalty and ambassadorship.

In July 2009, the team collected the brand's first prize awarded by co-marketers from across a wide range of industries. In Cannes 2010 the Let's Colour project was the talk of La Croissette. And then to think – it's only just begun!

Getting Focused

And Then Staying That Way

MOLSON *Coors*

JENNIFER DAVIDSON – GLOBAL SENIOR MARKETING DIRECTOR,
MOLSON COORS

Jennifer Davidson, a Canadian by birth but world citizen by day, is one of a rare breed of global brand leaders that, when she comes to visit your market for the day, you wish could stay a little longer to help more.

When Molson Coors decided that their beer business and core brands needed to operate on a truly global basis, they turned to Jennifer to make it happen for their largest brand, *Coors Light.*

A classically trained marketer with over 15-years' experience at tier one consumer packaged goods and drinks companies, Jennifer is recognized by her peers as a brand builder with a global orientation and a track record of driving significant growth for the brands she has had under her responsibility. She started her career at Unilever Canada where she managed a broad range of home and personal care brands.

Davidson has a natural drive to align brand strategies and make sure that they really focus. She knows the risk of vanilla strategies that do not make real choices and plans that keep evolving with the seasons. She is adamant that a list of 10 priorities is not a strategy:

'We've got our Coors Light long-range global plan where we set the roadmap for the next three years. We probably have 20 things we could do, but we've distilled it down to five big things that we focus on. These are the big initiatives that are common to all regions. We need to stay focused to guard against 'creep".

When there is disagreement on points of strategy or approach, Jennifer's inclination is to challenge her colleagues to recognize all the things they do agree on, and then propose a way forward that adds value for each region.

Davidson is the founding member and leader of the Coors Light Global Brand Leadership Team (CLGBLT) – the company's first cross regional global brand team. This team is charged with accelerating the brand's global growth and driving increased alignment on strategy and approach.

The group got off to a running start when in a matter of months it agreed a single global brand vision, strategy and short list of priorities to focus on in the first year.

Jennifer's rigorous approach for driving focus and getting strategic alignment can aid many a marketer on the key to focusing on the right things as a brand leader. A firm proponent of locking down a single global vision early and then communicating this broadly, she is always careful to balance this 'leadership clarity' with mindfulness and recognition of the different realities on the ground in differing markets:

'Our brand is at a different stage of development in new and emerging markets. The danger we need to watch out for is that we export inappropriate materials from a mature market to a new developing one for the sake of achieving efficiencies. The local culture and consumer needs to be at the heart of all decisions and adjustments need to be made to ensure relevance.'

Davidson's passion for agreement of vision and strategy is also reflected in her quest for clarity on how progress is measured. The CLGBLT quickly adopted a performance dashboard of both hard and soft industry-acceptable measures. Hard measures tracked market success, pricing and cost synergies. Brand equity measures were also included. The scorecard allows the team to share best practices, learn from each other and improve speed of roll out of best performing programs to other markets.

The result was that the Coors Light global team from the start took both an integrated marketing and general business perspective to building the business and achieving synergies. *'We've worked hard to develop a new global brand success dashboard. It's a work in progress – we continue to evaluate to ensure it tells the story of our brand in each market and that it drives action.'*

About 18 months after the creation of the global brand leadership team, Jennifer and her colleagues decided to even further focus their efforts on the bigger truly global initiatives. By creating more space for more local interpretation of the global vision in new markets, they empowered brilliant execution at the local level. Now that the single brand vision was effectively established and accepted it was time to get out of the way. The guardrails were clear and now creativity could flourish in local markets.

Jennifer Davidson's principles go a long way in helping marketers understand the process of attaining focus for the global positioning of a brand.

ALIGNING PRIORITIES
AND TARGETS

Who can't admire Jennifer's drive to focus on alignment at global level before allowing the strategy to cascade across the organization?

Imagine you've just been appointed the new global brand head of a major service firm. So far you've done everything by the book. First you ensured that you understood the lay of the land. Next, you connected with key stakeholders across the company. Subsequently, you managed to inspire the organization to rally behind a new brand vision that armed the brand with a much stronger purpose.

You've just completed a round-the-world tour to create excitement and buy-in for your new vision. When you return to your desk, jubilant and jet-lagged, the emails start flooding your inbox. Colleagues all over the world are offering suggestions and real-life plans of what they'll do to bring alive the new brand vision.

Clearly, everyone around the organization is exhilarated and ready to follow. As you review the multiple ideas and action plans, you realize that everyone is working with the vision. Yay! Problem is, they're developing their own approaches, uncoordinated, but best suited for his or her market. Oops, this can't be right!

Unfortunately, the above is a typical scenario. In these organizations, everyone does what he or she does best: invents a singular plan. The result? An assortment of different brand initiatives that are unrelated, duplicative and unleveraged (plus, a whole lot of confused, demotivated managers who feel that no one recognizes their initiatives, and who are desperate for more direction).

Or consider this alternative (but also very common) scenario:
It's the end of a two-day away summit. Brand leaders from all over the world have worked diligently together to think through the global brand's challenges and opportunities. Together, they've helped prioritize next year's global brand objectives. The agreed-upon plan is a real step forward toward global collaboration. A feeling of genuine accomplishment fills the room. As the group revisits its list of ten agreed priorities, and the names of the individuals who've volunteered to lead each initiative, the global brand leader poses one last check question (we think someone must have whispered it into his ear):

'I just want to know, as you all look at this list of priorities we have all just agreed to, can you please raise your arm if any of the priorities stated here in any way contradict your personal targets and objectives?'

Hands shoot up urgently into the air, signaling a lot of severely unaligned targets.

Which generally means that a few months later, when push comes to shove, and resources are scarce (and they always are), the new priorities will always lose. Coming back home to a boss who has other targets in mind, the people in the room end up trapped between two fronts, leading to later confusion and frustration.

The results from our ongoing *Leading Global Brands* study find that in general, most global, regional and local marketers agree that there's insufficient alignment and focus in their team's priorities. Why aren't people focusing more on the things that really matter? When you think about it, this is quite a statement. Now imagine the potential upsides of getting this focus and alignment right.

In contrast, effective global marketing organizations often have planning processes that force the alignment of goals and strategies across the organization, while driving the strategic focus required to get there.

So why is this so difficult to achieve? Is it more difficult today than in the past? We think so. Naturally, some people will always struggle to prioritize their work. But in today's global marketing arena, with increased trans-parency and near-total exposure to a brand's global issues, it's become nearly impossible for many managers to sort the important versus the urgent – and occasionally Just Say No to countries that are seeking their support. Add to this the complexity of dealing with a matrix organization, where functional lines cross brand lines, and you have a killer recipe for non-alignment.

Our *Leading Global Brands* study often finds a lack of alignment across a global marketing strategy's stated goals. Example: when we recently asked the top eight leaders of one organization to list its company's top five goals, only two points made it onto all lists. The remainder was a motley assortment of personal or local objectives that had somehow crept onto the global agenda without full alignment.

Focus On Alignment

As the organization globalizes, many marketers around the world who were accustomed to working in relative isolation must now align their work with others'. The implication? The days of making unilateral decisions are over. They now have to consider their choices within the context of a global strategy.

As it migrates down the organization, strategic alignment *must* be explicitly cascaded through the strategy. Meaning that the regional and local brand strategy needs to explicitly state how it links back up to the global strategy (and vice versa). Moreover, management should use the same metrics to measure success, and ensure that individual targets are aligned to promote delivery of the strategy.

Finally, focus is all about making sure that a company's goals match the personal targets of those key individuals who need to make the strategy happen. Sadly, the opposite occurs all the time. Later, we'll address how to nip this problem in the bud.

What to Look For

A quantitative benchmark survey should specifically ask stakeholders if the vision, mission and strategy of global business and marketing are crystal-clear to them, and to others on the team. Ask employees to rank their top three to five priorities. Next, ask for a brief description of each to ensure you really understand what they mean. In the quantitative survey, use a long list to provide prompts, from which respondents select the most important three.

Is everyone clear on their own marketing targets, and how they're measured? Here, drill down specifically to uncover whether each individual feels there's full, enough or insufficient alignment between their targets. What do they consider their global marketing objectives to be? Is there good alignment between the goals of key individuals, their teams, the different regions and the overall global marketing plan?

To achieve focus, metrics are crucial. In your assessment ask: Are people clear about how the company measures success? Do they believe that the company measures global, regional and local business success against a common set of metrics and common key performance indicators?

So what does it take to get this right? How do you best drive focus across some of the most matrixed, complex multidisciplinary organizations? Here are some suggestions:

Focus On The Business Brief

At the highest level, leaders need to focus on the right strategy. 'What business are we truly in?' should be the morning song and midnight cry of every CMO worth his or her salt. (Nor would it hurt for global brand leaders every now and again to ask themselves – and their teams – this same question.)

Focus On Language & Metrics

Nowadays, in most of the companies we work with, the business strategy cascade communication process looks something like this:

Day 1: The Chairman talks to the shareholders and press, and communicates key targets, as well as the company's most important growth and focus areas.

Day 2: The Chairman and all other board members fan out across the global organization, and cascade this same strategy to the company's top-1000 leaders and managers. These regional presentations are often accompanied by a drill down to regional goals that contribute to the overall strategy and objectives.

That's usually where it stops. But the most successful global marketing companies we've studied tell another story. Some CMOs have also conducted some very impressive follow-up presentations to their leadership team. In turn, the team drills down and explains how marketing will contribute to the overall business growth strategy. Revenue growth? Here's what we're planning at a penetration, share and repeat usage level. Global expansion?

Here's the portfolio approach we'll apply in the emerging markets. These explanations create a completely transparent bridge between the business brief language and its implications for the marketing function.

But what about language *within* the marketing function? Especially in organizations that are the product of mergers or acquisitions, we often find company-wide inconsistencies among such basic marketing terms as revenue, share, penetration, loyalty, and so forth. Big deal, you think? Yup, we believe it's a *very* big deal.

Typically, post-merger, the finance team immediately dashes across the globe to ensure the alignment of all financial metrics (and also that, in the next annual report, all measures add up nicely).

Unfortunately, marketing sometimes drops the ball at this crucial stage. Marketers have often conducted consumer insight mapping and market research at a completely local, or at a regional basis. There's no comparable data on key metrics, such as brand equity strength at a global level. Aligning language across marketing takes work, and many individuals in the organization consider it unimportant (they half-believe that the bureaucracy is playing favorites by making things easier for the global brand team only). Language differences can lead to scenarios in which key markets fail to recognize that they're dealing with the same key competitive challenges. After a merger, companies should adjust language and establish definitions in order to align basic terminology. Who bears responsibility for these adjustments and definitions? The CMO.

Harmonizing market research and brand tracking data is especially important in today's globalization era. These standardized metrics permit local and global marketing teams to divide their labor, while still measuring effect together. Common metrics are also crucial to uncovering the intricate balance between short-term tactical and long-term strategic success.

The common division of labor? Local teams lead brand activation in communication and promotions. Typically, their rewards are based exclusively on short-term results metrics, such as market share, total sales and sometimes profit. At the same time, the global team is also responsible for

'Our model was about focusing on things where we saw a reasonable chance of success, and then just doing whatever it took to be successful in those areas. It was about *prioritization* and *focus.*'

STEPHEN QUINN - CMO, WALMART

building long-term brand health and developing innovation. Naturally, local teams know it's essential to allot significant resources on behalf of long-term brand health.

Yet in the end, it's often just too tempting for local marketers to decide that the commercial that global developed and sent over to help improve the brand's long term equity values can wait a few more months. And if they don't think it can, their sales colleagues will be more than ready to remind them. And if no one can decipher the absence of progress on brand health because the metrics for measuring brand health are globally incomparable… well, maybe that's not such a bad thing for now.

The flipside is also true. In some organizations, the simple launch and on-time delivery of a product to its launching markets is the most critical metric against which global teams are evaluated. Subsequently, when three months before roll out, test results reveal that the team has to reformulate the product before it even stands a chance of succeeding in the U.K. – means launching late and missing a target date – it's tempting to pretend that all is well and sell in the innovation…when it's not completely up to scratch.

The only way to address this effectively? Ensure that global and local teams share some of the same metrics. We've worked with companies where the heads of local marketing teams are rewarded on the basis of *global*, rather than local, results. Another good idea: reward the global team if and when a product continues to do well in year two.

Focus On The Consumer

To drive, establish and sustain a common language, metrics and strategy alignment, we suggest starting with the consumer.

Says Nigel Gilbert of the Lloyds Banking Group, *'I think that understanding what has changed in the consumer mindset is absolutely essential, and the availability of data gives you the opportunity to know much more. Brands are all about experience. How can we ensure that we're not only driving that experience in as far as we can, but that we're measuring that experience from the perspective of the consumer?'*

No matter how global and complex the company is, taking the consumer as the starting point forces the company to begin from a common place...and work up from there.

Thus, we always recommend that the organizations we work with pay special attention (and give real priority) to the alignment of consumer research data and suppliers across the globe. Granted, it takes work, along with the attendant loss of comparable historical data for a few markets... but the upsides of comparing across categories and geographies are so significant that we've never heard any CMO claim to regret commissioning the work.

Aligning research, and eliminating duplication across the organization, typically delivers significant cost savings. Making these savings available to local marketers may ease the pain of moving to new metrics. One added bonus? By defining what should be measured, and which agency should become the preferred global supplier, companies go through an extremely useful strategy and team building exercise for the top research managers across the firm.

Focus On Market Reality

Another great way to drive internal alignment in strategy is by forcing everyone who's responsible for developing marketing plans to take a hard look outside. Again, it may sound obvious, but creating a common planning system that asks every market to analyze the market context, consumers, competitors and customers *in the same way* always helps increase alignment.

Over the years, we've done many such joint market analyses. Our clients are always surprised to find how similar their market circumstances are across the globe. Granted, significant differences exist among nascent, fast-growing and mature markets. That said, we have yet to come across any brands whose markets failed to permit them to be bucketed into three to five clusters of similar market dynamics.

Focus On Planning Processes

In any matrixed, multi-national organization, alignment will always be a journey, not a destination. That said, a few early wins are always possible.

Leveraging a company's planning system is among the most effective means of pulling down low-hanging fruit. First, companies should link the annual *budget* process to the annual marketing planning process. (As we mentioned earlier, quite a few companies out there still haven't mastered this concept.)

Next, why not develop, adapt, and then embed the global marketing planning process in such a way that the different categories or brands working on the same market can plan their activities based on a set of overall business or global goals? For example, let's work from top to bottom:

The Corporate Business Plan

The starting point of all marketing strategies is typically the corporate business plan, developed for, or by, the CEO and Board. This plan not only gives guidance, it sets objectives for all other disciplines and business regions.

If the company is active in multiple categories, the company's CMO will typically work alongside heads of categories to develop an overall marketing plan that defines the strategic roles of each of the categories, usually in general business terms such as 'grow aggressively,' or 'maintain.'

The Global Category Strategy

Each category leader should then submit category strategies that contribute to the overall strategic business objectives of the company, as well as deliver agreed growth and profitability numbers.

Thus, the Category Planning process kicks off with a clear set of top-down strategic objectives, both in financial performance as well as overall corporate strategic intent for the category. Assuming the company operates multiple brands within each category, it's the category leaders' responsibility to work with their global brand heads to agree upon the category portfolio strategy, and the roles that each global brand needs to play. In our minds, the category strategy is thus the most critical document to cascade and communicate within the company. It gives everyone the opportunity to place their work in a consumer and market context – and helps them relate to the external market reality that everyone perceives as the 'real world.'

The Global Brand Strategy

In sum, great global brands plan always and immediately define what the business is asking of them from a strategic perspective. The global brand strategy kicks things off by strategically aligning the overall business and portfolio role that the brand should play with the brand's long-term vision and purpose in consumer terms. As a planning base, this is crucial.

Once you're developing strategies at a global brand level, it's essential to integrate realistically the global, longer term and strategic and equity building objectives with the short-term market reality on the competitive and customer front that local managers face. All too often, the two feel separate, and fail to support one another, resulting in a blurring of focus.

For example, we've found that many of the best global brand strategies specifically list the statuses and key developments within their most important countries, say the top five markets. This grounds the strategy, and heightens its acceptability as the foundation for all further global brand planning.

Great global brand strategies typically identify the key thrusts that the brand must pursue over the next two to three years. These thrusts typically identify all important development work on the global strategic drivers of the brand, including vision, innovation and communication platform development, and perhaps third party alliances. Caution: these global strategies must never become too tactical or short-term. Strong global brand leaders lock down what's fixed…while leaving the rest for the local plans to fill-in.

The Local Brand Plan

Every local market plan begins by reiterating the overall longer-term brand objectives. It then goes on to explain the role of the specific market in making the plan come true.

The local brand or market plan should be highly tactical, e.g., over one year (though we've even seen half-year plans for very volatile markets such as mobile telephony, that spell out a brand's objectives and what programs the brand will deliver against these objectives). This is where plans should list activation programs, local retailer customer management strategies and tactical and promotional pricing programs for the upcoming year.

Of course, the local, one-year marketing plan is the briefing for that work on the brand in that geography. It's unfair to expect anyone to read multiple strategies. Thus, the local marketing leader is responsible for explaining to all key stakeholders how the strategy fits with the overall business, category and global brand strategy.

One final point on what makes a great global marketing strategy? Aside from the need for great content, ensure the strategy strikes the right tone of voice. The best global marketing strategies are written compellingly and as briefings.

Alignment Framework

Alignment on a brand positioning around the globe is a big challenge. Nobody we know would argue with that. However much work the global brand director put in it, however much stakeholder management was done upfront, you can safely bet a nice case of Puligny Montrachet wine that within hours after the launch, you'll hear some of the following responses: *'It's all well and nice that we aspire to become a 'lovemark', but in my country our competitors are beating us on both price and quality, and you think that transforming into an open, happy and warm brand will solve that problem? Please – give me a break!'*

Or what about this one? *'Now you want to talk about masculinity, adventure and freedom? Do you mind if I first educate our target audience a little and explain to them this category – which, by the way, is completely new to them?'*

And this one probably sums things up the best: *'I would love to do a campaign around 'adding color to people's lives,' but in my country, I first have to explain that using our brands will not kill you from poisonous ingredients.'*

Naturally, all these responses make sense. In most cases, they're driven not by a local marketer's lack of will but rather, by either one or both of the following issues:

1 THE PROMISE AND THE FOOTPRINT OF THE BRAND DIFFERS SIGNIFICANTLY PER MARKET.
2 THE MARKETS ARE AT VERY DIFFERENT STAGES OF DEVELOPMENT.

Let's explore both.

The Promise And The Footprint

We believe a brand promise can be made at four levels:

Level 1: The *functional* promise tells you what the brand does for you. For example this product is the safest, washes the whitest, is the cheapest, and so forth.

Level 2: The *emotional* promise tells you how the brand makes you feel. Examples: 'Cool,' 'Adventurous,' 'Authentic,' and 'Carefree.'

Level 3: The *aspirational* promise tells you what you are telling the outside world about yourself. For example, 'a good mother,' 'a winner,' or a 'responsible citizen.'

Level 4: The *societal* promise tells you what the brand contributes to the world. Well known examples are Dove's 'debunking the myth of beauty,' 'unleashing the artist in everyone,' or 'putting a smile on each kid's face.'

Bear in mind two rules:

1 You can only progress to the next level if you've completed the previous one. Here, completing means that the target audience recalls that promise – and believes that you deliver on it.
2 Even if you rise to the next level, you still need to maintain your promise and position on the lower levels.

Example: If, on your functional promise, you claim that your product is the healthiest for kids; on an emotional level, that it's all about 'doing the right thing for your children'; on an aspirational level, that it's all about others perceiving you as a good mother, then you can certainly communicate or activate around 'good motherhood' (a Mother of the Month contest?). That said, if a year down the line private label is perceived to be functionally on a par with your brand, then you can no longer rely on the aspirational foot-print of your brand to help it grow.

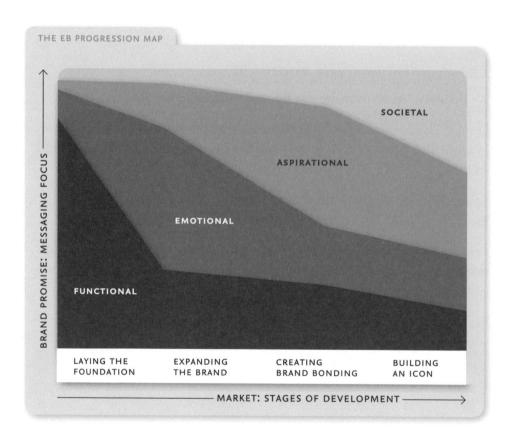

THE EB PROGRESSION MAP

BRAND PROMISE: MESSAGING FOCUS

SOCIETAL

ASPIRATIONAL

EMOTIONAL

FUNCTIONAL

LAYING THE FOUNDATION   EXPANDING THE BRAND   CREATING BRAND BONDING   BUILDING AN ICON

MARKET: STAGES OF DEVELOPMENT

Earlier in this book, we made a strong case for purposeful positioning, especially for global brands. Here's another reason: If you develop a purposeful positioning, the societal promise becomes extremely clear. At which point it's all about defining and detailing how the brand is constructed, starting at functional level, before evolving into emotional and aspirational levels, to finally extend the footprint into a societal – e.g. purposeful – level.

As a global brand leader, your task at hand is to demonstrate where each market *currently* sits on the Progression Map. And to make clear that every market is on the way to the same destination. There is only one shared destiny: the societal promise. Once a progression map is clear – and mappable to all markets – discussions tend to be less about the destination and more about the stage of development.

But wait – there's another dimension, too.

Action Required Based On Stages Of Market Development

Level 1: Laying the Foundation. The category and brand aren't established in the marketplace. As brand leader, your job is to increase consumer understanding of how to use the products within the category, as well as the category benefits.

Level 2: Expanding the Brand. The category is established, but you're a new entrant into the category. Your job, then, is to improve your position within the category, and increase your market share.

Level 3: Creating Brand Bonding. The market is mature, but the communication around brand values is weak. In this market situation, the task at hand is to maximize the badge value of your brand; increase aspirational and brand values-based communication; and extend the brand footprint accordingly.

Level 4: Building an Icon. The market is mature, competition is intense and marketing is sophisticated. You want to develop a 'lighthouse' brand identity.

By assessing which messaging, or brand-building activities, build highest ROI, the Progression Map can help you determine per market cluster where the brand is currently plotted and, subsequently, what the roadmap to the desired purposeful positioning should look like.

We've seldom seen a tool that so effectively aligns a global brand team, and that facilitates the ultra-important 'seeking similarities' mindset.

Companies like Unilever, Philips, and Diageo have made clustering their markets standard planning practice in order to facilitate closer collaboration, and promote speed and scale advantages. This fairly recent development signifies an important migration away from the traditional organizing-around-regional-geographies (about which we'll say more in the next chapter).

Clustering around market development brand maturity stages, permits global brand teams to simplify their planning, while developing bigger and bolder initiatives across markets. Now, instead of dealing with some 56 markets, a global brand team can work with representatives of each significant cluster to identify strategic growth drivers and develop, or roll out, programs that have proven to work for that strategic cluster.

Many of the winning global marketing teams we work with focus exclusively on developing programs that can be leveraged across the markets within a certain cluster. Silvia Lagnado of Bacardi proposes one such example when she discusses the 'create once, deploy many' model: *'We push very hard for toolboxes or repeatable models because that is where the synergy is, and that is where the speed is.'*

But if strategy is about choices, it's as much about defining *what* to do as it is about deciding what *not* to do...then vigorously defending that position.

Focus On Quality

Our next chapter is all about structure, roles and responsibilities, operating principles and ways of working. Right now, however, it probably makes sense to issue the following warning: Always make sure that the global team's priority list is sufficiently focused so that you can produce the highest possible quality work.

Ensure, too, that others perceive that the global team you lead over-delivers on quality. By taking on too much, we can almost guarantee that you'll spread your global resources too thin, and under-deliver. We like to say, *'You can smell quality a mile away.'* Consider the enormous example, and role, that a global CMO or brand leader team plays in the organization - we can't emphasize this enough - before saying 'yes' to new things.

Lee Ann Daly, CMO, Thomson Reuters: *'So many people put too much hay on their forks ... we need to under-promise and over-deliver.'*

That said, creating and sustaining quality is a huge challenge. As we mentioned at the start of this chapter, global brand teams enjoy the perception that they're servicing the needs of key markets...but then find it very difficult to say 'No' to a question from Equador, Iceland or Luxemburg. The global brand leaders we most respect have enormous discipline and restraint in what they take on, and what they demand of their global teams. If their team's work is lacking in any way, it sets a poor example for the rest of the organization - and invariably comes back to haunt the team in eventual discussions about who does what.

So You're Focused...Now What?

We believe that Ann Ness, Vice-President Corporate Brand Management, Cargill, hits the nail on the head when she says, *'The second hardest thing for a business to do is focus.'* This may come across as puzzling, that is, until you take in the real zinger of an insight embodied in her next line: *'The hardest thing to do is to stay focused.'*

Staying focused can be a challenge. Leaders tend to underestimate how long it takes to embed learning, or ingrain behavior change. Egbert van Acht of Philips relates his effort to upgrade his team's affinity for insight development: *'We spent a year training people deeply on insights. What is an insight? How do you get insights? How do you validate insights? Is it a global insight? Then we spent the next year training everyone on global propositions. The biggest mistake was to be impatient about this. We went a little too fast and we had to pull the handbrake because the maturity of insights was not there yet. So we took another six months before we moved to the next phase.'*

External pressures, too, can kidnap even the best-laid plans. Silvia Lagnado makes an insightful and candid comment: '*I think the biggest problem we have, is that post-launch we take the money away too quickly and move on to something else. Even in year two, 80 percent of the volume is still trial, not yet repeat. So the biggest lesson here is that year two is the one that matters. And we often don't have enough rigor to check that year two support is where it should be.*'

If a winning CMO like Lagnado can confess to this pitfall, we should *all* be alert to this risk.

What Success Looks Like

Karin Koonings of Starbucks admits, '*There's always going to be some tension between what the head office thinks needs to happen, what the regions think need to happen, and what the countries think need to happen. That's why developing a global brand blueprint is an important step of quantifying and getting one common view around the state of the brand, the state of the business, the state of global support, and what the local markets feel the priorities need to be.*'

As we noted earlier, human beings are territorial. We're hardwired to justify our existence (or in this case, our jobs). It takes global marketing leaders who are at ease in their own skin, and confident in their own capabilities, to make the best calls on behalf of their organizations, by assigning resources and work where they make the most sense.

Peter Vaughn of American Express clearly has this in mind when he warns of '*the danger of (global marketers) getting too close to the end of the executional funnel before handing your work over to the local marketers – especially when the sourcebooks/guidelines are so prescriptive in terms of identity, color palette, typography, language and imagery. Our challenge as a global team is to be very clear in our strategy and focus, and then let go.*'

Have we mentioned the often-overlooked imperative to find a balance when regarding the timeframe of your focus?

Nigel Hollis, Chief Global Analyst, Millward Brown, makes this observation: '*Brands and brand equity are fascinating to me because it's such an ill-understood area and it seems that many of the people charged with being responsible for brands don't really understand what they're being charged with. Conceptually they may do, but they often end up doing things that just seem to undermine the power of the brand and what really drives sales in the longer term. How do you persuade people to do the right thing for the long term when it may actually reduce the sales they generate for their country in the short term? It's that tension between long and short term that's fascinating to me.'*

And Lest We Lose our Focus... A Few Final Words

Jonathan Moore of Sara Lee offers this practical tip to get cracking: 'Looking *back, I think it's easy to fall into the trap of focusing on the 10 percent of non-alignment. So, if you have 10 percent alignment and 10 percent absolute misalignment and 80 percent agreement in between, don't get distracted by the things that just don't fit. Just say, let us just park what we can't align on at the moment, and remind ourselves what we can align on, because that might be enough to move forward anyway.'*

Tim Wright, President, Future Group, GlaxoSmithKline Consumer Healthcare, adds valuable advice: *'The primary tenet of the GSK model is consultation, not consensus. The way we run our core team meetings is that we consult with the core countries. We want the best country managers to work with us to create the best solutions for growth, but we don't look for consensus with them because if you do, you just take all the sharp edges off any innovation and advertising.'*

Once you get started, trust and transparency will keep you trucking, or better still, speeding along.

TAKING COORS LIGHT GLOBAL

The Coors heritage goes back to 1873 when Adolf Coors made a commitment to brew only the finest quality beers in the Rockies. Coors transformed into an international brewer in the 1970s when the company started expanding both its product line and distribution. Today the brand is sold all over the world.

The 20th century saw a massive takeover and merger wave pass through the beer industry. Everyone was getting either bigger or getting out. And murmurs of a merger between the two major brewers Molson and Coors became reality in February 2005 with the establishment of Molson Coors. The new company was bigger and even more ambitious about the global growth of its brands.

By 2006 senior leaders and marketers across the business had been starting to increase international collaboration by means of new body; the Brand and Innovation Council, consisting of the CMOs of the business units. By the fall of 2007, Jennifer Davidson was chosen as the council's first dedicated Director and the development of a global brand agenda started in earnest.

Coors Light was chosen as the first brand to 'go more global' and Jennifer, at this point still based in her native Toronto, was asked to lead the process. Davidson had the credibility and experience required because she had previously been responsible for the brand in Canada, the beer's second largest market. In early 2008, she worked closely with several colleagues from other markets to develop the brand's first global brand positioning or Brand Identity Model as it was called in Molson Coors. The pieces were beginning to fall into place.

By mid 2008 Molson Coors decided to further step up the focus on global growth with the creation of Molson Coors International. Now based at HQ in Denver, Jennifer was tapped for the role of creating a Coors Light global brand council and developing the brand's first focused global growth plan. The brief was to develop an aligned global brand strategy with clearly defined focus areas of strategic growth.

Jennifer understood that she needed to move beyond the previous informal collaboration model. Her peers respected the fact that she had led the marketing team of Coors in Canada and that she was close to the brand, at the same time Davidson knew that she needed to tread carefully as the brand was being managed extremely successfully in many local markets and the global team didn't want to disrupt this successful model.

Coors Light's Rich Heritage

Davidson quickly clarified that the aim was not to indulge in a heavy-handed, empire-building exercise. Working with her senior leadership team, her idea was to work with and through the business units, and grow global organically with everyone contributing. She wanted to start by creating the right team to shepherd the company from a local stance to a global outlook and perspective.

So it was that in early 2009, Jennifer brought together for the first time the people she considered crucial for Coors Light global growth. The Coors Light Global Brand Leadership Team (CLGBLT) was founded at a seminal 'Global Summit' hosted in the foothills of the Colorado mountains in Golden, CO.

The agenda was simple, but had never been done before in the company; Jennifer's goal was to 'shift a loose coalition of Directors and VPs from a volunteer army to an aligned leadership team'. The challenge was to agree a global strategy for the next three years that created clarity on what the brand should focus on, defining what was important and should be worked on at an enterprise level, and who would lead each initiative.

Now human beings are territorial by nature, and some bit of territory comes with every job. Jennifer was aware of what was at stake: *'It's a huge challenge because you feel the time and money pressures to get going, but we needed to do this as a team. This wasn't going to work if it was just a centre-driven initiative. Building Co-*

ors Light into a global brand had to start from the ground up – in the business units. The Coors Light leaders in each of the business units are a key reason for our early success. They had a global orientation and they believed in and drove our enterprise ambitions. Their experience and support was crucial.'

The Golden Summit was a big success. During the course of two intense days the team signed off the final positioning, gelled around a common mission for the brand, set a strategic growth agenda that focused efforts on nine priority thrusts and created clear accountabilities. The new global leadership team also agreed how it would be working together for the next year. A special beer can listing the brand's mission and focus areas was created and distributed to key stakeholders across the business.

Over the next few months, the Coors Light team worked hard to embed the foundational building blocks of managing a global brand into the operational subconsciousness of the organization.

Slowly but surely, people moved away from a mindset of projecting and protecting differences, to one of promoting similarities and laddering up to a common perspective of what the product and brand could be.

The start of the year saw the deployment of a brand stewardship tool to help educate colleagues on what the brand stands for. The first step was socialization of the global brand positioning. This happened formally in regional team meetings and informally with all members of the global team taking real ownership of the strategy and the commitment to bring it to life with every person on their team – internal, agencies and distributors.

The global brand leadership team also set itself firm objectives for achieving significant savings on packaging, advertising production and other discretionary marketing costs. A new behavior change took root and marketers were proactively looking at ways to reduce non-working dollars.

At the same time there was a concerted effort to bring more focus as the brand globalized. To drive focus for the global brand team, whatever didn't add value was eliminated from the agenda. The idea was to focus on fewer but bigger things.

That Summer marked the development and socialization of a global brand scorecard, comprising a mix of hard financial measures and softer equity tracking measures reviewed quarterly. 'Scorecarding allows you to benchmark your brand. It gives you a common language so that everybody knows what they're working towards.'

This was followed by colleagues creating a Coors Light digital toolbox – a prerequisite for effectively sharing assets across the global marketing organization. Jennifer emphasized its importance: *'One of the first things we looked at was creating a toolbox to organize our assets. You need a library; and then you need some kind of search mechanism that allows the local teams to go in and look for the things that they need. A toolbox is critical.'*

The global marketing machine was beginning to hum. Next there was a move to align global packaging and graphics in all key markets, resulting in significant savings. And in November, the GTM (go-to-market) launch model was developed for international markets based on success drivers from existing markets.

After almost two years of closer collaboration, results have been very positive, and the global collaboration model is still progressing. In May, 2010 Coors Light achieved the #1 brand position in Canada; and China has now joined the Coors Light global leadership team – a significant milestone. A sub-team consisting of marketers from the key markets of U.S., U.K. and Canada was created to ensure even closer alignment and more frequent contact.

Already the creation of a focused strategy has made a significant difference. There are now clearly agreed global brand mandates for positioning, packaging and product. The innovation program has been restructured to focus on fewer and bigger programs. Millions of dollars of cost synergies have been realized in Supply Chain and Commercial, and advertising is being leveraged across markets. And on the business front, Coors Light is on track to hit all its global growth targets including expansion into new international markets.

It's amazing what a little focus can do.

Up The Organization

And Down All Dysfunctions

Sony Ericsson

LENNARD HOORNIK - CORPORATE VP,
GLOBAL HEAD OF MARKETING, SONY ERICSSON

Lennard Hoornik, Corporate Vice-President, Global Head of Marketing, Sony Ericsson, checks every single box for the role of Global Brand CEO.

A graduate of the Haagse Hogeschool in the Netherlands, and a denizen of five countries all over the world, Lennard was appointed Head of Global Marketing at Sony Ericsson in 2008.

Having started his career with marketing and sales roles at Sony all across Europe, Lennard joined Sony Ericsson as Vice President of marketing during the early days of the 2001 joint venture. His responsibilities included launching the new Sony Ericsson brand in the European, Middle Eastern and African (EMEA) regions.

Subsequently, Lennard took charge of the new global customer unit at Vodafone, Sony Ericsson's largest global customer. Next, he was appointed to lead and grow the Singapore-based business in the fast-growing Asia-Pacific region.

A fast-thinking, fast-talking entrepreneur who challenges partners and team members alike by throwing out audacious business goals (and seeing what sticks), Lennard's character fits perfectly with the kinetic world of mobile telephones.

When Lennard stepped up as Head of Global Marketing, Sony Ericsson was struggling to maintain its market position. Nokia was the clear market leader; Samsung had recently introduced a handful of strong phone models; and HTC had also decided it wanted to compete. Then, shortly after Lennard's appointment, Apple decided to join the party by rolling out the iPhone.

In the face of extreme competitive and financial pressure, and in order to drive efficiency, in Q2 2008, Sony Ericsson announced a restructuring. The subsequent company-wide reorganization focused on streamlining the organizational structure and reducing fixed costs. Among Lennard's tasks was the need to reduce the overall marketing headcount, and recalibrate the marketing organization to increase global leverage and effectiveness.

A new global brand vision for growth – one designed to bring to life the new Sony Ericsson marketing strategy that Lennard and his new global marketing leadership team had developed – inspired the organizational transformation that ensued. Sony Ericsson's new marketing organization design was now far more streamlined, significantly increasing global marketing's role while redefining new global ways of working.
From the start, Lennard made it a mission for reconnect marketing both to consumers and the business.

'I think a key challenge for marketing today is to get closer to the day-to-day business. When I took the role of head of marketing for Sony Ericsson globally I said to my team, 'The first thing I'd like you to do every time you meet with me is to report the current health of your products, business and key markets'. I also regularly ask such questions as, 'How are our programs succeeding in the market? What is your forecast going forward? And what actions are we planning to improve our results?'

'The focus of our discussions, therefore, quickly shifts more toward the current business health and less toward being overly brand-skewed. It's important that everyone in our company understands that we feel just as accountable as they do for building our overall business strategy and making money.'

Since his appointment, Lennard has reoriented marketing at Sony Ericsson and built a global marketing organization that is much more *'fit for purpose'* for delivering a winning Sony Ericsson marketing strategy. After several years of significant losses, the company recently reported its second quarter of profit.

Never one to rest on his laurels, today Lennard and his team are working on the next round of developments: forging strategic global partnership alliances and enabling markets to work with global brand platforms to develop winning local strategies.

STRUCTURE FOLLOWS
STRATEGY

When he began his new job at Sony Ericsson, Lennard Hoornik's brief was clear: cut as many people as all the other disciplines are doing. Costs needed to drop quickly. *Oh... And fix the brand!*

The most important decision Lennard made before landing in London to claim his seat at the table: Calling the CEO to ask if he could take another month before deciding and announcing where precisely he'd reduce marketing headcount. First, though, he would develop a global marketing vision and strategy.

Structure follows strategy. This adage sounds so logical, yet most organizations forget, or ignore, it. The result? Marketers and their peers lacking a once-solid, integrated perspective. Increasingly, they share power with functional leaders. More and more, they've split up business units to increase their focus on narrow groups of products; created 'bridge' functions to co-ordinate existing functions; or added specialist capabilities to address new consumer media channels.

Either anecdotally, or via our observations and research, we believe that more than a few marketers spend as much as 80 percent of their day in meetings to coordinate their plans and programs with those of other internal groups. As we laid out in Chapters four and five, we believe as much in building good connections across the company as the next guy, but clearly this isn't the best use of marketers' time and energy. The result: Significant reductions in marketers' abilities to connect to outside reality with consumer needs – or to think objectively about how best to create value.

This won't change anytime soon. In the future, market globalization will drive increased organizational globalization. Our prediction? The sheer number of mergers that drive scale and global reach; *plus* an increase in strategic partnerships that deliver more holistic solutions and consumer experiences; plus the amount of internal regional and global integrations... will only snowball in the future.

Some of the underlying drivers of these marketing changes: A recent *McKinsey Quarterly* article revealed that consumer goods companies have seen an average revenue growth at the top ten companies from $13 billion in 1990 to $47 billion in 2009. Also these companies' average footprint expanded from 112 to 160 countries!

Consumers are increasing the number and variety of social networking sites and communication channels they use. When seismic change occurs at both the sender and receiver ends of the traditional communications model, you can imagine the ensuing chaos that overlays the organizational model.

And CMOs are changing organizational structures because they want to be closer to what's really happening in the markets. David Wilkie, Managing Director, Marketing 50, a community of CMOs from many of the world's most respected brands, signals the following trend: *'CMOs are tearing up their org charts, removing the 'regional marketing' layer and compressing their organizations to become a shallow hourglass: centers of excellence at HQ and capable resources in the field – with little in between. Speed and being nimble with resource has become the new operating mantra.'*

We've studied all areas of global marketing. Our findings consistently show that organization, roles and responsibility, and global behaviors are without doubt one of the knottiest global marketing leadership challenges out there. Yet few global marketers have the stomach or the energy to tackle the subject.

One consistent insight? Almost *all* global marketing leaders (and quite a few of their bosses and board colleagues) admit that they initially underestimated the importance of addressing the organization. All too often they waited too long to think seriously about marketing organizational structure, roles and responsibilities and operating models.

To which we reply: *Ignore this subject at your peril!*

What To Look For

As part of an assessment, we recommend spending time uncovering how well the current global marketing organization is working. After reviewing the state of connections across the company, the level of clarity and inspiration around the global brand vision and strategy and the amount of clarity about the brand's key objectives, zoom in on the effectiveness of the organizational structure and operating model.

Ask people to describe their roles and responsibilities. Next, ask everyone, from the CMO to the most junior marketing associate in Jakarta, the following question:

Is it clear to you and your colleagues precisely where your personal responsibilities start and stop?

As a query, it may sound simple, but it's imperative. Yet astonishingly, our *Leading Global Brands* benchmarking survey across 250-plus global brands finds that on average, only 53 percent answer a consensual Yes.

Next, probe to see if the organizational structure is clear to each and every individual. Do team members understand where they fit within the organization? Who's above them? Who's below them? Who's parallel to them, e.g., working on the same brands but from a different perspective? Typically the results are disappointing. On average, only 54 percent agree that they understand how the organizational structure built around them works. But in the leading global marketing organizations we see scores of almost 80 percent. Thus, getting this right is very achievable.

How can there be such big differences? And how can huge organizations get this so *wrong*? Especially when practically everyone agrees that it needs to go *right*?

The waste is often hidden. It is only when you take a real close look at what the marketers in your team are spending time on, and when you see how many e-mails being written are about turf wars, that you come to realize what the incredible size of this energy leak is.

If structure defines the pieces of the global marketing engine, then the operating model – the processes that define how the engine pieces work together – comprises the oil that makes the engine run smoothly.

As organizations become more global and matrixed, these operating models become more complicated. Who needs to sign off on what? How often should players meet? When they meet, what should they discuss? In our experience, whenever we design a new global marketing organization to increase global leverage, or become fit for growth, the operating model deserves equal if not more attention as the new structure.

We've been present at many reorganizations at a stage where one of the traditional strategy consultants (Bain, BCG, McKinsey, Mercer and Hay, all of whom we've had the pleasure of working alongside) has done the preliminary work of strategy, cost and headcount analyses. These consultants have then typically formulated recommendations that specify how many people can be cut across *all* disciplines, including marketing.

We invariably enter the scene at the point where a CMO next needs to decide on and then implement the new global marketing structure and operating model.

That's usually when the CMO decides that it's one thing to uncover the common overlap between local, regional and global roles – but it's another to determine precisely *who* in this brand new constellation needs to be doing *what*.

And that's usually when the CMO decides that they need more detailed knowledge on how global marketing organizations actually function.

'Sweating the details' as Helen Duce, one of our partners-in-crime puts it *'is precisely what's needed.'* Before redefining the roles, it's very important to understand precisely what's done in every role. Otherwise important actions may fall between the cracks.

Role Clarity Versus Breadth

In late 2001, when we first started out benchmarking global marketing organizations, drilling down into precisely who does what, and how marketers feel about the breadth of their responsibilities, we made a faulty assumption.

Once we understood the importance of role clarity in motivating marketers, especially those working in complex global organizations, we began honing in on the subject. The bigger the role the better, we thought! Whether it concerned positioning, pricing, product innovation or packaging, we thought, *'Why would someone pony up US$100,000 to attend a fancy business school, and then settle for a job with anything less than responsibility for the full marketing mix?'*

Boy, were we ever off-base.

In today's highly complex global marketing organization, full 'P' responsibility is no longer even an option. And clearly the marketers who work there know it. It's not the *breadth* of the marketing responsibilities that drives job satisfaction, but the underlying *clarity* about the role. This finding still takes a whole lot of CMOs by surprise, too.

We find that the organizations with the most highly motivated marketers have done a superlative job in laying out precisely not just who needs to do what, but also defining what are out-of-the-role specs.

The latter in particular is often a sticking point. Jo Ryman, our colleague warns: *'Companies are terrific at adding responsibilities to people's lists...and often terrible at stripping away responsibilities from people!'*

You wouldn't believe how often people tell us stories about the development of a new product innovation when suddenly, at the eleventh hour, the project leader receives an email with 'input' from someone he or she had no idea was involved (or for that matter, even interested). Talk about taking the wind out of your sails.

Says Silvia Lagnado, *'One of the biggest pitfalls to avoid is lack of clarity around decision-making. I have learned the hard way and now whenever I see the possibility of misunderstandings, I address it up front. There is no bigger energy drain than organizational ambiguity.'*

Building Role Clarity

Once we understood the importance of role clarity in motivating especially marketers working in complex global organizations, we began honing in on the subject. Via our proprietary benchmarking, we've been able to gather some useful insights about how to best create clarity around roles for marketers.

As an example, let's take a Unilever or P&G marketer who's responsible for a detergent brand in Portugal.

Objectively, and right off the bat, we'd say that his or her responsibilities are, in fact, limited. Ultimately, after reviewing each one of the elements within the traditional marketing mix, and our marketer's inability to make any significant changes, we'd conclude that these local marketing manager roles far more closely resemble those of a category or customer marketing manager than the 'traditional' 6P *Brand Manager* we learned about at school from Kotler, Ries and Trout and friends.

That said, these P&G and Unilever local marketers are generally among the most highly motivated marketers in our surveys. Why? Because they're extremely clear about what the company and their colleagues expect from them. They know they're playing an important role in the total mix. And their company and leaders explicitly recognize how critical their work on the last ten yards of distribution is to everyone's overall success.

Now, contrast this scenario to a local marketer working in Pharmaceuticals. It's a market hounded by local legislation and national restrictions that make it nearly impossible for a global marketer to tell the local marketer what to do. A decade ago, we supported the global brand positioning development and launch of a new women's contraceptive, *NuvaRing*.

It didn't take us very long to realize that local marketers perceived the ad hoc involvement by HQ 'expert' staff as 'meddling' – and even an impediment to local marketing success. The globally diverse legislation around the marketing of contraceptives made it impossible for the company to define a simple global marketing operating model that succinctly defined when HQ would, or wouldn't, get involved.

'For me the best global marketing leaders are the ones that *recognize their own limited influence.* They are strong on strategy and communicate well, but then focus on making the local marketers successful.'

FOLKERT KAMPHUIS, GLOBAL COO OF ANIMAL HEALTH, NOVARTIS

The end result: frustrated marketers on both sides of the line. HQ genuinely wanted to help. Local merely wanted clarity – to know how to plan their projects, create realistic timelines, and deliver on what they'd promised to sales.

It was only after we created a joint task force that included critical representatives from the U.S. and other key markets that we developed and rolled out a streamlined go-to-market plan for the first pilot countries.

Philip Gladman of Diageo pulls no punches: *'If you haven't got clarity between the local marketing and the global marketing teams about respective roles and responsibilities and if you aren't absolutely and utterly sure about who does what, you are headed for disaster.'*

Unlocking The Value Of Global Marketing Organizations

Industry experts used to say that global marketing was akin to a pendulum clock, and that Coca-Cola was a terrific example of how important responsibilities swing over time between global and local.

But if we listen to Marc Mathieu of Coke, clearly he feels the pendulum is at a standstill. *'Global brands have a higher propensity to make a difference, and therefore also a higher propensity to create competitive advantage...'*

For us, one thing is clear; the pendulum is good and stuck in the *global* position and it's not swinging back any time soon. Every single trend that's led to a more globalized approach to marketing – consumer transparency via the Internet; global competitors who are reengineering and improving less expensive solutions (and in a matter of months, too) – appear irreversible.

Even for a brand that needs to be managed to quite a large extent at local level – think of food brands that are deeply rooted in local eating cultures and habits – the ambition will always be to seek new, more global platforms. Platforms like Snacks, Health & Wellness, Organic, Slow and Fair Trade have no reference in any country's roots, and thus can benefit via a globally harmonized approach.

Our *Leading Global Brands* study also shows that an overwhelming majority of respondents believe that the role of global brands will only increase. Moreover, these global brands will increasingly be controlled by central marketing teams. Are you getting the picture?

That said, we believe that increasing the global marketing team's effectiveness is only half the solution.

Up With Local

All too often, global marketing leaders mistakenly believe that by focusing on improving their global marketing approach, and their global marketing team's effectiveness only they can dramatically improve success. Or that successful better marketing alone will drive competitive advantage for the years to come.

Naturally, we *do* believe in the power of the global brand and effective global brand teams. But let's be clear: increasing global marketing's effectiveness in no way reduces the power and importance of local marketing to a company's overall success. Some global marketers mistakenly conclude that increased global marketing effectiveness may well go hand in hand with decreased local marketing effectiveness. Not a good trade-off!

Bluntly stated, we believe that only those global marketing organizations that can quickly and dramatically improve both their *global* and *local* marketing effectiveness will succeed in the future.

Why? Because the very same trends that have led to globalization also enable consumers to demand more of what they want, *when* they need it and *where* they need it (oh, and more cheaply, too). Notice, if you will, how this centers around *local markets*?

Satisfying tomorrow's immensely more demanding local consumer requires dramatic local insights, brand new partnerships and total brand experience. Think AppleCare, where product usage and store, online, phone and social media customer care coalesce to provide consumers with a total brand experience that genuinely improves service and builds incredibly powerful brand loyalty. Think Zappos, where consumers honestly believe they've just made a new friend in customer service (and Zappos is just getting started, too!)

Once one competitor figures this out, the others players will look as though they're trying to sell you stone-age menhirs wrapped in banana leaves as eco-friendly solutions.

As we wrote in our **'what'** chapter, we believe that offering total brand experiences is the future of successful brands. To get this right, all brands, whether local or global, need to dramatically increase their ability to build total branded experience solutions. This entails connecting with consumers at every relevant touchpoint, and working with many new partners such as retailers, transportation companies, media owners, and so forth, to interpret and instantaneously leverage any new consumer understanding.

Since all consumers are, in effect, local, this expertise matters most at the local level. Local marketers will need to choose which retailers to partner with, so that they can offer consumers better overall need-state solutions. Local marketers will also need to ensure that the organization shares its overall knowledge about a consumer's preferences across all touchpoints to improve its offerings. Finally, local marketers will need to understand how to bridge the last mile between the company and all the touchpoints with the consumer in the most effective, efficient ways possible.

We never said it would be easy.

RECOGNIZING LOCAL

Telling local marketers how important their work is something that HQ often forgets. When we discuss the roles and motivations of local marketers with global brand heads and CMOs, we often recommend over-communicating and using every opportunity to talk to the troops in the field.

Some may argue that the more global, traditional HQ brand development work like positioning, innovation and the development of communication platforms may ultimately have a greater impact on long-term global brand success. But every CMO knows that if a concept doesn't land, it might as well not exist.

It's typically pretty easy for the CMO or global brand leader to walk around HQ, pat the 50 global and central brand developers on their shoulders, and tell them what a great job they're doing. Much more difficult is convincing five hundred or even five thousand faraway local marketers that you recognize the importance of their jobs.

INSPIRING LOCAL

Despite its lack of glamour, we'd argue that among the most dynamic, exciting areas of marketing these days is, in fact, local marketing.
How teams develop first-rate positioning, packaging or television hasn't changed terribly much since 1950. But three years ago, social media, collaborative filtering for CPG goods, and Red Laser didn't even exist.

Great global brands should be as dexterous on a local marketing scale as they are on a global level. If local marketers have to rethink positioning and portfolio strategies, the truth is, they're not spending enough time on excelling at local activation. Our belief? Only those global marketing organizations in which global and local recognize each other's separate but interdependent roles will win in the future.

SYNCING GLOBAL AND LOCAL ROLES

Thus, local and global will probably need to migrate even farther apart. Each will specialize in its respective skills. The future scenario will be akin to the differences between R&D and marketing. Both contribute to ultimate consumer solutions, yet neither claims they could do the other's work. When both groups excel at their roles and trust and build on each other's contribution, an organization will have truly – finally! – unlocked the value of global marketing.

We think (and hope) that very soon, the discussions inside companies about who does what will vanish. (No one in his or her right mind has the time for such fruitless debates. They're *far* too busy attempting to do their part in the best way possible.)

Having said this, it will be hugely important to understand and perfect the interface between the two – and to better sync how they work together: Think of an extraordinary soccer team in action, and you'll understand at once why people dub it 'The Beautiful Game.' Everyone knows his role. Everyone plays his part to perfection, stroking and passing the ball from one player to another, bringing it up the field in one fluid surge until a single athlete unleashes one unstoppable shot. The defense and the offense have entirely separate roles. They never pretend otherwise.

By transferring this analogy to a global marketing machine, you'll see why you need a similar self-awareness and discipline if you want to bring a new product to market and roll it out quickly and globally, in the most effective, efficient way possible.

Degrees Of Globalization

Let's first recognize the traditional local to global spectrum. Naturally, no organization 'fits' precisely into any of these stages of local-global, but it makes sense to understand the sliding scale.

Almost all global marketing organizations have a past (often many takeovers ago) where local operating companies had full national autonomy. Marketers in the market did precisely as they saw fit. There was no contact with either regional or global marketing groups. Subsequently, no one leveraged any learning across markets nor realized any benefits of scale.

Informal cooperation is often the first step of any collaboration where countries informally share knowledge and learnings on an ad-hoc basis. Local and global marketers are aware of each other's existence but there is no obligation to adopt practices from each other. Amongst those who are sharing, there is an 'export mindset – this has worked for us' and those listening pick and choose or take a germ of an idea and re-create it back home.

The next step of collaboration may entail *informal or uncoordinated networks* around certain highly prioritized practice areas. For example, there may be a global marketing meeting that focuses on the basics of 'digital marketing,' where internal and external experts exchange stories and learning. Or a group of emerging markets come together to share business cases and success factors. At this stage, both parties are still on the fence as to whether or not to adopt any common or best practices.

At some point, corporate will step in and appoint a coordinator, who'll ensure that all parties share best (and worst) practices. This coordinator may review work across markets and choose examples to share with all other markets. This represents the simplest form of *coordinated marketing knowledge management*.

Over time, an individual in the center or a big market will typically rally for evolving the role of central even further...to be led, of course, by that person. *Global marketing management* is when significant investments in central brand or marketing resources come forth. The newly appointed central marketer will most likely develop the first global brand vision and strategy. Without formal power, this strategy only works if the largest markets feel it serves their own interests.

In the next stage of centralization, an *empowered global marketing group* has the muscle to veto any significant country programs that the global team feels are not aligned with the global marketing or brand strategy. Eager to avoid this embarrassing situation, local, regional and global marketers usually engage in an intensive consultation. Central and local typically then shake hands on a clear division of labor, with agreed hand-off points and metrics to ensure that the whole works as a 'total' team.

Finally, there are companies where a *Global Brand Vice-President* has complete decision-making power over all important marketing mix elements. Local marketing reports to central marketing, rather than to their geographic group. This is more the exception than the rule.

Alternate Global Marketing Roles

What role should global marketing play? The traditional spectrum shows that this choice is seldom a black-or-white, all-or-nothing decision.

Particularly over recent years, many global marketing organizations, and specifically their CMOs, have struggled with the question: Who should be doing what? Or, as we've heard more recently: *'I know we need to be doing things more globally, but which things? And where do we draw the line?'*

Structure should follow strategy and so the vision, ambition and strategy dictate the structural role of global marketing. We need to first understand what the overall global marketing environment looks like, as well as the key strategic objectives of the business.

We typically consider four fundamentally different roles that global marketing can play along two dimensions.

The WHAT And HOW Dimensions

THE WHAT

A high score on the 'What' axis implies that the group designs and delivers content – brand strategy, equity and product mix is centralized with little or no local tailoring. In these companies marketing mixes are often developed centrally and often manufacturing is also centralized. Luxury goods are often marketed this way. A very high score implies that almost everything and sometimes even the total mix – all the way down to point of sale materials – is fixed globally.

THE HOW

A high score on the 'How' axis indicates that centralized marketing group drives processes and builds capabilities which are seen as essential to facilitating growth objectives and gaining competitive advantage. Centrally developed key marketing processes (such as Country Marketing Planning or Innovation Process Management) drive alignment between global and local, and build marketing capabilities to establish a common way of working.

Should central marketing create the actual marketing mix and drive it through? Or should it facilitate country marketing by championing consistent, global processes that build capability in local teams? The answer is often a combination that is appropriate for an industry external context and a company's internal context, ambition and strategy.

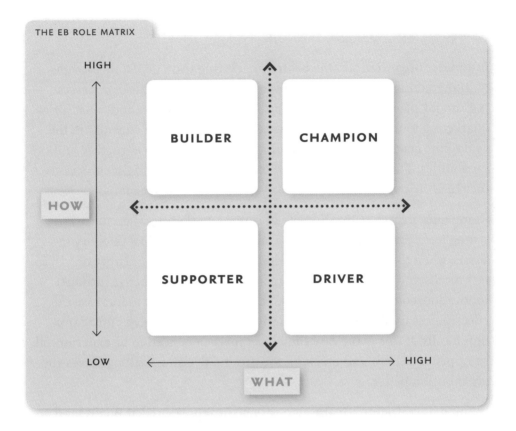

The 4 Roles

1 - SUPPORTER

In some industries like Banking or Computers and Electronics, other functions such as Finance, Sales or R&D drive the business, not Marketing. In this case, Marketing is merely Communications ('Marcom') – whose role is to create awareness for products and services after they have been launched with little influence on the product development process. Responsibilities typically include PR, Sponsorships and Corporate marketing. In a direct selling company for example, the Sales function drives the organization and Marketing provides brochures, selling materials and incentives to support Sales. The role of the central marketing group serves to buttress the rest of the organization with programs that help 'sell' solutions, as well as educate the company on the advantages of better understanding consumer needs and trends. In these companies, Marketing is seldom represented at the highest Board level.

2 - BUILDER

In Builder organizations, the central marketing team generally provides local marketing teams with venues for sharing best practice, processes (e.g., brand-planning), tools (standard briefing templates), and capabilities (marketing foundation courses). By acting as an internal consultant, the goal of the central group is to build local marketing infrastructure and capabilities. This ensures that local marketers make the right choices, as they're ultimately responsible for key marketing mix decisions.

Companies may elect for this role of central marketing when there is strong local competition, there is a lack of common global category insights, when there is high market complexity in legal, regulatory or technical standards and when there is a high speed of change (product innovation, competitive activities). There is often a need to increase the effectiveness of marketing and a desire for flexibility, speed and adaptation locally. If this is the case then local marketers need to be experienced, equipped to act fast and quick on the ground decision making serves the organization better.

In these organizations, marketing may be unrepresented at Board level. The Head of Marketing will most likely be a combined role as in Commercial Head i.e. Head of Sales and Marketing.

3 - DRIVER

The purpose of global marketing in the Driver organization is typically to build consistently strong, billion-dollar-plus brands and manage for efficiencies. The large global team is responsible for developing the full brand mix which is consistently implemented in all countries. All marketing services are situated centrally.

The Driver role is appropriate for organizations in mature categories, where there is a moderate level of global competition, where they share common global category insights, where markets are fairly homogenous and where the brand ultimately drives the business. Luxury brands are run this way, mainly to preserve the exclusiveness of the brand.

In these organizations local teams focus on how to 'land the mix' and create pull in their market. In Driver companies, a CMO typically sits on the Board, and reports directly to the CEO.

4 - CHAMPION

In Champion organizations, brands often compete in mature markets with low levels of growth and must perform against sophisticated global and local brands. There may be a global category insight but this needs to be adapted for the local market. Moreover, there is high complexity across markets i.e. they are in different stages of growth, legal and regulatory standards are different, etc.

Thus, significant expertise at market level is mission-critical in translating global mixes into winning local propositions. The global mix may be designed but leeway is provided for fine-tuning the mix to be more relevant and competitive locally. To maximize the advantage of scale and expertise, global marketing in Champion organizations collaborate to deliver better output than individual markets could achieve. These brands win their competitive battles with a superior marketing mix facilitated by marketing excellence – e.g. common processes and skills. All learning training, processes and tools are centrally led and deployed. In this organization, the CMO sits on the board and reports directly to the CEO.

Transitioning to New Roles

Adopting a new global marketing structure and operating model takes time. To more effectively embed new ways of working, we've come up with a few practical guidelines:

The Plan Is Nothing – Planning Is Everything

Organizational change always feels as though it goes too fast at the top, too slow at the bottom. This is normal. Keep the receiving-end perspective in mind. Bear in mind, too, that early planning and great engagement is often more important than picture-perfect structure and process design. Creating a coalition for change, and using co-creation and open, authentic communication are essential techniques to ensure that the organization remains healthy post-design. And remember the edges: marketing's very nature is to interface with many parts of the business. Be mindful of the implications.

During the early stages of reorganization, typically very little can be communicated because of legal restrictions and confidentiality around reductions in headcount, changing job grades or moving people between jobs. For those at the bottom of the organization, this is a miserable, fear-filled, doubt-inducing period *(Is my job secure?)*. It's often when the most talented individuals choose to leave for safer shores. Those who stay behind are less productive and even less committed.

At the start of any reorganization project, we therefore insist on developing an engagement strategy as part of the overall reorganization project plan. This should start the *same day as* the organizational redesign work. During the early stages, typically the only thing that can be communicated is progress and good intent...but at least this fills the void. (It could be a simple weekly e-mail newsletter or better yet, an entire engagement mix of internal communications, including webcasts, blogs, town hall meetings with Q&A sessions, consultation calls, dedicated intranet sites, and so forth.) To some degree, this comforts those affected by the change with a newfound sense of openness and some understanding of progress.

Go Beyond Structure

Naturally, structural changes alone can never address a company's key challenges. A reorganization plan needs to address what changes are required in the operating model; the people; the experience and expertise that are required; and the processes and skills to be developed.

On people: Grasp the opportunity to build the right mindsets and behaviors as you embed the structural and process changes. Increasing people's personal and team effectiveness rewards both the individual and the company.

On processes: Focus on the interfaces. Sweat the details of each and every role on the map. Marketing organizational changes should immediately be reflected in the product development and brand planning processes.

On skills: Be mindful to celebrate and build the capabilities required of each new role.

Embedding Is The Start...Not The End Point

Organizational design reminds us of marriage. It's not about planning a great wedding, but about spending the rest of your lives together! Embedding begins at the planning stage with creating a coalition and executing a communications strategy. Create a cascade approach; use the leadership team to first explain why change is forthcoming; then explain how the organization and its processes will transform itself to address these challenges.

Sweat the details at all levels in *live* action – applying the change to real life business cases in real time – in order to ensure that the team truly lives the new model.

Build in sufficient feedback and adjustment mechanisms, for example by creating shadow and pilot projects.

Be very careful about this! In our experience, all the focus, resources and budget go into the initial designing of a new organizational structure. This often shortchanges the embedding phase of the reorganization. No matter how prettily they're presented, new organization structures sent out by mail don't land!

Amanda Mackenzie, CMO Aviva; *'You have to get buy in from the top. .... get the processes, the governance, the structures, and have your operating model in place. That discipline is absolutely essential if you're trying to push a change management program through a global, diverse, federated organization. Thirdly, there is no substitute for being very resolute, but keep your stakeholders informed!'* Remember that tools to lock down roles aren't actually the output, they're the process that leads you to the right decisions. More than anything else, the quality of the discussions between key stakeholders is what really counts. Bear in mind that organizational redesign is never finished. It's a living, breathing entity that needs an embedded process for ongoing tweaks and adjustments.

Finally: If there are tough conversations that need to happen, make them happen early. That's what senior people are for. Leaders who fail to resolve issues, or who choose to sweep them under the nearest rug, always see the issues reappear later. By then, typically, they've gotten worse.

Embedding New Roles: Behaving Globally

Let's assume you've created clarity around new global marketing structure, roles and responsibilities, and even the operating model. We know it doesn't happen easily, but play along with us for a few moments.

Creating clarity isn't all that's required.

Often there's an even more important question to address, namely: *Do the people who matter around the organization believe it's the right organization and operating model for the business? Will the structure assuredly enable the delivery of the stated strategy?*

'Now hold on a second,' we can hear you protest. *'Not only do I have to create clarity around structure, you mean I also have to convince everyone and their uncle that the model we have chosen is the right one?'*

Yes.

An important finding of our work over the years? The critical importance of leadership behavior on the adoption and credibility of a new operating model. Too often, key stakeholders trample new rules, confusing and de-motivating the lower managers. Which is why we ask as part of our benchmarking whether or not people feel that everyone in the marketing organization is behaving consistently with the operating model. On average only 11 percent fully agree with this statement!

Let's take a typical example that we often confront: An organization is globalizing in response to increased market transparency, converging consumer demand and competitive scale threats. In her wisdom (and incidentally, we almost always agree with this), the CMO convinces the CEO that from now on, the regional marketers should no longer report to local general managers, but instead, into global marketing.
You don't need to be a genius to understand who (almost instinctively)

dislikes the result of this decision. First, the General Managers that lead the regions lose their ability to influence marketing decisions through a direct line. They now need to accept the wisdom and decisions of global marketing, as well as the loss of an important report. Second, regional marketers themselves need to buy into the concept of global taking decisions, as well as the wholly new responsibility of helping to *implement* versus *develop* strategies.

After a new structure or new way of working is announced, people who believe the decision was misguided or against their own personal interests may set out to prove everyone else (or at least the CMO) wrong. If this doesn't happen, it would be the exception, so plan on it.

When this happens, the CMO or global brand head has to act quickly and resolutely because the credibility and survival of the whole new operating model is on the line.

If other stakeholders are looking on from the sidelines (and let's assume they're *always* looking on) and if they perceive any gap between how the CEO and CMO react to this challenge, your new marketing organization is pretty much doomed to fail.

We remember all too well the disastrous effect of Unilever's leadership ambivalence when the company first began promoting a global brand approach in 2001. (This took place when two Chairmen, one Dutch, the other Irish, led the company.) Evidently, as one Chairman went around emphasizing the importance of the new more global operating model, the other Chairman made it a point to insist that local marketing directors refuse to compromise for the sake of overall global success. Unilever resolved the ensuing mayhem only when its first single CEO and Chairman, Patrick Cescau, came on board.

Even today, we nearly always find that organizations tolerate individuals up high who confuse and demotivate others by knowingly contradicting the new operating model. Any CMO or global brand head worth his or her salt will rout this behavior and respectfully but resolutely remove the offending party.

Hiring For The Role

Against this backdrop, the individuals you hire, and the traits you seek in region and country marketing roles, take on critical importance.

Listen to Peter Vaughn of American Express: *'If you've decided that you're going to do most of your product, marketing and brand strategy centrally, you're not going to want to hire someone who's only interested in doing just that into a local marketing role. You're going to want to hire somebody whose passion is about delivering the strategy in the most robust and locally relevant way possible.'*

What Success Looks Like

Deciding who does what is never easy and expends a lot of energy. But once an organization clarifies its decision-making processes, it can move forward speedily and effectively. Recalls Aline Santos of Unilever, *'Once our DIG GBT started working as an effective decision-making body, things started moving. And people started following through. It became untenable to say one thing in a meeting and then do another outside the meeting.'*

Human nature is what it is. Expect recidivism, e.g. occasional slides back into old habits and mindsets. That said, management's timely reinforcement always serves to embed mental constructs and promulgate behavior change.

What are the rewards for all this heavy lifting? Is it *really* worth the effort? Yes. When alignment takes root, and people perceive organizational challenges through a common lens, a marketing machine begins to sing. A company that's accomplished its objectives can take enormous comfort in a well-oiled marketing machine: one that transports them to where they need to go – smoothly.

ORGANIZING SONY ERICSSON
FOR GLOBAL SUCCESS

Sony Ericsson

In 2001 the prominent Japanese consumer electronics company Sony and Ericsson – the Swedish telecommunications company – established a new joint venture and created Sony Ericsson – a new mobile telephone company.

The joint venture seemed like the perfect marriage; matching Sony's consumer electronics and design expertise with Ericsson's technological and hardware dominance in the communications sector.

The company quickly reaped the benefits of the joint venture. Within five years Sony Ericsson had emerged as the fourth-largest mobile phone manufacturer in the world. It spearheaded industry-changing innovations such as the Walkman and Cyber-shot telephone series.

But after big initial successes the tide started turning. By 2008, competition had become intense, Apple had just launched its first iPhone, and financial pressure was mounting. The company was restructuring across the board to regain profitability, increase efficiency and address the industry globalization trend. Lennard Hoornik, who had just taken on the mantle of Head of Global Marketing, knew the challenge was tough.

But in the eye of the crisis, the marketing leader saw a chance to develop a new global brand vision, build a new *fit for growth team*, roll-out a new marketing strategy and re-model the organization. By 2010 Sony Ericsson pleased the markets with the first two quarterly profits in many years and a very attractive line of new phone models and marketing programs that are recapturing consumer favor.

Lennard Hoornik came over to London as Global Head of Marketing from Singapore where he had been leading the company's business growth in the aggressive Asia-Pacific region. Sensing that marketing had become too removed from the business, he quickly set about reconnecting and making clear to the rest of the organization that marketing understood its role; building the brand through marketing programs and communication to serve the business.

Ensuring that he had the right people on the bus first, and moving fast, Hoornik quickly assembled a small team of the best HQ and regional marketers to develop the new brand vision and global marketing strategy.

'Speed is of the essence in this business. It now all goes so quickly. So where normally people probably took a year to roll out a brand, now we have to do it in a third of the time.'

Starting with a global marketing effectiveness *PulseCheck,* Hoornik quickly built an understanding of all the key opportunities, challenges, and needs of the company, as well as the readiness for growth of the new more global marketing organization. By quickly reaching out to all major stakeholders across the business, Lennard and his team ensured that everyone knew marketing was connected again.

'How much time you spend talking and listening in the company is very important. In fact, it's crucial. You're managing expectations, not just with your own group but also sideways – and up.'

The results were pleasantly positive. People in the organization were highly motivated and inspired. They displayed high energy levels and enthusiasm about working on the Sony Ericsson brand. They were positive and encouraging about a more global approach to building the brand and leveraging a more global strategy to make relevant for local markets.

The idea of arming everyone with a global marketing model with global marketing communications and tools to support local implementation received tremendous support. But people were looking for changes in the organization to eliminate roadblocks, confusion and duplication, and for new ways of working to enable the brand vision to be translated into reality.

Once it was clear what business requirements the new global marketing strategy needed to address, Hoornik challenged a dedicated team of internal and external experts to redesign the marketing organization, cutting overall headcount numbers and making it *'fit for purpose'* for the new strategy.

The organizational transformation of marketing across global and regions would involve streamlined marketing structures and newly defined global marketing roles, processes, and ways of functioning. In the new world, global would take complete ownership of developing the Sony Ericsson brand vision as well as the global communication campaigns. The number of regional marketers was significantly reduced and those who remained were asked to focus on helping local marketers develop winning local activation plans to implement the global strategy.

Lennard laid out his key priorities and asked his team to work out the next level of detail for the strategy and the global marketing organizational structure. To ensure successful embedding of the new organization and help people succeed in their

Sony Ericsson 2010

newly defined marketing roles, there was a need to build marketing capability in some core expertise areas at the same time as the new ways of working were being rolled out.

The grand idea was to re-communicate the new Sony Ericsson brand vision and strategy and at the same time offer tools to local marketing and sales teams to succeed in the fast moving mobile communications industry. Sony Ericsson wanted its people to talk more about communication solutions to serve the consumers and customers and focus less on the hardware features and specs. With new and much better designed models on the way, there was an opportunity to make a bang and achieve maximum market impact for 2010. The goal was clear: the new program had to be dynamic yet simple.

During 2009, global marketing designed and then rapidly rolled out a new marketing planning program and tools that helped strengthen expertise, capability and the marketing infrastructure in all key 'must-win' Market Unit (MU) teams.

To translate and adapt the global brand vision and strategy into a winning tactical market program, local marketers were supported as they assessed their key consumer, competitive and retail dynamics and then developed their next year's plan. A two-day marketing capability workshop incorporating focused 'learning by doing' was designed to identify compelling consumer insights, develop winning propositions, as well as embed a common language and approach across the total organization.

Senior marketers from global and regional teams participated in all of the top 10 'Gold' market workshops. *The ResultsFactory* Workshop was launched in vital market units, such as the U.K., Iberia, Russia, and China.

Workshops were timed to have maximum influence on each market's planning for first half of 2010. The markets chosen for the workshop were the top-of-the-line local markets so that large-scale impact could be seen and if positive, could be immediately duplicated by smaller markets.

ResultsFactory attendees always included key delegates from marketing and sales, as well as the local general manager. Everyone attending the workshop was asked to contribute in-depth through their analysis of the local market's specific opportunities and challenges and submit their program suggestions to the country heads who then clustered and aligned inputs and added rigor and a leadership perspective.

Every workshop included an immersion session with shoppers and mobile phone store managers to allow participants to discover insights or solutions to energize and make the local markets more ready and competition wise. These insights were then applied to the key opportunities and challenges to be addressed in the 2010 plan.

A global or regional participant led a brain-storming session on execution tool-kits, media and digital guidelines and support packages. This set the foundation for the creation of an integrated marketing and sales 2010 roadmap. Roles and responsibilities and agendas were finalized and the workshops all ended with a final opportunity and risk evaluation study.

The new local marketing plans displayed a much clearer coherence with the overall global strategy and there has been a marked success upturn.

Almost two years after the more global structure and ways of working were adopted, the structure and ways of working are being evolved further to recognize the successful embedding of the global brand approach. Now that the Sony Ericsson brand has been firmly re-established and local programs are displaying high levels of alignment with the global brand vision, global guidelines are being relaxed and more say is being delegated to local teams to even better ensure local implementation with relevance.

The transformation in Sony Ericsson's global marketing structure and ways of working have helped the company to re-emerge stronger than ever to tackle the challenges of the dynamic mobile communications industry.

Building
Capability

And Then Letting Go

P&G

JIM STENGEL - GMO PROCTER & GAMBLE (2001-2008)

Jim Stengel is one of the most recognized and successful CMOs of the last decade.

In late 2008, Jim surprised the marketing world by leaving his prestigious role as Global Marketing Officer (GMO) at Procter & Gamble, one of the world's most admired brand-building companies. This bold and unusual move was Jim's first step on a new mission: Sharing his passion for growing brands through a focus on higher ideals.

Jim grew up in Pennsylvania, in a family of six children. He holds a BA from Franklin & Marshall College and an MBA from Pennsylvania State University. These days, Jim and his wife Kathleen divide their time between Cincinnati, Ohio and Coronado, California.

Try having a polite, superficial, two-minute-long conversation with Jim about brands. It's impossible. Eternally questing, he loves nothing more than to question, probe, brainstorm and fire himself up about everything from economic demand theories to insights about Latin American cooking habits. All this at the speed of light, too. Persuasive to the point that most listeners can't help but end up agreeing with him, Jim can make a new marketing concept sound as compelling and innovative as the invention of sliced bread.

As the Global Marketing Officer of $83B Procter & Gamble, Jim oversaw an $8B advertising budget while maintaining organizational responsibility for nearly 7,000 people. In 2008, P&G was honored as the 2008 Cannes International Advertising Festival Advertiser of the Year for the first time in company history – a tribute to Jim's extraordinary leadership. Asked what he enjoyed most about the GMO role, Jim, a genuine global citizen, is quick to reply: 'What stimulated me was the power of sharing totally inspirational work and ideas across cultures and across boundaries. I would get such energy out of a visit to China and discover something that I thought could work somewhere else. So, to me, it was all about getting out there and understanding what was working, what was elevating consumers, elevating customers. And then, to try and spread that.'

Surprisingly, Jim didn't start his illustrious career at P&G. It wasn't until

1983 that he left Time-Life books to join the Cincinnati-based company. Before his 2001 promotion to P&G's top advertising and marketing position, Jim had P&L responsibility for the company's European Baby Care business, and held positions of gradually ascending responsibility in P&G's developing markets, Cosmetic, and Food businesses.

Jim may have been widely recognized for his work alongside CEO A.G. Lafley on revamping P&G's innovation approach, but he'll most likely be best remembered for reinvigorating P&G's marketing capability, culture and ways of working after the company suffered several years of decline in marketing performance and confidence. During his tenure as GMO, he spearheaded the complete transformation of the marketing discipline, once again firmly establishing P&G as among the most renowned brand-building companies in the world.

How? By doing a few things really well and putting the consumer first in everything P&G did – which served to reinvigorate the organization's consumer-driven culture. Under Jim's watch, Procter marketers re-dialed up their focus on understanding and serving consumers' needs.

Another key focus: To capture, codify and spread marketing best practices quickly, and to redefine how everyone inside the company perceived the role of marketing. Jim and his team also developed and instigated a framework that enabled P&G to teach and effectively transfer knowledge about brand-building across the world, across all categories.

As Jim later told us: *'You need to have the vision and the courage to prepare the people and the company for the future. Let's not think about the next year or two, but let's think about preparing the company for 2015 or 2020. What capabilities will we need? What do we need the agency model to look like? Where do we think media is going?'*

The results of Jim's capability building investment are self-evident. Today, P&G boasts a stable of 22 brands, each of which has racked up more than US$1 billion in sales. Eighteen additional brands are each valued at between US$500 million and US$1 billion in business volume.

And maybe most importantly of all...the company has rediscovered its marketing mojo!

Reflecting on his seven-year role at the helm of the P&G marketing machine, Jim Stengel comments, *'Probably my two biggest legacies were in having a big impact in shaping a culture of more purpose-driven, innovative brand building, and putting in place strategies and designs for future organizational capability which to this day are still being executed.'*

Since venturing out almost two years ago, Jim has taken on a variety of ambitious new roles. As a consultant, he inspires brand and business leaders across the globe to achieve higher performance by rethinking their marketing. As an author, Jim serves as a catalyst to help companies attain higher performance by focusing on higher ideals. And, as an Adjunct Professor at the UCLA Anderson School of Management, today Jim is inspiring a new generation of marketing leaders to redefine the very meaning of marketing.

Always a pioneer of applying new technology, Jim was among the first senior executives to understand the value of connecting via new media – and to communicate with younger audiences through new channels. His Facebook page explains his personal philosophy in language anyone young and old can understand: *'I believe marketing must rethink its purpose to achieve far better results. We must apply life's lessons – generosity, love, humor, empathy and service – so that marketing inspires life and life inspires marketing.'*

BUILDING GLOBAL MARKETING CAPABILITY

If Focus is about creating clarity for everyone in the organization about the business and brand objectives; and Organize is about making clear who does what; then Build is about arming everyone in the organization with the information, skills and tools they need to succeed.

And then letting go. Getting out of the way.

Stengel recognized the value of building the ultimate marketing machine. To prepare P&G for accelerated growth and maximum benefits, and to ensure marketing fully leveraged the company's scale, he spent as much time focusing on building global marketing capability as he did on the product marketing mix and performance.

Asked what he believes determines the effectiveness of a global marketing organization, Jim quickly mentions one of his key priorities: *building capability*. How else can a large and (almost by definition) somewhat bureaucratic global marketing organization trounce an agile local competitor? Why be global if you can't swiftly identify, then share, a winning product concept or market program across multiple countries?

For Greg Welch of Spencer Stuart, few organizational imperatives are as crucial as building marketing capability: *'Really taking the trouble and the time and energy to figure out, what is it that makes individuals in the team, and the organization as a whole, successful? Then giving them not only the feedback but also the processes, tools and information to get their job done and keep growing themselves.'*

Building global marketing capability is about laying the groundwork for effective global marketing collaboration. Call it whatever you want – table stakes, or the hygiene factor. It's about compensating for being less small and agile than a local competitor. It's about driving competitive advantage by equipping your marketers for success by leveraging your organizational scale and experience across your global market network.

The Art Of Letting Go

In the previous chapter, we discussed at what point a global marketer should pass the baton to local. Does global focus exclusively on vision, positioning and communication platforms, or does the handover take place much further down the marking mix? Many CMOs and global marketers of our acquaintance struggle with this question. And, as we indicated earlier, significant market, competitive, and cultural conditions can drive this particular decision.

That said, we also recognize this isn't quite what you'd call a rational decision-making process. Global marketers who have developed what they believe is a winning concept are understandably wary of letting go and allowing others to seize and run with the idea – only to (just perhaps) get it wrong. Smart CMOs won't demand too much from a local marketing organization whose skills and competencies are nascent or immature.

At the same time, most global marketing leaders recognize that merely rolling out a cookie-cutter solution across the globe is, more often than not, a recipe for disaster. If a given solution fails to combine the global mix with local translation and expertise to make the company's solutions and programs locally relevant, a competitive global company is neglecting to leverage its total ability. To do otherwise requires *real* local marketing excellence.

If a company has established – and harmonized across the company – a shared marketing language and base set of skills and competencies, then in practice, passing ideas and programs back, forth, up, down and all across the organization becomes a whole lot easier.

Or, to put it another way: If you and others speak the same language, and think and act similarly, you're more likely to invest in a timely way in helping them learn from your experience.

Therefore, building global marketing capability becomes as much about building marketing excellence as it is about enabling the global team to let go.

Badly Needed

Successful CMOs find the time and resources they need to develop key competitive skills and competencies. Seldom if ever will they delegate these responsibilities to HR, or to a training manager. Instead, they're actively involved in leveraging what they've developed as a key leadership tool.

This much is clear to us: marketing capability programs are crucial - across industries, geographies and marketing seniority levels.

In 2008, we ran a dedicated *Leading Global Brands Asia* study. (We wanted to better understand the global marketing opportunities and challenges in this fast-growing region.)

The Asia-Pacific region runs the gamut from emerging to mature economies. Not surprisingly, the depth of marketing capability tends to run in lockstep with the level of market maturity. That said, what we discovered about global marketing capability development was dramatic:

Fewer than half (46 percent) of Asia-based respondents agreed that global and regional teams provided country marketers with the right tools to do their jobs well. Only 37 percent believed they had the right tools in hand to carry out their jobs. And fewer than $1/3^{rd}$ of all respondents (31 percent) claimed they were privy to best practices. In one strikingly candid admission, only 28 percent of respondents believed that regional teams did a capable job of helping them by building skills in-country.

Which is all the more reason to lay the groundwork for building marketing capability. With this foundation in place, organizations are freed to eventually launch important brand initiatives.

You might recall that Kerris Bright of AkzoNobel was behind the major re-launch of the Dulux brand. Kerris stresses that during the first few years, she focused on preparing the organization for change, but, '*Only after laying the strategic foundation, a common language, common process, a common market segmentation so that people look at and explain the market in the same way, can we now accelerate and activate the gate. If we had not laid the foundation first, we would be on shaky ground.*'

Marc Mathieu of Coca-Cola concurs: '*When I was heading Global Brand Marketing at Coke, I made 'The Coca-Cola Way of Marketing' a big priority. We recalibrated all our key marketing processes and ensured that we had a consistency in approach across all brands and regions.*'

Change Leadership

But if most people agree that building capability is among the pre-requisites of achieving consistency and effectiveness across the globe, why aren't more organizations engaged in what seems to be a fairly straightforward (if work-intensive) exercise? Why hasn't *every* organization done it?

Without new capabilities, step-change transformation is impossible. If you fail to articulate new capabilities from the get-go, and establish a plan for their future development, you cannot transform your newly slimmed-down company. An organization that fails to develop a positive, forward-looking future vision will invariably shrink under the pressure of cost-cutting. (And as one management guru famously said, '*No company has ever shrunk its way to success.*') Cost-cutting solutions that ignore internal imperatives to develop new capabilities and skill sets drain organizations of the very skills they need to survive these same solutions intact. Let's be mindful of the goal, after all: to do *more* with less...not less with less.

Bear in mind, too, the huge efficiency factor. Reinventing ideas and programs costs money; thinking through new strategies for identical visions wastes precious time; and making the same mistakes across the globe is expensive in more ways than one. Savvy, capable global marketing organizations recognize the upsides of building a common marketing language and approach, and making both available to everyone who faces the same challenges and opportunities.

Example: The Marketing Director of a category leadership brand in Russia calls to say that for the first time a retailer's private label product is mounting a serious attack on his brand. As usual, the retailer is both an essential partner and, now, also a ferocious competitor. How should an organization best respond to the threat? The responses are often anecdotal, e.g.,

'Didn't we once try that somewhere else?' or *'Who was it who was facing the same decision last year?'* or worse, *'I feel I'm reinventing the wheel here!'*

Few things are more demotivating to a local or global marketer than knowing he or she can't access crucial expertise or experience within a company (or alternatively, in some cases, has no idea how). We've often heard people saying with a sigh, *'If only my company knew what it knows!'*

Finally, an important element of leadership revolves around attracting, developing and retaining talent. Time and again, studies show that companies that invest in developing their talents, skills and competencies boast higher employee motivation and retention levels. In the end, what could be more expensive than a team of veteran employees who leave the company because organization was unwilling to invest in their growth?

In short, from many leadership perspectives, building marketing capabilities makes a great deal of sense. So how to start? In this chapter, we'll be discussing both the *what* and *how* of marketing excellence.

What To Look For

Typically, we recommend assessing whether or not a global marketing organization is effectively identifying (or *harvesting*, as we call it), and then leveraging, its best practices and experience across the company with a dedicated marketing excellence benchmark study.

A marketing excellence assessment checks that employees at every single level across the discipline, plus adjoining and cooperative disciplines, are both well-informed and well-armed for success. It's important to aggregate and analyze at geographical, functional and seniority levels. Do people feel as though the organization is taking care of them? Drill down to individual country and brand levels to better understand the answers.

Starting at an overall, almost cultural level, ask: Do people feel as though they're members of a *learning organization*? To put it another way, does the organization roll out its successes globally? Are systems in place that prevent the repetition of mistakes? Is management capturing and sharing best practices? Do local and regional marketers feel that their ideas, suggestions and experiences are reflected across the overall global strategy? In short, the hypothetical question is worth repeating: Does the company know what it knows?

A thorough assessment also addresses the question of whether people feel the company is making an effort to help them succeed. Are these efforts effective? If not, why not? For instance, one question in our assessment specifically asks local marketers whether regional, and/or global marketing are helping them build brand expertise. And whether local marketers feel that the tools that regional and global marketing teams have given them facilitate their jobs.

WHAT Capabilities *To Build*

At a minimum, a global marketing community must possess functional expertise or capabilities. (These are baseline table stakes that simply allow you to play the game. Yet sometimes even these basic capabilities are lacking!) Thus, every single traditional marketing and communications function – from deploying market research; to developing consumer insights; to deepening your distribution; to leveraging your channel; to competitive intelligence; to intelligent pricing; to sponsorships; to management-marketing and advertising; to leveraging social media – should be part of an arsenal you can wield with confidence and fluency.

But back to basics. To build marketing capability, what should we focus on?

COMMON LANGUAGE

Everything starts with developing and embedding a common marketing language. If I don't understand you, and you don't understand me, well, our conversation won't get very far. If we're using a markedly different language to describe similar circumstances, consumer need-states, habits, attitudes, benefits, positioning and so forth, then we can't even *begin* to identify best practices and sharing tools.

Most of the big global marketing companies have established foundational, practical courses and programs to help new employees ease the leap from a university to an office. Since these same companies promote from within, language isn't a problem.

Such programs are particularly important for companies that hire market-ers only after they've spent their five years of post-university training on the job at companies like Kraft, Nestle or P&G. The same is true for entire industries where marketing is not typically in the lead – including telecom, financial and technology companies. It's essential to align immediately the language of their marketers.

BASIC MARKETING SKILLS & PROCESSES

Many organizations pointedly offer basic marketing skills programs to ensure that all employees understand and agree upon the organization's approach. These programs can also include on-board cross-discipline moves, e.g., a development manager who's just been transferred to market-ing for the next few years – as well as basic processes like briefings, project management, time management, budgeting and team management.

In short, these programs typically cover the basic skills required to prepare a manager for a junior role in marketing, when the real learning starts.

CATEGORY/MARKET EXPERTISE

As mentioned, many organizations have developed market immersions or category specific training programs. This way, every marketer has the benefit of absorbing the expertise that the company has accumulated over the years. Over the past decade, we've helped leaders in companies as diverse as Starbucks, Novartis and technology company, TomTom, share their market expertise across their firms. Ranging from a *'Beauty Academy'* to a *'Foods Excellerator,'* these market immersion programs typically focus on sharing in-depth expertise on market specific consumer habits and attitudes, competitor strategy, retail dynamics and activation learning.

The target managers in these programs are typically senior. Their 'students' are new team members who are proficient in marketing, but who've come to the firm armed with external marketing experience. Sometimes they're even internal colleagues who are focusing on building brands in a new market.

BRAND CLARITY & CONSISTENCY

Earlier in this book, we focused on brand vision and strategy. As we all know, marketers and their colleagues in sales, research and development may be working on several brands at the same time. Sometimes the *company* is the brand. In general, though, each and every brand has its own proprietary story to tell, and promise to make (and deliver against).

Almost all the brands we've studied have some sort of brand immersion program in place. Most equip people working on the brand to start building it at 200 miles per hour! Some global brand leaders create brand immersion intranet websites, brand books and videos. Still others hit the road running with brand engagement workshops. These programs are typically available online 24/7, or duplicated annually to accommodate the significant movement typically found in marketing. All are founded on the same premise: to ensure that everyone understands where the brand comes from, and where it's heading.

MARKETING PLANNING TOOLS

Once you've clarified the brand, and the basics around the market in which you work, marketing strategy discussions typically turn to brand planning. In other words given our overall marketing growth or brand vision, what can we in Research, or Germany, or Sales do next year to help drive the vision? (In our chapter on *Focus*, we emphasized the importance of a rigorous brand planning process, one that forces alignment across disciplines, geographies and down the organization.)

These marketing planning processes serve to align *the objectives* of marketing plans across markets and disciplines. So let's discuss the value of creating marketing tools that help leverage scale in strategy and tactics. These days, the best global marketers collaborate with lead countries to develop guidelines and/or toolsets that can ensure that local marketers quickly duplicate proven marketing tactics. After all, if a tactic has worked well in the past in a similar market, why bother reinventing the wheel?

Often organizations will have clustered markets into three or four development stages. They'll have designed and developed market-specific programs dedicated to the most relevant brand objectives. For example, despite their significant market differences, India, China and Russia may receive training in marketing programs that have been proven, or specifically developed, to win share in fast-growing environments where traditional retail isn't yet established.

We've worked with clients to develop specific product launch toolkits or programs designed to ensure that local marketers can apply tactics with minimal adaptation. In 2004, Dove Pro-Age was among the first beauty-category launches ever whose program – from trade magazine advertisements to generating buzz to help with new shelf space allocation across a multiple number of formats – was available on a DVD developed by the global team.

Caution: These kits run the risk of becoming overly prescriptive. (They may even offend local marketers if too little room is left for local interpretation.) Prepare and design them well – with the help of one key country in each cluster – and you'll trump these risks via significant efficiencies and increased quality.

The best toolkits typically involve some sort of quiz or questionnaire to help local markets select which tool components may work best for their market.

WHAT Skills To Build

Many organizations have set up marketing skills programs that reflect the progression of their marketers from assistants … to marketing managers. These courses generally cover the first five to seven years of an individual's career.

Among the topics most basic Marketing '101' programs offer are brand planning; consumer connections; competitor analysis; interpreting market data; promotion planning; idea brainstorming; briefing and evaluating creative ideas; basics of positioning; and annual calendar event-planning development.

Marketing '201' programs typically target marketers who have a few years' experience under their belts. They focus on deepening these same skills to reflect these marketers' seniority and responsibility. They also tack on a few crucial – and relevant – subjects. Via a full 'war gaming' module that forces executives to step into their competitors' shoes, then walk through a variety of scenarios designed to uncover new opportunities and challenges, these programs can deftly target competitor and market analysis, master brand positioning development, as well as the fundamentals of brand stretch and architecture. Additional modules often include sponsorships; Finance for Marketers; program ROI measurement; Category Management; assortment pricing; and Shopper Insights – while activation and promotion development are ratcheted up a notch through modules on fully integrated communication that encompass all touchpoints in 360-degree programs.

Additionally, companies also offer advanced marketing programs at the Director level. These programs also target experienced marketers who need a quick immersion or refresher course. These programs also focus on Portfolio Management and Strategic Partnering, not to mention modules that fold in other full marketing mix components, including Innovation and full Communication Platform development.

Hot Topics

If these subjects comprise the staples of a marketing skills training program, where does that leave subjects that can't leverage either internal experience or expertise?

'It's very difficult to become incredibly well-rounded these days,' says Greg Welch of Spencer Stuart. (This skilled headhunter should know.) *'You've got to understand multi-cultural marketing. You've got to understand digital and social media. And sustainability is quickly becoming table stakes rather than competitive advantage.'*

Among the questions that practically all brands struggle with? What agencies should they partner with? How can they optimally integrate online and offline touchpoints? What percentage of spend should they place online versus offline? How can they measure effectiveness? (This doesn't even begin to cover the multitude of questions surrounding Twitter, Facebook, and other social media.)

Digital & Social Media is by far the hottest topic for last, this and probably next year. In the digital field, we've worked with content and channel experts ranging from Google to MSN to AOL to develop programs that immerse marketers in the digital world, especially more senior marketers who are less well-versed in new media than their junior counterparts. In many cases, we believe today's leaders aren't fully leveraging the medium *enough* (their children are too young; while they're often too advanced in age). Some of our most exciting and effective programs leverage reverse-mentoring techniques, coupling senior marketing managers with young marketers in order to expose seasoned leaders to the new universe of social media.

Experience Branding has also become a huge topic. Marketers are realizing that the acceleration of convergence across touchpoints has made a fully integrated brand experience possible, and in many cases, essential to developing competitive advantage and consumer loyalty.

In order to offer consumers more comprehensive solutions, *Strategic Partnering* is quickly becoming a subject that marketers are pursuing aggressively as well. One such area? Collaborative innovation with suppliers. We often find that a lack of internal alignment – for example, between marketing and development or purchasing and supply chain – poses big challenges to healthy partnerships.

HOW To Build Global Marketing Capability

There are many ways companies can develop, deliver and embed global marketing excellence. We stress the importance of matching the delivery vehicle to the materials, thereby creating an overall learning and sharing environment. In this scenario, people walk away equipped with real action plans they can apply not next year, not when they graduate to a new job, but *right now.*

Among the best ways effective global marketing excellence building can work?

FOSTERING A LEARNING CULTURE

Everything starts with a company's culture. Change is a long-term exercise. Influence is, too. Both have to happen. A learning culture is best fostered and demonstrated via example. If the CMO can convince the CEO or Chairman to lead by example, news will spread quickly. As they travel through the world, CMOs and global brand leaders can make an enormous impact merely by demonstrating support and promoting a learning culture.

By making it a point to visit local research, never forgetting to probe beyond the 'polite questioning' level, and openly supporting initiatives devoted to increased understanding, CMOs will quickly communicate that an openness to learning is a strength, not a weakness or vulnerability.

But if the company's culture is entrepreneurial and Lone Wolf-like, it's often difficult to embed marketing excellence. In these environments, central marketing and support teams should offer training on a demand-only basis. This means that central marketing should invest time resources and time only *if* and *when* individuals or market units decide they *need* the training.

INTEGRATING WITH BUSINESS PLANNING & THE BUDGET CALENDAR

By far the most effective means to ensure that learning isn't just understood, but applied, is to embed important marketing skills and capability building into the company's regular planning processes.

Is there a better time to learn budget planning than during your preparations for the budgeting process? Why not learn about media planning as you're getting ready to brainstorm about your country's media planning?

Sad to say, this rarely happens. If it does, it's seldom done well.

A few years ago, we helped Unilever develop and embed their new local marketing planning process into 32 'hot spot' markets around the world. This new Brand Marketing Planning (BMP) process was one element of an overall approach that the Unilever Marketing Academy developed and rolled out. Special about the new approach was that it forced local managers to combine their reality on the ground (retail, competitive and of course, consumer) with the brand's longer term vision. Today, this process has been folded into the formal planning process for all national market planning, global brand strategic planning and global category planning.

We used this roll out into the 32 hot spots as a training moment to embed key strategic marketing skills, e.g., consumer shopping behavior analysis, customer and retail planning, and integrated brand communication planning and development. It took two full years – a trial year followed by a full-blast roll out year. After that, the new process was fully embedded and felt like as though this had always been the Unilever way of doing brand planning.

IN-COMPANY STRUCTURED PROGRAMS

The easy way? Send your high potentials to riotously expensive programs at INSEAD, Kellogg or Harvard. But when your newly inspired potentials return to the office, their Inboxes will be overloaded, and their colleagues typically indifferent. It takes a big man or woman to pull the whole department together and say *'We need to now do things differently! Listen to me!'* Not exactly what we'd call an ideal scenario for change-initiation. Change of any size requires momentum – a quality in which chic business schools don't exactly specialize. Our colleague Elana Gold: *'You have to ask yourself the question: if I send this talented team member for two weeks to Fontainebleau, who will really benefit from that, besides that team member him/herself?'*

By institutionalizing capability in-house, you can avoid this vacuum pitfall. Structured marketing programs like a *Marketing University or Academy* are often closely linked to marketers' career progressions. Their participation is best linked to (pending) promotions into new, more senior, marketing roles – as well as personal development plans and targets.

SPECIAL AWARDS & FELLOWSHIPS

Structured programs usually encompass the basics skill sets or the *'Company X Way of Marketing.'* By leveraging Awards, Centers of Excellence and Fellowships, many CMOs and heads of global brands go a step further by promoting learning, and the deepening of relevant expertise.

We propose that companies mount a (healthy, wholesome, un-nasty) annual internal competition, during which markets and HQ developers strive for recognition of the quality of their work. These competitions are a great way to inspire, showcase and celebrate great work at all levels. (Please note the words 'at all levels'!)

At the end of this chapter, we'll take a look at how Procter & Gamble's Jim Stengel and his team reinstated the Harley Procter program to recognize specialized marketing expertise. Fellows gain special recognition, plus time and budget to travel as they continue to develop and share their expertise with colleagues across the company. We might add here that recognizing individuals goes a long way toward motivating and retaining long-time talent, some of whom are perhaps unwilling or unable to make further career moves.

MARKETING ON GLOBAL BRAND INTRANETS

'If you're serious about leveraging marketing capability,' says Marianne Schoenauer, Director, Marketing Knowledge Management at Unilever, 'you need to first establish a robust way to identify best practices in the marketplace, then actually analyzing them in a rigorous manner, then codifying them, and finally, making them accessible to people to learn from and most importantly: use.'

She elaborates: 'Accessibility isn't just putting something somewhere and saying, hey, there you are! It's putting it in a place where you can find it, when you want it, in a form you can access and use easily. At Unilever, it is all part of our online learning program. Knowledge and expertise are institutional products of any large organization. And make no mistake - no company can survive for long without a strategy for capturing and leveraging the institutional knowledge.'

Marianne should know. Over the years, she and her team have transformed Unilever into a knowledge management powerhouse. How? By constructing a world-class marketing intranet system that captures and shares knowledge at both brand and category level.

When well-executed, these intranet sites can serve as one-stop solution shops for marketers all over the world. Over the last five years, they've become critically important central resources for expertise, strategic planning tools, relevant training programs and best practice examples from other markets.

The most-used resources on these sites are tools. *'When we launched the new platform,'* recalls Egbert van Acht of Philips, *'we realized that we needed to bring new training and tools into the company. You cannot expect people to change how they behave if you don't show them how and give them the tools.'*

The best brand intranet sites often include a significant on-boarding immersion program to accommodate the enormous number of people who are joining any global brand throughout any point in the year. A global brand site typically takes the target audience through the vision, positioning and longer-term strategy, thereby establishing inspiration and focus. Nowadays, many of these sites also provide leadership presentation kits that local marketing directors can use to run a workshop or session alongside their local teams.

That said, a lot of large companies have lagged behind in the area of marketing knowledge management. All too often, junior managers operate these brand intranet initiatives, using the lame briefing, *'Please put our brand book online and share some case studies from countries.'* In our experience, an initiative won't work unless the team leading it brings knowledge and change management, coupled with significant brand experience.

CMOs often forget that the quality benchmarks for these intranets are external. Merely establishing a site doesn't necessarily represent a big step forward. Remember: Marketers will compare a site's user-friendliness and ease of access to information sites like Google and Wikipedia! A site has only one chance to make a good first impression. Repel your users with a poor intranet resource, and you'll have a tough time getting them back.

NEWSLETTERS WITH CASE STUDIES

From our perspective, case studies are among the best ways of sharing best practices, expertise and new planning processes. Shared newsletters, workshops and even webcasts that celebrate 'heroes' who can then 'own' great work will make a big difference in the lives of the people you're trying to influence. Ensure that every case study offers an example and tells a real story, but also leaves users with a codified approach, or tool, that local marketers can apply to their own businesses. Case studies needn't be *only* best practices. People can learn from failures as well as from successes. And remember, don't underestimate the power of codifying a case study. Finally, some companies and even global brands offer their key markets temporary access to SWAT teams, or ad-hoc expertise teams who can fly into Vietnam one day, Russia and Nigeria the next. These teams can help address an urgent local issue that impacts the whole company.

Principles Of Effective Capability Building

Building marketing excellence. General, across-the-board training. Why have these two areas long been marketing's ignored, underfunded, too-often-outsourced stepchildren? At the first sign of budget pressure, these bare-minimum teaching attempts are often cut off at the knees. Remember though that today, the most successful global marketing leaders don't just use marketing learning experiences to drive increased efficiency, they consider these experiences an integral part of enhancing job performance.

So, what does it take to get it right? If you're planning on investing significantly in the development of global marketing capability, what lessons can you learn from other experienced leaders and companies? What should you do? What shouldn't you do?
Below is a summary of some of our most important findings:

DRIVING THE BUSINESS STRATEGY

Companies should introduce each and every program with a clear, simple explanation of how the module links to the overall business strategy. Our advice? Communicate this information to all participants *before* they begin the training (and again at the start and the conclusion of the program). This information should include a definition of the business or brand strategy, as well as an explanation of why participants should learn and begin applying these new skills immediately. When, say, a company CEO makes this same link in an introduction presentation or video, it can be a supremely empowering and inspirational boost that drives program effectiveness.

STRATEGY AND GOVERNANCE

Yes, it's tempting to *just get on with it* by developing quick modules that satisfy some urgent tactical need – but don't go there. Hastily launched

'The CMO role is about
capability building;
it's about building forums and
knowledge transfer and best
practice transfer.'

NICK FELL - MARKETING DIRECTOR, SABMILLER

marketing capability initiatives often fall by the wayside. Why? Their existence, approach and focus didn't have time to sufficiently embed itself in the organization.

Often capability programs can isolate themselves from the business, thereby losing the latter's respect, or sense of relevance. Before companies invest too much in program development, we always recommend working to win alignment around an agreed capability development strategy.

The best marketing capability development strategies work from the overall global business or global brand vision. They start by developing a list of marketing skills and capabilities that ensure the delivery of that vision. Any capability gaps in terms of skills, competencies and processes will become clear when participants contrast this list with an honest assessment or benchmarking.

By including key business stakeholders *and* topic experts both inside and outside the company, organizations can develop a learning strategy that addresses both urgent and important business needs. For example, Procter & Gamble interviewed all its aligned agencies to discover how they felt about working with P&G's marketers. A strong marketing excellence strategy always includes a model for governance over time. Without the direct involvement (even if it's only advisory) of key business leaders, the program can become overly isolated from day-to-day business.

FIT FOR PURPOSE

Participants must feel that the program is far from cookie-cutter, but is instead dedicated to their personal or global brand use. We always include just enough external best practice cases to ensure an outside-in perspective…while simultaneously including as many internal case studies as possible to show that participants can apply what they learn to the industry, or even brand, in question.

LEADERS TRAIN LEADERS

The best training programs feature substantial and visible top marketing leadership involvement. Marketing learning can't be delegated. The most successful programs are those with a CMO or CEO involved in, and committed to, the marketing learning program's development, implementation, objectives, progress and results.

BUILDING ON EXISTING PROGRAMS

A surefire way to get to a negative ROI on marketing excellence programs is to start from scratch with content development. Unfortunately, many companies do just this (thereby throwing the baby out with the bathwater by scratching previously unsuccessful attempts). We insist on reviewing available materials, then reprocessing as much as possible, often in a completely new context. This not only respects the work of others who may still be within shouting distance, but ensures that the company doesn't toss out an important heritage.

BUILD ON EXISTING MOMENTUM

At the moment of its launch, any change initiative should map where the energy, focus, and momentum is within a company. Energy and momentum will always amass around any make-or-break priority projects in an annual plan. Our advice: Use them. If the top 50 executives of the company gather for an offsite in the Rocky Mountains, request a two-hour slot in which you announce your capability program, then explain how it links to the strategy that's being discussed at the offsite.

Take the top priority projects of this year's annual plan, and link support and/or improve them, using the tools of your capability program. By doing so, you immediately demonstrate the relevance of your program and add value, thereby creating a level of attention otherwise unobtainable without very high costs on a stand-alone basis.

LIVE-ACTION LEARNING

Learning by doing is extremely powerful. Leaders and participants can apply processes and tools to real business challenges and opportunities. (The result? It's time *on* business, not time *away* from business.) This kind of relevance drives faster results. One of our clients pulls together teams for 'White Space Innovation,' wherein marketers and interdisciplinary colleagues learn new tools or processes before applying them for several months to a real-life issue. Moreover, with the help of a professional facilitator and a senior leader, the team continuously attempts to improve these efforts.

Program timing is essential. Optimally, companies should deliver a program when they glimpse an immediate need to deliver a critical skill. Example: a brand-planning program should be delivered before or during the planning process, not three months after implementation.

COMMUNITIES OF PRACTICE

In order to create a unified vision, global companies such as P&G, Philips, and Coca-Cola set up communities of practice where groups of like-minded individuals coalesce to learn from one another. To establish and maintain a successful community of practice network, pick an influential host who top management has empowered; ensure that the subject is a hot-button topic (for example 'How to Launch Innovation During a Recession,'); share all relevant e-technology; maintain information; and reward and motivate participants for their trouble with recognition and even awards.

E-LEARNING

In many companies, e-learning is an increasingly significant element of skill development. That said, it works best when it's blended with other more collaborative learning methods. For example, a webinar can be put to good use as part of a follow-up to topics previously raised in more focused marketing learning programs.

As we mentioned earlier, marketers new to a company might use intranet-based webinars to learn about a company's language and tools. At the same time, hires should also attend a facilitated course early on their careers not only to meet their counterparts, but to begin building important informal networks. As with all other programs, e-learning should be engaging and interactive. Simple multiple choice testing isn't nearly as effective as hands-on learning.

Many companies make the mistake of training exclusively on an individual basis...meaning that one week, organizations may train a single team member, then, several months later, train two or three others.

Yes, it's essential to create informal network opportunities across business units and countries. But it's even more advantageous to train people in their natural teams. For example, by taking a whole innovation team through a structured program (including Research and Development, the creative agency, the marketers and the assembled customer managers), you'll ensure that individuals immediately apply their new learning to the projects they're working on, along the way building significant team skills.

F.R.E.S.H. LEARNING FOR EFFECTIVENESS

Over the years we've adopted some simple rules to help in the design. Our colleague Elana Gold: *'Marketing programs work best when they're F.R.E.S.H.: Fun, Relevant, Engaging, Simple, and Hands-on. These principles ensure that marketers get the most from the program. They also guarantee a higher rate of successful long-lasting behavioral changes and meaningful results.'*

Fun...well, that one is crucial. Like a great novel or film, a learning experience should grab someone from the get-go, especially if it's relevant to building the business at hand. If participants perceive a program as fun, they'll be more engaged. They'll retain more information, too. Through the use of engaging elements that spark creative innovation and action, programs should also offer marketers exhilarating new ways of collaborating with consumers and customers.

'Adults learn better when it is fun learning,' says Ronny Vansteenkiste, VP of Organization & Leadership Development at Avaya. *'It makes learning memorable and makes the insights last longer. When overlooked, you can count on a wasted day for your participants as they will not retain information.'*

As we noted earlier, relevance is also crucial. Does the training program offer new solutions to new challenges? Does it connect to today's business realities? Programs must also be relevant to various individual learning styles. Some people learn best via theory, while others may require practical application. Oh – and make sure you speak the language of whomever's in the audience.

We once worked with Philips on their *'Brand Matters'* program, which focused on engaging the sales function with the brand by showing them how the brand could help them achieve their targets. We began by demonstrating only the engine specifications of four different types of cars (we didn't name the brands). We listed the different horsepower, top speeds, and cylinder volumes, then asked which car Philips' sales force members preferred. We then unveiled the car brands that matched the specifications. Of course, people's preferences immediately and dramatically shifted! For team members long-accustomed to rattling off specs while bypassing the brand, it was not only a valuable exercise, but a powerful means of showcasing the value of branding.

Engaging a company in marketing learning means broadening involvement to groups *beyond* marketing. (Building a customer marketing plan by offering different programs to the marketing and sales organizations doesn't exactly encourage collaboration between teams.) Our suggestion? Bring together both functions and link the training to personal, multi-functional team and business ambitions.

Keep things simple. Programs needn't be complex to impart their message. Simplicity is a crucial didactical tool. If people remember three specific datapoints six months after a 48-hour training session, you're doing pretty well. That said, make a concerted effort to ensure that they remember the three things you *want* them to remember. This can be achieved only through focus and simplicity.

Hands-on program design allows marketers to train and learn while addressing relevant business issues. It balances big-idea external examples with internal ones. Internal examples offer the most proof that change is possible, while a hands-on program gives marketers the opportunity to play an integral part in that change.

Measure...And Get Results

Ultimately, every marketing learning program should demonstrate measurable changes in market performance. CEOs and CMOs can monitor the time it takes to adopt new ways of working across the organization, as well as their impact on market share and profits.

Innovators in Marketing Learning are proactively driving increased transparency on effectiveness, Return on Investment and the long-term impact of their programs. They should remember to celebrate projects that have been supported by live-action training as examples of how integrated marketing learning can directly affect results.

Remember to use both pre- and post-program evaluations to monitor and correct program contents. Leverage annual tracking studies to conclusively show increases in retention and inspiration. Many organizations now benchmark their Marketing Learning programs to ensure they're above, or on a par with, world-class programs.

A Few Caveats And Pitfalls

So what's the catch? Why aren't organizations falling over themselves in a rush to build marketing capability?

Well, we do want to offer up a couple of reality checks.

Warns Nigel Gilbert of Lloyds Banking Group, *'Recognize that not every organization has a marketing-literate culture. Many are very successful cultures built on delivering high levels of efficiency and profit. But they are not necessarily about understanding the power of brands, or of fulfilling customer need. So don't be fooled by the language that's used. First you must recognize the culture that exists.'*

Nigel offers a cautionary note: There will always be twice as many worthy causes to support, and twice as many candidates for an operational budget than it can reasonably fund. Even with all the corporate will in the world, capability building is a slow-burn initiative. At its earliest, it will show returns on investment over the next year, but certainly not within the next quarter. Battle-hardened marketing leaders know that the way to ring-fence capability-building budgets is to ensure that the priority doesn't just form part of their personal agenda. Instead, it must become part of someone else's agenda too.

The second caveat revolves around measurement: How does one accurately track the success of a marketing capability development program? Sure, a company can handily commission a baseline survey to ascertain benchmark competency levels. But, human nature being what it is, there will always be the temptation to 'play the system,' especially if program results link to salary increments or bonuses.

What Success Looks Like

It goes without saying that Jim Stengel of Procter & Gamble succeeded, and better still, could enjoy the fruits of his hard work on capability building sooner rather than later. If the CMO of one of the world's largest consumer goods companies considers one of his key priorities to be capability building, surely that speaks volumes to the rest of the world's marketing leaders, right?

Nick Fell of SABMiller: *'It's about supporting capability building in a culture of learning from results, and analyzing what worked and what didn't work, and understanding what's transferable and what's not.'*

Displaying a sharp ear for the sound-byte, SABMiller's Nick Fell says, *'You're building institutional capacity, you're building a legacy of processes, tools, ways of thinking, ways of coming to decisions which will outlive you and which are sustainable by many different people in many different cultures in many different environments. You're building a machine. You're building, in fact, the fabric of the organization.'*

By developing an awareness of how individuals learn, and by codifying processes that permit organizations to preserve the best while reinventing the rest, marketing leaders can help their organizations pull away from the pack... on the back of a well-tuned, finely honed marketing machine.

(RE)BUILDING GLOBAL MARKETING EXCELLENCE AT PROCTER & GAMBLE

In 2008, when Jim Stengel left what is unquestionably one of world's most prestigious global marketing jobs – Global Marketing Officer at Procter & Gamble – the company was, once again, at its marketing pinnacle. Almost all of the company's billion-dollar brands were again growing revenue and share. P&G's marketing morale and confidence was up and still growing.

Just seven years earlier, things had looked very different.

As Jim was making his move from his previous position leading the Baby Care business in Europe, he knew how much hard work lay ahead. Ever since the company's financial troubles, and its major 1998 reorganization, P&G's marketing discipline seemed to have lost its bearings. Among the problems? Many of the company's power brands were losing share. P&G was dropping its strong connections with consumers and their needs. Marketing expertise appeared to be dwindling. And within P&G's traditionally proud marketing discipline, morale was at an all-time low.

But Jim was confident he could turn this boat around. Moreover, he could also rely on the support of CEO Lafley (his discussions with the CEO before taking the job had assured him of that).

CONNECT

Jim began to rebuild P&G's marketing capabilities as he would any other critical challenge. First, he connected with the target group to truly understand what was going on in their minds (only this time the consumer was not a German homemaker discussing how she juggled her work, hobbies, a husband and a newborn. Instead, P&G senior managers and marketing colleagues all over the world were weighing in on what they felt was needed to revamp the quality of marketing).

With a rigor typically reserved for the company's mega-brands, Jim commissioned quantitative and qualitative internal research, as well as external benchmarking, to zero in on the essence of what was thriving - and what needed urgent revamping. P&G shadowed colleagues worldwide to understand how the best marketing managers spend their time, and how the most effective marketers think and act differently.

Among the key insights that quickly began floating to the top? Marketers were rushing through their roles. Worse, some weren't in their positions long enough to observe, or even learn from, the results of their own brand-planning decisions.

Spending time connecting with consumers was fast diminishing. Instead marketers were devoting time to non-essential marketing activities such as project planning and meeting after meeting after meeting.

Another dilemma: Marketers no longer felt that P&G was training them in the 'P&G way.' Thanks to widespread cost-cutting and reorganization, the marketing programs that for decades had created P&G's top-of-the-line reputation for all marketing graduates had been severely compromised.

INSPIRE
So why was marketing morale so down in the dumps? Answer: Because marketers no longer felt as though they were at the heart of the company. Colleagues from other disciplines were assuming marketing leadership roles in emerging new fields. Many marketers felt powerless. It felt as though the company was transforming right under their feet.

P&G – how the company perceived marketing, and in turn, how marketers performed – had to change, quickly and meaningfully, too.

Right off the bat, Jim knew he had to reformulate and communicate a compelling vision for the role of marketing and brands. Together with a team comprised of the company's best marketers, Jim developed a vision for the future, one in which P&G celebrated the company's legendarily rich marketing expertise heritage, and restated its ambition to become once again the world's best marketing company. With the commitment and support of CEO, A.G. Lafley, marketers soon felt reenergized – and from the top, too. It made a big difference.

FOCUS
Preliminary research and analysis also revealed that P&G was in danger of losing some of the most famous marketing processes that had made the company so immensely successful.

Perhaps the most important of these was the famous 'one-page memo.' For decades, this document forced marketers to distill their thoughts and focus their strategies on a single page of parchment. Moreover, the memo had to be communicated – and understood – across the global company. Not just the one-page memo, but other key planning disciplines, tools and processes that forced strategic focus, had slowly given way to elaborate ways of working.

Billion Dollar Brands

It was time for focused planning and communication to make a comeback. Starting at the very top, the company migrated to a strategic language, one that focused everyone's plans around a structured brand building framework that included three key components: Who was the target consumer? What was the desired brand equity? How would a program work? The organization swiftly adopted the language – and it had an immediate alignment effect.

ORGANIZE

In the years leading up to Jim's appointment, the marketing discipline was in a continuous state of flux. The reduction in headcount left some marketers in charge of activities that often lay beyond their expertise, such as global program and project management, packaging development coordination, and other non-core marketing responsibilities. As you can imagine, this often resulted in quality issues, as well as ambivalence among marketers around the exact scope of their discipline at P&G. Plus, what about innovation? What about spending time – and connecting – with consumers? For that matter, what had happened to crucial expertise? The short answer: No one in the company 'owned' it anymore.

The new marketing leadership team responded quickly by creating 'Centers of Excellence' for core marketing skill areas, like advertising and media planning.

Jim Stengel: *'What keeps marketers up at night is a lack of understanding around what they should be accountable for: How are they going to be measured? How are they going to be rewarded?'*
Jim moved rapidly to define what was within – or else beyond – the scope of the marketing discipline. He increased tenure by several years so that marketers could learn from their own decisions. He also redefined role success metrics to clarify what was important, and who was responsible for what.

BUILD

But by far the most painful message of the overall marketing organizational effectiveness assessment was this: P&G marketers were under the impression that the marketing training powerhouse they'd joined straight out of business school didn't seem to care about them as individuals or careerists.

What had happened to managerial one-on-one coaching? How had marketing training courses lost their priority and luster? It was as if someone, somewhere, had kidnapped P&G's heart and soul.

Stengel and the team decided there was no better way to boost the importance and quality of marketing than to restore that heart, that soul. The company established a marketing university – and soon after was offering high-quality training programs to marketers at all levels.

Management also took pains to create long-term career paths for marketers in order to restore prestige to those who'd chosen to pursue marketing over general business. Sure, marketers could always aspire to the chief marketing officer job, but otherwise there was scant opportunity for advancement. So P&G resurrected its Harley Procter program to recognize marketers who'd acquired a high level of relevant expertise and were comfortable sharing that same expertise, and providing training, as internal consultants.

For what should a CMO be held accountable? Jim's reply is instantaneous:

'In my mind, a CMO should be measured on four things: 1. You should be accountable for business results. 2. You should understand which parts of your brand equity drive consideration and preference, and be incentivized to build those aspects. 3. You should also be incentivized to build the functional capabilities your organization needs for the future (e.g. best-in-class shopper marketing). 4. You should be accountable for marketing talent recruitment and development, as well as the networks of expertise you surround your team with.'

Today, P&G's results speak for themselves. Thanks to Jim Stengel's inspiring leadership, Procter is once again on top of the marketing world. As for those much-coveted marketers? They're among the most highly motivated professionals in the industry.

Characteristics Of The Global Brand CEO

What It Takes (And Why!)

VISA

ANTONIO LUCIO - CMO, VISA INTERNATIONAL

Antonio Lucio, CMO, VISA International, may be one of the most creative and global thinkers in marketing today. Antonio's dynamic vision of marketing, which melds local customer-centricity with global brand clarity, was honed over a 25-year career of leadership positions in global marketing and brand management experience for companies including PepsiCo, Kraft and Procter & Gamble.

Global is second nature to Antonio, who was born in Spain, raised in Puerto Rico, educated in the United States and is fluent in English, Spanish and Portuguese.

His successful strategic approach to marketing makes Antonio a frequent keynote speaker at international business conferences, as well as a sought-after contributor to marketing and business publications in the U.S. and abroad. He thoroughly enjoys debating global marketing topics, and uses his passion and insight to inspire others to take non-traditional paths to marketing success.

As VISA's Chief Marketing Officer, Antonio is a member of the VISA operating committee and responsible for the VISA brand, positioning, architecture and all consumer and business to business communication globally. He is responsible for the overall marketing budget and leads all efforts in consumer, financial institutions, merchant and innovation marketing as well as providing global marketing services in sponsorships, MROI, brand integrity and database management.

Antonio joined VISA just prior to its initial public offering (IPO), the largest in U.S. history. Assuming an executive leadership role at a mature company in the midst of such extraordinary change required Antonio to bring a distinctive point of view to the task, along with a laser focus on outcomes to match the company's new priorities and an emphasis on incorporating the latest digital techniques.

His first task was to refocus and optimize the marketing function to match his customer-centric vision, resulting in a new global marketing organizational structure at the same time; he instituted rigorous controls and accountability measures appropriate for a publicly-traded company.

One of Antonio's core objectives was to make VISA's marketing programs 'glocal.' In his view, key to VISA's future growth, would be its ability to drive local brand equity while delivering global operational synergies, efficiencies and sustainable shareholder value.

From Seoul to Sao Paulo to San Francisco, his approach required the brand to maintain a distinctly local interpretation without sacrificing the consistency and clarity of its global voice.

Delivery of this vision also required optimizing VISA's global media buying to drive efficiencies while centralizing the creative process and reducing five agencies to one. He restructured the organization to sharpen focus on key priorities and innovation and implemented a rigid global measurement model, Marketing Return on Investment (MROI) which would serve as the basis for all marketing decisions moving forward.

Antonio accomplished this by implementing 'Media First', a bold shift in the creative process that makes consumer-centric media planning 'step-one.' For VISA, Antonio determined that the media consumption behavior of its audience would be used as a compass to guide creative development. This approach mandated a deep understanding of media within the context of buying decisions - in VISA's case, cardholders using VISA instead of cash or checks.

That approach bore fruit in VISA's first-ever global advertising campaign – More people go with VISA. The campaign delivered on the glocal strategy with a single global message that could be executed locally for maximum relevance. It created cost-saving efficiencies for VISA that also supported its core growth strategy to migrate consumer and business spending from cash and check to VISA.

In the form of VISA's global Go World marketing campaign in support of the Vancouver 2010 Winter Olympic Games, the 'Media First' approach showcased its true potential. VISA moved 40% of its marketing weight in support of the Olympic Games to digital.

As new ways to interact with consumers continue to evolve, Antonio suggests that all marketers need to revisit the consumer through experiential observation: more time spent out of the office facing 'real' consumers within the complexities of their real world, and incorporating emotional, cultural, cognitive and physiological variables into their consumer insights, as well as using today's digital tools to not only reach consumers, but to listen to them and gain insight from their conversations in social networks.

In a recent publication Lucio writes 'In many ways, the CMO plays a CEO role within the marketing organization. Not only will he need to own the role of Chief Brand Experience Officer, he will also have to become Chief Marketing Personnel Officer, Chief Marketing Resource Allocation Officer and Chief Evangelist & Alignment Officer.'

Obviously, we could not agree more. This chapter digs deeper into what it takes to be a winning global marketing leader and sets out some of the most important roles to play.

SUCCESSFUL GLOBAL
MARKETING TRAITS

CONNECT

BUILD

INSPIRE

Universal Truth
Purposeful Positioning
Total Experience

ORGANIZE

FOCUS

So what is it about Antonio Lucio's mindset, behaviors and leadership style that fuelled such organizational achievement? Sure, in a behemoth organization like P&G, nothing comes down to one man – yet at the same time, no one will disagree that Jim Stengel created a huge impact on the success of one of the world's largest companies (and not just any company, either).

Back to VISA. With the help of a winning team, and supported by a great CEO, Antonio influenced the approach to marketing for several hundred marketing leaders around the VISA world (and no, they weren't exactly begging for someone to come in and redefine their jobs). It was a formidable achievement. So what made Antonio so successful, first at Pepsi International, and then at VISA? For that matter, how did Jim Stengel accomplish what he did at P&G? What's the secret behind Silvia Lagnado's success? How did Rob Malcolm reshape Diageo's approach to marketing?

Do successful global marketers share common traits? What characteristics do the world's most effective brand leaders – and those who recruit them – consider to be most important? And if we're eager to ace the global marketing leadership role ourselves, what personal attributes can we adapt and/or emulate?

Global Brand CEO DNA

If we perch on the shoulders of the giants performing this role today, the answer becomes abundantly clear. So let's go ahead and consider the personal traits that characterize today's most successful global marketing leaders.

The first one concerns *who* they are – *not* how they act. It encompasses their character strengths, as well as what experience and perspective they bring to the job.

It all begins with an individual's DNA. Marketing may be in the midst of radical change, but some foundations remain the same. Like this one: Good marketing is predicated on great insights. And unless you immerse yourself completely in the world of consumers, those insights will be sorely lacking.

UP CLOSE WITH CONSUMERS

Jim Stengel of P&G puts it this way: *'I had a curiosity about our work as a company. I loved what I was doing and am still curious to learn more. And whatever I learned, I shared. I had a constant energy to discover. I think global marketers need that level of energy and capacity.'*

Jonathan Moore of Sara Lee once ran a Euro 2B global detergent brand. Asked what he feels are the keys to global marketing leadership success, he responds, *'... I think it takes a combination of an inquisitive mind and an ambition to want to achieve something. Coupled with the willingness to explore, embrace and champion different ways to get there. You have to love working with all types of people, and be especially fascinated to understand your consumers!'*

Anthony Ruys, former Chairman of Heineken, explains how company founder Freddy Heineken, set a lasting example: *'Freddy Heineken always said 'What would the consumer say about that?' Right after my appointment, I went around the world to learn more about the young adult consumer. I wanted everyone at the company to grasp just how important it was that we understand this market. In many countries I sat in on local research about young adults, usually without them knowing my job title, so that I heard the naked truth. After a number of months, the ball started rolling, and more and more initiatives emerged.'*

Clearly, no matter how senior his or her role, a marketing leader has to exhibit a fiery passion and curiosity about what precisely drives consumers. What are their habits and attitudes? What are their unspoken needs? How can we improve their lives with products and services? We believe there's little room for technocratic marketing leaders. If the credo is 'live by example,' then surely the top person needs to maintain an oversized interest in what makes consumers tick.

Jim Stengel honed his modus operandi to a fine art during his tenure at P&G. He transformed the concept of consumer immersions, hardwiring the practice into the organization's marketing playbook. And no matter how time-crunched his travel schedule was, he led by example. *'At P&G, we developed an approach: Begin with the consumer who's important to you. And learn about her life before you run out and execute. For example, do a deep dive on the media in her life. To me, that is a provocative event. People start to see the consumer is in control, that she is choosing, that she feels more empowered than ever. She feels overwhelmed, but she wants choice; she wants it all. We have to find a way to market that fits into her life in a way that she accepts. So it may start with a shop-along or live-along; it could be a day in the life. We must be much more innovative about how we get marketers, in an honest and natural way, to experience how brands are part of consumers' lives. That, to me, is where marketing is going.'*

COURAGEOUS AND LEADING BY EXAMPLE

Did we mention the new marketing leadership job also requires courage? You can't just develop intellectual plans at HQ, and hope that someone, somewhere, recognizes your sheer razzle-dazzle. No: the role demands getting out there, interacting, willingly trying out new things and often taking big risks. If you don't, how can you expect yourself to come up with potentially transformative innovations?

Consumers are more critical than ever before. The perils are obvious. Tex Gunning of AkzoNobel concedes that *'building brands in the new world is an entirely different game than I've ever seen in my life, ever. What you now have to do is create brands that resonate in this space, with consumers' new values. The risk with this is that the resonance is picked up wrongly as incongruent;*

or the attitude of the brand or the intentions of the people who are managing the brand are second-guessed or doubted.'

One of our first – and favorite – consumer connect leadership moments was with the Chairman of Campina (now known as FrieslandCampina), a huge dairy company in Europe. Campina asked us to help them internally launch their new master brand positioning, before developing, rolling out and running their new internal marketing academy. The underlying idea? At launch, every marketer would learn what the new brand symbolized. Next, with the support of new marketing academy programs, the company asked us to equip them to successfully launch and apply the brand in their respective markets. Appropriately, the academy's first program was *consumer connections*. We decided to challenge the complete company by making an example of their most senior leader.

The company chairman was a seasoned, amicable, gentle, 'typical' executive who traveled frequently around Europe, visiting local dairies and retailers. In general, he worked from the back seat of a chauffeur-driven car. When he was in residence, the car was situated in plain sight at HQ – a clear signal he was in the office. Everyone could see that the back seat was packed with newspapers, business documents and, not least, a big box of cigars. Clearly, this wasn't someone who interacted much with the company's end consumer.

That said, the chairman was extremely open-minded about doing a consumer connect program to set an example for his troops.

Fast forward to the opening day of the global marketing event. The brand and marketing academy launch programs centered around their annual global marketing event. For two days, the top 150 marketers and product developers would sit cheek-by-jowl in the same room.

As the event kicked off, all the marketers appeared eager to get on with things. They sat up ramrod-straight, primed to listen politely to what they assumed would be the chairman's 'standard' 10-minute-long opening. Usually he clarified the company's financial goals, as well as his employee expectations. Well, imagine the marketers' surprise when instead of seeing a PowerPoint chart devoted to projected revenues, they found themselves gazing at a huge, wall-to-wall picture of Martha – a 40 – something Dutch homemaker. The picture was full face, not particularly flattering, real... and oddly touching.

For the next half-hour, the chairman talked about Martha and her day-to-day life. He described how Martha ran her household with a double-shift-working husband and three children. He revealed intimacies only a friend or family member would know, cataloguing not just the various roles that dairy products played in Martha's life, but what her needs were around cooking, nutrition, even assembling desserts for her kids.

We so enjoyed watching the faces of the marketers in the room morph from surprise, to joviality, to astonishment, to shame, as they realized that their chairman – a guy who spend most of his time in the ivory tower of his blue Mercedes – actually knew more about the company's core consumers than practically everyone in the room. The experience was profound – and led to a highly successful kick-start of the Campina consumer connect program.

RAW INTELLECT

If you were to ask us to name one fundamental thing that's changed about marketing over the past decade, we'd have to say that it's become more complex. What used to be based on gut calls has morphed into a science of measuring and adapting. Too much consumer data is available. At the ready are many promotional and communication tools that provide real-time measurements of what's working and what's not.

In short, marketing is going through a major identity crisis. Brand love. Consumer intimacy. Both are still crucial. Yet today, quantitative analysis, econometric modeling, real-time message monitoring and adaptation are all elements of the marketer's toolset.

As Nigel Gilbert, CMO of Lloyds Banking Group, the U.K.'s largest financial institution, puts it, *'The CMO role today is so much more complicated than it was just ten years ago. When I think back, and compare it then to today, I sometimes wonder how my teams keep up. It is intellectually challenging and extremely stimulating to play at the top of the league. I know that many of my team members are motivated by the challenge to do this better than our competitors - to analyze better, get to better insights, develop better solutions and implement with superiority.'*

'There's no more room for that old flying-by-the-seat-of-your-pants attitude', says Greg Welch: *'These people are overachievers. They're wicked smart.'*

DISCIPLINED AND HEALTHY

Let's play Dr. Andrew Weil for a moment (and forgive us if the following seems out-of-place in a marketing book). The global CMO role we're talking about can easily make its practitioners, well, *ill.* If you're undisciplined about exercise, diet, sleep routines, and alcohol consumption, you may not survive a global marketing position. All too often we've seen clients who've spent years burning the candle at both ends, and who are facing serious health or emotional issues that can be blamed entirely on utter physical exhaustion.

Quite seriously, this is nothing to laugh about. Notwithstanding recent developments in videoconferencing, the job's travel demands mean that fewer and fewer marketers are even interested in joining a global marketing team. There are too few women (and even fewer mothers) in senior global marketing roles. The skies that global marketing leaders need to travel have become, accidentally, a glass ceiling.

Diversity and health are pressing issues. Several companies we know of have instituted health monitoring and counseling programs to help their employees cope with the demands of their key global jobs.

Yet in the end, maintaining equilibrium is up to the leaders themselves. Fortunately, the majority of our most successful clients live pretty self-disciplined lives. As Nick Fell of SABMiller puts it, *'I think you need someone who's got enormous personal resilience – because it takes three months to work out what the hell is going on, two months to work out what you want to do, two months to convince people of the right things to do, and then two months after that you've found out whether you're right or not because you'll get results of some sort.'*

From rumor or experience, most people will concur that many global marketing leaders aren't exactly small-timers in the big ego department. (In fact, quite a few *love* creating buzz and controversy around their own personal brands.) But we believe that although 'celebrity' CMOs who skip from company to company tend to create a lot of fuss, they're not necessarily the most successful global marketing leaders.

In truth, some of the most successful global marketers at all levels keep their egos in serious check. What could be more mature (or 'level 5,' as Jim Collins would put it) than giving away the credit for business growth by letting other key stakeholders own the biggest ideas and take responsibility for the big launches? After all, there is no global market to conquer – simply a number of large local markets where your brand needs to triumph. If the leaders of these local markets win, the global marketing brand wins. The CMO wins. Period. Yes, it's that simple.

Greg Welch of Spencer Stuart puts it like this: '*There are some common DNA qualities around most of the folks who are doing the job really well…a kind of 'high EQ, low ego' quality.*'

Neil Punwani, Global Brand Director at Fanta, agrees: '*You have to acknowledge the fact that you are trying to move a huge amount of people across a really wide variety of markets. So, the first thing is to keep it really simple. Keep it to three or four key strategic priorities or plans that are written in very easy-to-understand language, and then every time you talk to a market, every time you present to a group, always start with the foundation of those three or four strategies. You may alter your view slightly as you go along and learn more, but never underestimate the benefit of repetition and the benefit of simplicity in global marketing. The reality is, you're going to get a completely different level of execution in Kenya than you are in the US or in Germany. So, one of the things that we did was to design a program with the idea that it would be executed at different levels in different markets -- and that meant kind of a more modular approach to global marketing programs.*'

EXPERIENCE 'CREDS'

One factor cannot be 'bought' by importing a famous CMO from another company: the credibility and respect that derives from a lifetime spent knee-deep in the trenches. 'What helped you get the job done?' we regularly ask global marketing leaders. The typical response: *'I've been there myself.'*
In sum, these leaders truly understand what they're asking from local and regional marketing leaders. Experience also means that they can look anyone in the eye and say, *'I have been there, done that, and I think you now need to trust me – this is doable.'*

Maybe even more crucially, these leaders bring with them a deep network of important relationships. (Think about it: how else, with a single phone call, can you request a favor, and ask someone to trust you to run with a new program?) Time and again, we find that a major cause behind global marketers failing in their new roles is an absence of real in-depth relationships. Rob Malcolm at Diageo told us that over 90 percent of the top 50 leaders and marketers at Diageo had worked together for over ten years. Not only that, but they'd all served at least once in regional, global or category roles.

Tim Wright of GSK is a good example. When GSK decided to create its first-ever global marketing group, the company hand-picked some of the most successful business leaders to staff the global group: *'A successful marketer needs operational credibility. You can't just appreciate marketing as a science. You need to appreciate its commercial potential. When we recruit, we look for marketing capability as well as operational capability and credibility. We want to ensure that they know their way around a business, and that they have credibility on a world stage. I don't really have a place for people who don't have operational capability. Who may have just a pure appreciation for marketing as a science as opposed to the commercial potential of the work we create.'*

Naturally, with these relationships comes responsibility, which makes them reciprocal. Sometimes a company needs to change directions entirely. By hiring its first non-Unilever CEO, Paul Polman, Unilever gave off a clear signal that things would be different from now on. At the same time, Unilever gained instant credibility. Polman had earned his stripes by building a career in Unilever's two most important categories – Food and Household

'The key to be a big-time CMO in this day is raw intellect combined with a velvet-clad hammer...'

GREG WELCH - GLOBAL PRACTICE LEADER, CONSUMER GOODS & SERVICES, SPENCER STUART

Care. (The big difference? He'd done it by working for Unilever's biggest competitors, Nestle and P&G!)

Global Brand CEO Mindset

The very best global marketing leaders perceive the world differently. Where others see challenges, they suss out opportunities. Rather than playing Brand Police, they empower their marketing colleagues around the world. They don't solve problems. They build systems that drive solutions. They're as happy serving the needs of the Chinese or U.S. marketing teams as they are leading their company's biggest-ever innovation projects. Their own egos matter less than serving their organization's needs. Did we mention that they also understand when a company demands true leadership?

SERVANT LEADERSHIP MINDSET

As we mentioned earlier, some years ago we borrowed Robert Greenleaf's term, 'Servant Leadership.' Why? Because in our opinion, it optimally sums up the mindsets of the best global marketing leaders. Greenleaf describes this role as one of 'Listening, empathy, healing, awareness, persuasion, conceptualization, foresight, stewardship, growth and building community.' Servant leaders recognize the dual roles they've been asked to play. They're agile enough to transition from one leadership style to another in seconds (sometimes even during the same meeting!).

Why do we emphasize the servant role? Says Peter Vaughn of American Express, *'To go deep into priority markets without pushing away the local marketers, you need to be very humble in your approach and explicitly acknowledge that you don't really know the markets as well as they do.'*

But let's make one thing clear: Servant leadership doesn't mean that Global Brand Leaders should sit back and await instruction from key countries (here, in fact, is where the 'leadership' component comes in). It goes without saying that leaders must listen to important stakeholders. They have to decide what strategies or priorities they should pursue. Global leadership is about weighing the options, then choosing the right path for the company, and not for any one individual country.

Greg Welch of Spencer Stuart opines: *'IQ really does matter, but the EQ notion is particularly important for CMOs. These are people that have the smarts and the ability to develop incredible, soft one-to-one relationships, but are also able to paint a vision for the bigger group. It takes time to build these enduring relationships. I think you need to be able to offer a compelling, different point of view.'*

We had the privilege of working with Silvia Lagnado as she was shaping the first global leadership role of Dove. As Silvia now recalls: *'I like the Servant Leadership concept for global brand leaders. You need to lead on vision and strategy, but serve on activation support and leveraging best practices. The term works well I think. The difficulty of connecting on the big brands is that the more people you listen to, the more opinions you get. The more you try to be sensitive to cultural nuances, the more you find them. To steer the right course for your brand, you need global brand leaders who are in touch with both the markets as well as their internal compass.'*

GLOBAL MINDSET

The best global marketing leaders are natural global citizens – and have been all their lives. They love nothing more than working their magic across borders. They believe in the serendipitous 'je ne sais quoi' quality that occurs only when people from many cultures mix and merge.

'They have a very large view of the world,' says John Seifert of Ogilvy. *'They have a very expansive, connected, thoughtful perspective on the outside environment, and can easily think about the role of the brand in that larger context... They are extraordinarily good listeners and ask great questions around the fundamentals of cultures and the business. They understand language and visualization. They know how to move people emotionally and rationally.'*

By now, it's very clear that the dynamics around global business in general – and global marketing in particular – have evolved dramatically. At the same time, the number of interested, involved stakeholders has increased exponentially. Which makes it essential that future marketing leaders maintain an open, rounded, global mindset.

Working with people of different backgrounds. Leading and motivating them to bring out their best. All crucial stuff – especially given that global marketing leaders tend to be isolated from far-flung team members, and seldom get the chance to stroll down the hallway to see how they're progressing. Karin Koonings of Starbucks sums up this conundrum: *'You've got to constantly ask yourself: How am I going to build a real team? How can I continue to build these relationships? And how can I really provide added value? If you're visiting local markets and you're just being taken on tours or having dinners as opposed to really helping the local team, you're not necessarily adding value.'*

Nick Kendall emphasizes the key challenges: *'How to blend unity and diversity; how to achieve focus and flexibility across countries and different skill sets.'*

PURPOSEFUL AND PASSIONATE MINDSET

If Servant Leadership describes how best to engage with the rest of the organization, the question remains: what does the global marketing leader stand for as a person? How does he or she communicate these qualities to important stakeholders? After all, more and more organizations look to the CMO to help define what the company represents, what it deems important, and how it does business.

As Marc Mathieu of Coca-Cola explains: *'More and more companies need to see their activities as part of a much larger responsibility…consider marketing in 3D: marketing for the triple bottom line of people, planet and profit. I think that the Marketing Leader of the future is the man or woman who leads with purpose. Who builds brands to be purposeful. Who recognizes that the brand's success will be about more than just sales. This will become more and more crucial!'*

Simon Clift of Unilever agrees that *'we all feel kind of helpless when we look at the problems in society or problems in the environment. Actually, at this level, rather than just standing helplessly by, you can influence the company to do the right thing, and I think that's tremendously exciting and frightening.'*

Ideally, the Servant Leader balances humility with passion and energy. When you're in a global marketing role working with local markets, it's important to remain mindful that your far-flung colleagues bring a lot to the table. After all, they're the ones who day after day live and breathe that culture, that consumer - and that market.

Among the most profound changes we've seen in marketing over the last decade is the enormous increase in accountability and financial transparency. Tomorrow's CMOs must be fully conversant in the language of the CEO and CFO. Not only to influence and help drive the business strategy, but to prove that marketing no longer merits its old-fashioned 'spender' label, that marketing is worthy of resources, and that marketing contributes significantly to growth and the bottom line.

As Peter Vaughn of American Express puts it, *'You need very good business sensibilities. It doesn't do marketers any good if they don't understand the fundamental drivers of the business and they don't understand what's going to actually make that business profitable. Early on in the first global role that I had, I underestimated the amount of investment I needed to make to really understand the business drivers in an individual country before trying to implement a global marketing strategy in that country. I also realized that I needed to spend a lot of time with the business leaders in that marketplace, and invest an enormous amount of time in focus groups with consumers understanding what their needs were and what their behavior might be.'*

Greg Welch of Spencer Stuart agrees that something fundamental has changed in the required mindset: *'The best marketers create an air of transparency around their marketing efforts. They're not afraid to show you how they're spending, what they anticipate, what the measures are, what the goals are … and putting it out there.'*

Global Brand CEO Roles

Effective global marketing leaders act – and prioritize their time – differently. They understand the intricacies of influencing and making decisions within a complex global environment, then act accordingly. Some of their actions are explicit and well-considered, while others occur naturally and instinctively.

Whenever we begin a new relationship, we often spend the day meeting one-on-one with our new clients in order to understand how, where (and also, on what) they spend their time. Reviewing their calendars over the past few months, and using pie charts, we quite literally encourage them to visualize how much time they've spent with markets, customers, outside experts and their own C-suite colleagues. Specifically, we zoom in on how much time they've spent with their CEOs and CFOs. Often we find that these latter two are under represented in the mix.

The pinnacle of a global marketing organization can be, and often is, a very lonely place. Yet it needn't be. Among the most common mistakes market-ers make as they ascend to these lofty treetops is ignoring the importance of locking down their responsibilities (not to mention a behavioral con-tract) with the CEO, and also building alignment with peers within the C-suite.

Lennard Hoornik of Sony Ericsson frames it as follows: '*How much time you spend upside and below is very important. It's really crucial. You're manag-ing expectations, not just with your own group but also sideways – and up. It's incredibly important to make sure that there's no light between what you say and what the CEO says – because marketing is often seen as the embodiment of the overall strategy of the company.*'

In industries like Pharmaceuticals, Electronics or Banking, where mar-keting isn't the organization's natural driver, it's imperative that board members fully understand what marketing can contribute – and that they support the focus and efforts that marketing affords. Do board members have the CMO's back? In companies where the CEO came from marketing, it's imperative to have full alignment on roles and priorities.

Warns Greg Welch of Spencer Stuart, '*The challenge for CMOs as they start in their role is to negotiate the space they need with their CEO and perhaps even with the Sales colleague and CFO. To do more internal connecting with key stakeholders around the business, so that they build confidence in others and earn the leeway they need to run marketing and lead their teams the way they should.*'

With proper alignment, however, CMOs and CEOs can perform their roles in effortless tandem. Greg Welch relays another story: '*I had a conversation with a talented marketer last week and he said, 'You know what, Greg? I am so enthused by where we're headed. I feel so good about where my CEO, my CFO and my company are going, that I wouldn't dare get off this train right now.'*

With the relatively recent onset of immediate and more precise marketing results, metrics and increased transparency surrounding program effectiveness, we're also seeing vast improvements in the relationship between the CMO and the CFO.

The strongest CMOs and global brand leaders embrace these new quantitative results and transparency. They actively seek out collaboration with the CFO and his or her team in order to develop, monitor and act on sensible success metrics. As we mentioned in Chapter 2, marketing accountability is a nascent field. The best CMOs realize that there's no shame in not knowing everything yesterday. But it's a sign of strength to develop increased effectiveness Key Performance Indicators through an open and accountable approach.

The result? Music to a business's ears.

THE 'CHEERLEADER-IN-CHARGE' ROLE

Great marketers are often great communicators. They're skilled narrators of the brand story. It's a rare talent – a gift, even – that colleagues often overlook and underestimate.

Instinctive, born-to-the-role marketers are alert to the essence of their brands. They also understand what resonates with colleagues, customers, and ever-changing consumers.

Needless to say, for global marketing leaders, this talent is worth its weight in gold. Jennifer Davidson of Molson Coors confirms the importance of stewarding a brand's mythology. Nick Fell of SABMiller agrees: *'The CMO's job is to be the internal storyteller, the myth-builder, and the capability builder.'*

Great marketers have to love to communicate and teach. If they don't, they can easily forget about connecting with their key stakeholders across the organization.

Perhaps we can learn most from the men and women of advertising (the ultimate storytellers!) who have seen many of their clients succeed and fail. *'The best global marketers are extremely good at consultative selling. They're phenomenal writers and presenters. They understand language and the power of communication to move people. They're inspiring. You want to follow them. They're unbelievably passionate and optimistic. But more than anything else, they have the ability to frame context. To articulate a point of view, then facilitate others to get behind it and execute the vision flawlessly.'*

These are the views of Ogilvy's John Seifert. He should know. Over the years, his agency has partnered up with legions of global marketing leaders to create countless memorable and outstanding brand campaigns.

Yet this Success Scenario demands a great CMO, an enlightened client and an inspiring agency. All of whom need to play their parts. Remember the old adage: clients get the advertising they deserve. In the quest to uncover competitive advantage and drive the brand, no marketing leader should leave any stone unturned.

THE 'PERFORMANCE COACH' ROLE

The very best marketing leaders have a world view that could best be termed 'panoramic,' as well as a people-centered approach that frames and enhances that perspective. They have full confidence in their abilities. They thoroughly embrace the broad demands of their charter. As a result, they strive to achieve their goals by empowering others. As advisor to the CEOs of large multinationals, David Gershon of the Empowerment Institute has helped us better understand how this works and how to integrate the empowerment methodology in our approach. All our programs relating to global marketing leaders today devote significant time and resources on their roles as performance coaches or, as we like to call them, empowered leaders.

Evidence clearly shows that the best global marketing leaders invest emotionally in their people. Says Greg Welch, *'The really good CMOs somehow seem to find the time to nourish, coach, provide feedback and improve the careers of their people. Those are the ones that I go to call and they're like, 'Greg, I'm not leaving this organization.'*

THE 'MEASUREMENT & ACCOUNTABILITY' ROLE

Many former CMOs and present-day marketers remain wary of marketing effectiveness measurement (and admittedly, it can be overwhelming). But the CMO of the future thoroughly embraces these new measurement tools.

What, precisely, should be measured? How do you measure a global marketer's success? Unusually (but perhaps not surprisingly, given the impossibility of isolating marketing cause-and-effect, as well as the practice's historic lack of rigor), people's opinions are divided.

Jim Stengel weighs in: *'First, short-term business results. Second, key measures of brand health that drive brand preference. And third, the ability to create a world-class marketing organization.'*

Rob Malcolm, formerly of Diageo, offers a different perspective: *'I would go for strength and uniformity of business growth and brand equity. And speed of global implementation. I would also ask: How many markets have plans targeted against our proven growth drivers? And I'd keep an eye on culture, and alignment.'*

Silvia Lagnado champions a slightly different model of metrics: *'I always look at global strength vs. local strength. Global share is total worldwide share. And local share is the average of your share in all the markets in which you play. So for instance, if you go into 10 markets and achieve 10% share in each of them, or I spread myself thin in 100 markets, but only achieve a 1% share in each of them, we'll both have the same global share. But you will have 10 strong brand positions. And I will have 100 weak ones.'*

All these are valid approaches. Each one works, too. Conclusion: It isn't precisely *what* you measure (the jury's still out on *that* one), but that you make it a point to consistently measure one or more things over time, while adapting your efforts based on the results.

The rest will take care of itself.

THE POET AND/OR FARMER ROLE

Obviously, the CMO's role is various. Its descriptors appear to fall into two camps: the operator and the thinker, e.g. the creative brand strategist. (Our belief? It's never one or the other).

Ann Ness at Cargill recognizes this duality. *'In order to be effective in this role, an individual needs to bring analytical skills as well as appreciation for the creative and artistic side of this work, and the ability to persuasively defend it and inspire persuasion and enrollment in the organization. So it is a specific combination of traits that can't be over-indexed in any one area.'*

In our opinion, CMOs and global brand leaders are the marketing industry's lightning rods. Which makes them responsible for both right-brain and left-brain activities - building effective global marketing organizations and overseeing the creative expression of brands.

Mike Linton, former CMO, Best Buy, and CMO, Ebay, dissects the role(s) as follows: *'I would say the CMO role is splintering into at least three versions of the role: I think there is the actual global CMO, or the super-CMO role that is actually running the consumer function or really running a big part of the company's efforts. There is the communications CMO role that is just taking whatever the company produces and, essentially, selling it. And then there is the analytical CMO that is actually managing the math of the CMO job.'*

As we mull over the CMO's evolving job responsibilities in today's rapidly globalizing marketing environment, we can't help but wonder: should today's global brand leaders be creatively focused poets *and* artists and numbers-driven, financially savvy managers devoted to building global marketing capability? In a roundtable discussion with three enormously influential CMOs, we kicked around the following question: Are you a Farmer, a Poet...or both?

Says Jim Stengel of Procter & Gamble, *'There's certainly a need for CMOs and the head of a global brand, like for example Pantene, to be good at both. Yet, when I was at P&G, I realized we were much more like operators than artists. And our recruiting system hired operators. The on-the-job experiences we gave to people were more operational. We valued the operational stuff of marketing more than the creative component. I felt that we would never become the kind of brand company that we could be without building up our creative capabilities. So I worked with AG Lafley, our CEO, and other P&G leaders to boost that capability.'*

Simon Clift of Unilever chimes in: *'I think the best marketers are people who are of course good at business but also value, cherish and protect 'flakier', more* off-the-wall brand people in their team. The companies we all most admire are driven by people who are good at business but also have a kind of passionate, almost unreasonable vision for their brand. So, yes, I think that you have to either be good at both the financial/managerial and creative aspects, or if you are better at one than the other, you have to be able to respect then manage and find support for the other thing you're less good at. I feel that the bad marketers are those who just don't understand the value of both.'

We also debated these specific descriptors. Are they valuable? Or do they simply distract from the essence of the argument?

Rob Malcolm of Diageo: 'The first part of my career was developing the love of brands and learning the discipline and craft of marketing. Some have called it the 'poetry' side of marketing. Then I moved into general management P&L roles, running markets, regions and categories. In these GM roles I had direct responsibilities for distributors, joint venture partners, supply operations, finance, information systems functions, and human resources. I never lost the belief in and passion for brands, but I learned that, when I was responsible for the entire value equation and the whole scope of the business, there are trade-offs that you have to make at the general management level. For me, the management responsibilities were absolutely indispensable later on, to be successful doing the global marketing and sales job I did at Diageo. I could not have done it successfully going straight through, along the marketing track alone.'

Jim Stengel: 'At P&G, we had discussions about the profiles of the people we needed, and also the career paths that were necessary to build the capabilities we wanted to build. The idea that we debated was to actually move to create two different career paths. One career path would lead to running a country, running a customer team, and eventually to being a candidate for a senior operational position. The other option would be a franchise leader. These people would have an affinity with a particular brand. It is about matching the person with his/her passion. Franchise leaders need to be travelers, co-innovators…incredible communicators. It's a very tough profile to find… I do think if a CMO or global brand leader cannot understand the farmer – the operationally minded, numbers-savvy marketer – and what's important to the operational business, he or she loses credibility.'

Let's be real: not every marketing leader can juggle such a broad set of competencies. Smart marketers understand that it's not an 'either-or' trade-off. The exceptional ones manage to combine the farmer and the poet. They identify and harvest the low-hanging fruit to deliver and celebrate early wins – while using the buffer they've just bought to double-down on the things that really matter.

Those who can find the balance typically go the distance.

THE 'UNLOCKING MARKETING CAPABILITY' ROLE

Not every marketing leader has the wherewithal to take a step back and objectively observe his or her organization – or evaluate it as a marketing machine, akin to a clock that needs to be precisely ticking. Most lack the confidence to project their presence within the organization more than one or two years down the road. Those who do find themselves freed up to adopt a more holistic view of what might well be their lasting contribution.

Rob Malcolm of Diageo: *'The first thing a CMO needs to do is a situation analysis, to discover what's the big business need or opportunity that they've got to tackle immediately. And then they need to ask, 'What is the organizational talent capability that I have to accomplish these goals?' You need both these answers straight in front of you.'*

One key decision that global marketing leaders must make (we believe it's a call that *all* business leaders should consider) is to determine quickly what the organization is – or should be – or should be good at. Which competencies are non-strategic, and can be outsourced?

'At P&G,' says Jim Stengel, *'we decided that we would never want consumer understanding outsourced; it has such a direct impact on our brand purpose and innovation pipeline.'*

Once CMOs have resolved these issues, they'll know how best to prioritize skill sets in a company's recruitment efforts. As our colleague Jo Ryman points out: *'Building organizational capability is all about thinking through structure, processes, roles and responsibilities. It's about how an organization equips each of its contributors for success. Address these issues properly, and the benefits will be almost immediate.'*

Obviously, the CMO role isn't for everyone. But for those who are up for it, the emotional payoff is ample reward for the time spent on the road.

IN SUMMARY...

Throughout this book, and specifically in this chapter, we've identified the characteristics, mindsets and behaviors that we feel comprise the winning global marketing leader. Thanks to a decade of working with the world's best marketing leaders, we've observed and analyzed these qualities – which we hope to pass along to the next generation.

Ultimately, the title of this book sums it up. If you asked us to come up with a single definition for success, we'd say that the most effective global marketing leaders must adopt the role of a *global brand CEO*.

Successful CMOs understand what it takes to be a CEO. Today, rather than carrying out the old brand development role, they're living that life now. To an unprecedented degree, today's CMO role is about thinking, inspiring, building capabilities, bringing along the whole team – and above all, leading. Can we add that it's also about ensuring that you've appointed functional experts within your team – and permitting them do the marketing while you devote your energies to being a true leader?

The CMO role has evolved to become more of a general management role. CMOs need to focus on the return to shareowners; on building an effective global marketing machine; and on measuring and re-allocating investments. For this kind of CMO, what's the next logical promotion? Becoming CEO.

LEADING VISA TO
GLOBAL BRAND GROWTH

VISA is both the world's largest payments technology company and one of its best-known brands. VISA's network links consumers, merchants, businesses, financial institutions and governments in more than 200 countries and territories. VISA technology is the power behind digital currency: Secure, convenient, reliable and fast, it is driving economic growth, fostering financial inclusion and rapidly replacing cash and checks.

The promise of VISA and the universal appeal of digital currency soon made VISA one of the world's most recognizable names. The company has built an enviable set of brand attributes including convenience, security and unsurpassed acceptance. On the strength of its network, products and brand, VISA in 2009 processed 62 billion transactions with a total value of US$4.4 trillion.

VISA had historically been a membership organization comprised of financial institutions and managed via several geographic regions. Its fundamental role as a payments technology provider was often obscured because of the focus by members on their own brands, and the VISA products they provided to customers.

That came into sharp focus as VISA began working toward a transition to a public company in 2008. What had been a set of affiliated regional organizations, sharing a common brand, was to be merged into a seamless, single company, with regional management reporting into a strong and centralized global leadership team. The marketing challenges that accompanied this shift were clear: Create global brand clarity and consistency to drive growth and shareholder value; establish a focus on consumers on par with financial institutions; and demonstrate transparency and accountability around the company's investment in marketing.

MERGING MARKETING STYLES

VISA's CEO and senior leadership team recognized that what would be effectively a new company needed a new approach to marketing, and that required a different kind of Chief Marketing Officer. The company turned to Antonio Lucio, a proven, innovative and dynamic senior marketing executive and a veteran of consumer giants P&G and PepsiCo.

Lucio understood that VISA needed a CMO who combined two styles: capability building and operations. He also recognized that, for marketing to make its contribution to VISA's success as a public company, he would need to retool the marketing organization to match this dual mission in a uniform global fashion.

The legacy of a regional approach meant VISA had six different brand expressions, five different advertising agencies and four different media agencies around the world. This created a high level of functional duplication across regions, increasing costs without increasing brand cohesiveness.

After consulting with VISA's CEO and board, it was agreed that the top priority for marketing was to replace that approach with a new global operating model that was far more effective, yet still allowed VISA to be responsive to the different needs of different local markets. To help develop this brand strategy, Lucio set out to define VISA in global terms, so that the company would have *'one global positioning statement…one global brand architecture and one global brand idea. We were going to have one way to measure performance,'* Lucio recalls. *'Everything else was local.'*

CONSOLIDATION WITH LOCALIZATION
VISA understood that such a radical change would likely meet with some resistance in various regions, because they were accustomed to operational autonomy. To help overcome that resistance, Lucio and his team built a business case based on the cost efficiencies VISA could attain via a reorganization in global marketing, along with the potential growth opportunities from addressing the needs of global-aware consumers.

At the same time, the plan had room for important aspects of localization. Rather than absolute control from company headquarters, VISA would establish a framework that consolidated resources while permitting individual countries to express local nuance and ingenuity in campaigns.

In the actual process of agency consolidation, each of the regions was encouraged to have its incumbent agency pitch for the global assignment. VISA challenged each agency to demonstrate how it would express the single brand idea across three product lines in five different countries. Finally, any ideas developed for the global brand campaign had to match, or beat, locally developed work in efficiency and effectiveness.

While this approach allowed significant flexibility within local regions, Lucio made it clear that the regions could not use that as an opportunity to retreat to full local autonomy. While members of the team were free to express diverse points of view during the formulation and development process, once the final path had been chosen, the marketing team across the globe had to commit to alignment with the path and become passionate about the new vision. In short, the marketing team was given a choice: Align to the new vision or move on. Most decided to

VISA accepted everywhere around the globe

stay. Some were encouraged to move on, under fair and equitable terms. Lucio's approach, and his insistence on absolute commitment, helped to craft a new collaborative, global marketing mindset within the larger framework of VISA's new, public-company identity.

LAUNCHING THE NEW BRAND

In March 2009, against the backdrop of one of the most economically challenging times in recent history, VISA introduced its first global advertising campaign under a single global theme – *'More People Go With VISA.'* The campaign enabled VISA, for the first time in its history, to communicate across all its regions using a single marketing message. Yet the campaign provided the regions with the ability to execute local programs adapted for maximum relevance and impact.

A crucial innovation was at the core of the campaign, one that supported Lucio's broader mandate to drive greater effectiveness and efficiencies within the marketing function. VISA deconstructed the traditional creative process and replaced it with a *'media first'* approach that established consumer-centric media planning as the initial step in creative development.

The approach maximizes consumer impact and brand relevance, leading to the development of more persuasive communications delivered through channels that amplify messaging and deliver innovation across emerging and traditional outlets.

Building on the strategic framework of *'More People Go with VISA,'* in 2010 VISA launched its first global marketing campaigns for both the Olympic Games (Go World) and the FIFA World Cup (Go Fans). A study by Survey Sampling International's (SSI) global panels after the FIFA World Cup showed that VISA was one of three sponsor brands that saw significant gains in global consumer awareness among both men and women.

To date, the global marketing platform has helped deliver against key metrics, such as building preference for VISA over cash and checks – a critical indicator of success in market.

VISA recently ranked number 18, 18 spots from its 2009 rank, on the BrandZ Top 100 – a list of the world's most valuable brands. *'You may have a global consolidated brand idea,'* says Lucio, *'But it has to be reinforced and refreshed continually with every action or otherwise it will die.'*

Your *First* 100 Days

The Art Of The Start

11

 GlaxoSmithKline

PETER KIRKBY – VP GLOBAL MARKETING EXCELLENCE,
GLAXOSMITHKLINE CONSUMER HEALTHCARE

Like many of the global marketing leaders profiled in this book, Peter Kirkby began his career in marketing by learning the profession at one of the marketing motherships – in his case Procter & Gamble. Educated in Bath, Peter worked for P&G for seven years – the first five from 1990 to 1995 in different brand management roles in the U.K., and the last two years in the Balkans based in Bucharest.

These days Peter is happily married to a P&G marketer, lives in the U.K., has two kids, and loves to relax by sailing competitively.

From 1997 to 2002, Peter left the client side to work as a marketing consultant working for clients across the U.K., Continental Europe and the U.S. In 2002, his client GSK tempted him to join the very team he was a consultant to by asking him what he wanted to do when he grew up. Switching back to the client side, Peter has remained there ever since because he likes to take charge quickly and see through what he starts.

After a few years on the *Aquafresh* toothpaste brand, Peter was quick to raise his hand when GSK decided to get more serious about its global brands and build a new dedicated global marketing organization to support global growth.

As Vice-President Marketing Strategy & Excellence for GlaxoSmithKline's Consumer Healthcare sector Future Group, today Peter oversees global consumer and market insight, strategy, brand and communications planning, digital marketing, agency management and the company's marketing capability program.

Kirkby: *'We weren't growing fast enough. Our focus had been on profit delivery, but that was clearly not a sustainable model long-term. So about five years ago, we challenged three teams to determine how best to accelerate growth in the company. All three teams came to the same conclusion: to drive growth we needed to step-change our innovation.'*

The teams recommended a *'more centralized, robust, and connected global marketing and R&D organization for our global brands - freeing up our regional and local brands - by essentially putting decision-making in the right places and at the right levels. The new global organization would need to concentrate and take the lead on driving the growth and innovation agenda on our global brands. In short, our brands needed to become 'future brands'. That's when the decision was taken to change the operating model.'*

Kirkby is a passionate believer in building capacities across global brands, countries and disciplines. In 2005, GSK introduced a new more centralized global marketing and R&D organization dubbed the 'Future Group.' At first created as a confederation of seven GSK global brands - including Aquafresh, Sensodyne, Alli, and Panadol – the new *Future Group* was responsible for taking the lead on driving the growth and innovation agenda.

Peter's role is to help accelerate brand growth and build the trust and effectiveness of the Future Group model. Called *Global Marketing Excellence,* his team enabled all the global brands to draw on specialist resources – whether it was insight, strategy, brand development, digital marketing, expert marketing (marketing for healthcare professionals) or marketing excellence.

Long dedicated to ensuring that central marketing teams never lose sight of local reality, and remain connected by listening and interacting with major markets, Peter quickly reached out to key stakeholders all across the business to gauge key market opportunities, challenges and priorities as they perceived them with a dedicated *PulseCheck.*

Fielded within the first three months of the group's founding the assessment's findings went a long way toward helping shape the first year's strategy. By repeating the PulseCheck annually ever since, Peter and the team have stayed connected to local markets and been able to measure quantitatively how effective the Future Group has been in addressing key stakeholder needs.

Peter's *Servant Leadership* mindset and actions in the first few months of the Future Group's existence did much to build key stakeholder confidence in the new group and win support for the more global approach. His insights and actions have made an important impact on the effectiveness of global marketing at GSK. This chapter will focus on some of the key consideration and actions to focus on during the first 3 months of taking on the new global marketing leadership role.

UP PERISCOPE:
LOOKING FORWARD

The previous 10 chapters have distilled the essence of our learning across 10 years in the business, supporting global marketing leaders as they build the *ultimate marketing machine.*

The ideas and suggestions on these pages describe not just *what* great marketing organizations focus their attention on, but more importantly from our perspective, *how* they go about doing it.

Taken in aggregate, these pages contain both our philosophy and approach, as well as a host of practical ideas and best practices gleaned from studying and working with over 50 of the world's biggest and best marketing organizations.

Now – allow us to wrap things up and end the book with a personal case study. Suspend reality for a few moments, and accompany us on an imaginary journey to see how you would handle the challenge of building the ultimate marketing machine...

Congratulations!

You've just been offered the CMO role. You're now the leader of an enormous global marketing community, and the steward of a brand with a long and impressive heritage.

There's only one problem. The brand happens to be in serious trouble right now.

Which is just maybe why they picked you for the role. Given your strong track record of proven results in all your previous local and regional marketing roles, as well as the respect you've garnered from your colleagues and peers at your previous employer (they checked of course), the CEO and Board are convinced that no better candidate exists who can get this global brand organization back on track. Oh, and fast, too, since the company has just announced cuts across the board to catch up with share-holder expectations. Basically, there's no time to waste.

Everything in you says, *'Take the job!!'* (and your headhunter says it's probably the best thing you'll ever be offered in this economy), but a small voice inside your head warns you to look before you leap. Through the grapevine, you hear word that someone at P&G was also offered the job, but that he turned it down on the grounds of *'Impossible expectations.'* So how will you move forward?

Well, let's start by acknowledging that we've seldom witnessed a weak start followed by a strong, triumphant finish. The reverse is also true. According to our colleague Robbie Millar: *'CMOs who conduct the proper analyses up front, and make all the right moves from the get-go, seldom end their tenure involuntarily, or with a whimper. Instead, they snowball forward…and bring their organizations to a higher plane.'*

For a decade now, we've studied the actions individuals can take before taking a job, and what they do during the first 100 days. Why? Because we believe they're critical. The good news? There's a clear and winning formula for success. The bad news? Knowing that doesn't make it any easier. Not surprisingly, our template includes a series of do's and don'ts. It also includes a clear roadmap e.g. a consecutive order of priorities and actions for you, as new global marketing leader, to focus on.

Your tenure at the top, your residence at the CMO desk doesn't have to expire within the average 18 months. Let's lift a glass. *Here's to your success!*

Start Before You Commit

The first success factor begins at the recruitment stage. It's this: Getting a crystal-clear perspective of what the board expects from the role. Doubtlessly, when the company first offered you the job, the CEO or COO had some concrete expectations about the role. But now, as you remember those preliminary interviews and meetings (and go so far as to reread the job description), you probably realize that the accountabilities you remember weren't as clear-cut as they first came across as being.

REACHING OUT TO THE BOARD

Spending sufficient time up front with the CEO, and maybe the CFO, to define and reach razor-sharp agreements around your exact responsibilities, accountabilities, and available resources, is essential.

Agree up front by what key performance indicators you'll be held accountable. Create full clarity on where the marketing budgets sit, how large they are, and who, precisely, has what influence over them.

Most importantly, before you start, gauge, discuss and force alignment across the Board on *what the role of (global) marketing will be* in order to help achieve the organization's overall business objectives and develop a shared vision on what success within your job looks like.

REACHING OUT BEYOND THE BOARD

But we suggest you take this one step further. Next, talk to an influential local marketing director and get an idea of the expectations at the local level – remember, success is delivered with, and through, local teams. During this step, we also suggest you firmly grasp what 'climate' you'll be stepping into as well.

During these conversations, we recommend focusing on three areas. Areas, we might add, for which any CMO should be clearly accountable. In descending order, these are:

GENERATING CONSUMER INSIGHTS

Consumer insights are the lifeblood of marketing. They're the inputs which fuel the key processes of innovation, communications and the customer experience. As CMO or global brand head, you're responsible for the enterprise capability to develop and define consumer insights, place value on them, then translate them into product and service innovations, stronger brands…and more satisfied customers. How is the gathering of consumer insights led and managed? In what way are insights a strategic capability? What are the insight targets, and how are the reporting lines run? Now's the time to find out.

BUILDING BRAND EQUITY

It's fairly straightforward: Ultimately, you'll be responsible for consumers' loyalty to your brand. As we know, we can measure this commitment in various ways but by whatever measure you choose, in order to create consumer preference and loyalty, it must reflect the perceived added value that marketing brings. Customers may love your brand. They may trust your service. They may recommend you to others. They may rely on you in a crisis. Regardless of the nature of the emotional bond, marketing's job is to create, nurture, monitor and strengthen it. Therefore, during these conversations, nail down the status quo, the level of understanding and the quality of metrics.

BUILDING MARKETING CAPABILITY

You may've just been approached to become the CMO or head of the global brand, but bear in mind you won't be in the job forever. Your duty to the shareholders is to leave behind a stronger marketing capability than the one that was in place when the company appointed you. Thus, you'll need to define the components of this capability, decide how to measure strength and improvement, and reach consensus on the remit you need to build this particular capability. Our colleague Roxanne Aquino recommends: *'Find out who knows what about the quality of the marketing capability. How is talent managed? How is the organization's overall marketing capability benchmarked against its competition? How well-integrated is the capability development agenda with the business growth agenda?'*

SPAN OF INFLUENCE

One particular characteristic of the CMO role is, we suspect, unique to marketing alone: No other job in the company has such a high range of influence mixed with such a low span of control over resources! Which is another way of emphasizing the crucial importance of influencing others.

Occasionally, CMOs and heads of global brands really *do* have full control of a large marketing budget for advertising and other key mix elements, including communications. Moreover, they'll focus on using these elements effectively and efficiently. But more often than not, budget control in fact rests with the operating units, meaning that your direct control over resources is low.

Many global CMOs have to become experts almost overnight in influencing country and business unit structures in order to divert them from narrower product and geography promotions – and convince them to devote resources to a new global brand-building campaign.

This high span of influence – remember: without having authority over them, you must excel at influencing many business units and functions – requires highly specific support structures. The CEO, the board of directors, and the heads of the operating units must offer their clear, visible, and active support. If you feel any hesitancy, or if history indicates conflict, be appropriately wary. Why will it be any different with you at the helm?

Okay, let's now suppose all conversations went well, and the answers you got back ticked all the boxes. You're excited. Sure, now and again, it sounds like too much is packed into just one job, but honestly? You believe you may well beat the odds on this role. You're the right person for the job.

You're positive.

Here's what we recommend you focus on from the moment that the ink on your contract is still drying.

'As I move along in my career,
I find that I am spending more
and more time talking about WHO
to involve in the decision-making
process and *HOW* we will
implement versus just *WHAT*
are we going to be doing.'

EGBERT VAN ACHT - CMO, PHILIPS CONSUMER LIFESTYLE 2008 - 2009

Start Before You Start

Once upon a time, companies enforced what was loosely dubbed '90-day probation period.' During this time, organizations gave new recruits both the time and the flexibility to settle in, build rapport with a buddy, and navigate their way around the system.

To succeed today, you have to fit in, perform – and do both on a blindingly tight schedule. Let's assume you did your preparations before you started. Now, to stay ahead of the curve, consider mentally starting your new role even as you physically wrap up your old one.

No one can perform at peak efficiency indefinitely. If this describes you, allow yourself to take a break. It can be as brief as you like, but it has to be total. Turn off that Blackberry. The more revitalized you feel upon your return, the more electrifying your impact will be in your new role.

As we've noted, the CMO role is among the most exhilarating, excruciating jobs extant. From the start, it demands all your mental, emotional and physical commitment. Some CMOs even prepare themselves for the job's rigors by equipping themselves with executive coaches and personal trainers to get into top shape for what lies ahead.

Now is also a good time to put into place and prepare your personal support infrastructure to ensure that your whole family is as prepared as you are for what's upcoming in your first 100 days on the job. Believe us: you'll need their understanding and support.

Finally, carefully use your last days of objective observing! Once you start, it will be a matter of days before the system kidnaps you, and you need to drink its Kool-Aid. Use these last days to notice everything there is to notice from the outside. Talk to people you respect, and whose external view intrigues you. They'll be more honest now than they will be after you start the job.

Next, before even setting foot in your new office, strive to become familiar with the key business issues, opportunities and challenges. Take on board a wide range of views from people who have a key interest in the business, and who know how it works backwards and forwards. Seek out knowledgeable external experts such as industry analysts, ex-employees, and journalists, as well as your reporter and agency friends. Figure out what questions you want to ask these key constituents. Take meetings and have lunches and dinners with the smartest, savviest observers possible.

If you prepare well, don't stint on your due diligence, and rest as though a normal night's sleep is not a thing of the past, you'll resemble the expert, targeted parachutist who floats down to land, then hits the ground running. Always remember: Your long-term effectiveness and ultimate impact will be hugely influenced by the actions you take over the next 100 days.

Start Right When You Start

Connect – Listen & Learn

First, reach out. On Day One, the most critical meeting you'll have is with your team. None of us ever gets a second chance to make a winning first impression. (Malcolm Gladwell's *Blink* offers research-based evidence that people form lasting impression within mere seconds of an interaction. Which is both sobering and scary.)

Over the next days, walk the corridors. Learn to find your way around not just the formal but also the informal communication networks within the company. Befriend a couple of 'lifers' and secretaries. We guarantee both history and perspective will jump to life. Ask them to 'bring you to the graveyard,' so you can discover why the bodies were buried.

You'll be tempted to hurriedly place your stamp on the work, and discuss your ideas at length. Try and resist the urge for now. Never badmouth a body of work even if everyone else seems to think it's sub-par. (You wouldn't have joined this company if you didn't think it had something going for it.)

Next, after just a few short days it's time to take leave of HQ and those ivory-tower offices. Get out. Be gone! Thoroughly immerse yourself in the markets. Demonstrate your willingness to meet with people on their turf. Be seen to want to deepen your understanding of local market nuances and realities. (Keep a record of your findings, too, and revisit them often.) You'll surprise yourself by what you can glean by asking the right questions. Focus on the biggest markets, but don't forget to communicate to key smaller markets that they count, too.

The topics on which you should focus your conversations? Let's define them in terms of 'the *what*' and 'the *how*'.

'THE WHAT'

Use every bit of your intellect and all your analytical powers to deep-dive into what we call The Five C's: the Consumer, the Channel, the Context, the Company, and the Competition.

Per C: what are the key drivers, and what are the main trends and developments? Analyze and ask, What are the apparent similarities across markets? Where do you, and key stakeholders, see, or perceive, fundamental differences?

Now study how the company responds to its market challenges and opportunities. Analyze the full marketing mix by critically assessing all key components, from the insights on which value propositions are built, to retail solutions, to strategic and tactical pricing, to the innovation funnel, and how well it's filled with horizon 1, 2, and 3 concepts.

With your fresh-born perspective, you'll see things more clearly than most people do. *Notice* everything you notice – and write it down (the simple phenomenon of noticing something means it's noteworthy, and worth pondering.) From a technical standpoint, the people you speak with will always know more than you do, but you might very well have a clearer perspective. Take note of the forest, and be grateful you aren't yet pre-occupied with the trees.

Our advice? Be relentless in your demand to get every single detail on the table. Leave no stone or pebble unturned. Others will respect for your thoroughness and professionalism. Oh – and if for some reason you don't understand something, ask again. If you still don't understand, don't assume it's your fault. Do the opposite. Ask people to come back another time, and clarify the issue in another way. It may very well help them revisit and/or revise a limiting belief or faulty assumption.

It's time to focus on the organization's global marketing effectiveness from a structure, processes and team perspective. Look to understand the state of relationships among global, regional and local brand teams, as well as those among functions (by focusing primarily, of course, on marketing, sales, and R&D).

How much understanding and respect exists among these teams and functions? To what extent are people on the team able to take 'a receiving end' perspective about their work? If they can, does someone recognize this? Do people work interdependently? Perhaps most importantly, *Is there real trust?*

Now it's time to visit the subjects of vision and inspiration around the brand. How strong and clear is the brand vision? Does it reflect the external reality as you perceived it before you jumped into the fray? To what extent is it borne from a universal truth and, at the same time, aligned with the overall company's roots, vision, mission and objectives? To what extent do stakeholders inside and outside the company buy into the vision? Are people *really* living the brand values? Have people thought through what the vision means to them personally, and to the projects on which they're working?

Next up? Strategy and alignment. Is there full clarity and alignment on priorities and the key performance indicators? What about the balance between (short-term) business building and (long-term) brand-equity building priorities and innovation investments? Are people's personal targets and incentives aligned with the company and brand goals? Can people truly define the brand's top priorities, and which strategic thrusts exist to deliver on them? Does everyone agree that these are the appropriate priorities? Regarding organization and ways of working, uncover how well the structure works for the business. Is everyone clear about their own and others' roles and responsibilities? Who are the (rising and potential) stars, and who should have left the business three or four CEOs ago?

Are people's behaviors in line with the present operating model? Do they feel they have the remit and resources to do their job well? What are the views of the local or business unit general managers and heads of marketing? Do these people actively support the global marketing operating model?

On the topic of marketing learning, find out how the organization captures, and rolls out, best practices. Also, does the culture encourage people to learn from mistakes, or sweep them covertly under the rug? Is there an infrastructure in place for learning and capability building?

Ensure that as you circle the globe twice to meet with all key markets, that you're always making an effort to understand their *'receiving end'* perspective – whether it's consumers, local, regional, and global brand marketers, sales, R&D or finance – and attempt to agree on a follow-up communication channel with your key stakeholders. Once you've reached out and listened to them, and they in turn understand that you're well-informed about the lay of the land, they may not only give you credit, but become more open to your ideas once you start talking about them.

Okay – the listening tour is officially over. Now it's time to do something essential: shape and share your vision on (the role of) global marketing.

Inspire – *Crystallizing And Communicating Your Vision*

Before you play the role of ambassador of the consumer voice, and focus the troops on competitive threats and opportunities, bear in mind that this is first and foremost about your view on the role of (global) marketing and the contribution it should bring to the company's mission and objectives.

Give market researchers a challenge, and their solution will involve market research. Present brand marketers with a problem and their solution will involve the brand. But market research, the brand, and the innovations are all means to an end, not an end in themselves.

By making it extremely clear how the marketing function serves the overall business mission and objectives, your vision should make abundantly clear how the brand is a means to an end. The CEO and CFO will love you for it. Your team will love you for it, too. Everyone's a fan of clarity of purpose – and a well-defined destination (if they're not, maybe they're in the wrong place). Remember that it's also your task to show the board, and the rest of the company, how valuable marketing is to helping achieve the business vision, while simultaneously valuing and recognizing your team at the highest level.

In Chapter 8, we explained our four archetypical roles for global marketing: the Supporter, the Builder, the Driver, and the Champion.

Now you must clearly communicate which role you feel global marketing should play in the future – and your vision of how big the gap is, versus the current state of affairs

Success in this area isn't only about the quality of your vision, but convincing others that you can expertly communicate it. Literally taking a page out of the P&G playbook, most impressive would be if you could communicate this vision to the board on a single page.

Once your colleagues are on board, it's time to start rallying your own troops. Plan a few significant kick-off events somewhere around your 100th day. People will be expecting you to begin taking a position. Do it, and do it with flair. Now is your moment to set all eyes in the same direction.

Focus – Identifying The Key Thrusts To Be Addressed

Needless to say, it'll take more than 100 days of listening to develop a plan of how, precisely, you'll achieve your stated vision and goals. To manage expectations, throughout your conversations it pays to state explicitly during your first 100 days that you have no interest in developing the plan on your own. The team that's executing the strategy should also develop the strategy. You've set the vision... and now, along with the team, you'll develop both the strategy and the milestones. If key stakeholders are genuinely involved in the development of the plan, they will also own it.

That said, it's important to provide as much clarity as possible about the guardrails that are in place for strategy development. What terms have you agreed with the CFO and CEO on regarding costs? Will you need to further centralize marketing? Outside of your direct control, what corporate initiatives should marketing be a part of? Lay everything out as early as possible.

Be transparent. Relay bad news up front, and if there are difficult messages to communicate, let the CEO do some of the heavy lifting on your behalf. If you begin with the difficult stuff, it may very well feel like smoother sailing from that point on.

Remember: at this stage, it's not about the details. It's much more about clarifying what you want to achieve in macro terms. The sooner you realize this, the more (and better) you'll be able to streamline efforts and focus energy in the entire organization.

Organize – Select The Players & Lock Down Remit

Now that you recognize the lay of the land, and where you want to go (including key priorities), it's high time to choose the team that will help you get there.

At this point in time, you should have met all the important players, and had the opportunity to discuss key individuals with several stakeholders. Now, you need to set the tone of all future work by announcing who's on the team. Make no mistake – everybody's been counting down to this day. Everyone in marketing is fully aware that there would come a day soon after your start (we hope not too soon after your start) where you'd clarify what types of people would be in charge on your watch.

Also, how will the group work as an ensemble cast? Are these the people you feel you could leave in charge of the shop when you take that vacation next year? All fun aside, this is perhaps the most important announcement you'll be making for a long time to come.

Explain why you've selected key people by highlighting those qualities or behaviors that you'd like others to begin replicating. Acknowledge performance beyond the brief as you empower people for new roles. By celebrating personal success at this point, you set the tone for everything that lies ahead. It's an extraordinary opportunity to shape how people work and perform.

A word of caution about all the people who may feel *'left behind,'* or who may perceive your appointments as evidence that somehow they've been performing poorly. This is potentially a great intervention moment, so use it well. Explain why, and why not. Explain what you are looking and hoping for from them in the year ahead. Pointedly recognize people who are serving in ideal roles, and shouldn't move – then make sure you communicate that a lack of movement or promotion should in no way be interpreted as a lack of performance, or a vote of no confidence.

Finally, there will be agents of resistance, maybe even saboteurs. At the end of the 100 days, you'll know who they are. Have a plan in place, agreed on in advance with the CEO, on how you'll be dealing with these people at the first inkling of resistance.

Seek out anyone who will be clearly compromised by the changes you're demanding, then remind them again why you are making those changes. Ask them how they want to proceed. Make it their personal responsibility to own these new circumstances, this new environment. If you come up against any – and we mean any – signs of rebellion, be decisive. In the end, humans are herd animals. If you allow just one individual to disrespect your vision, the herd may trample you sooner than you can imagine.

Build – *Define Crucial Capabilities for Success*

Now that the first 100 days are nearing their end, realize that you're nowhere near done Connecting, Inspiring, Focusing, and Organizing. These crucial drivers of global marketing effectiveness will keep commanding your attention forever. You'll have to keep circling through the wheel of drivers of global marketing effectiveness to keep improving global marketing effectiveness.

But now, beyond your first quarter, you can kick off one of the most gratifying parts of your work as CMO, or global brand leader. Start to *build for sustained impact.*

Global marketing leaders tell us every time that few things are more gratifying than leaving behind a better marketing organization. Just recall how Jim Stengel, Rob Malcolm and Simon Clift feel today about their legacies at P&G, Diageo, and Unilever.

Each one of these leaders speaks with enormous pride when they recall the team and ways of working they built up over the years. Each one knows he went far beyond launching a variety of successful innovations, or communication campaigns. Each one knows deep in his heart that if tomorrow everything changes again in the market, their teams will react forcefully and successfully.

Just imagine how you'd feel a few years from now if you made a similar impact on your team.

So right now, we challenge you: Start planning how to build that capability. And remember our colleague Stef Gans' favorite change management rule: *'You have to behave yourself into new thinking, instead of thinking yourself into new behaviors.'*

So determine how you will build the connections, the trust, the vision, the clarity around strategy and goals, the organization and operating model, and, not least, the training and sharing systems that make the effective global marketing organizations world-class.

In other words:

How will you build *the Ultimate Marketing Machine?*

CHECKING THE PULSE TO EQUIP
THE FUTURE GROUP FOR SUCCESS

Before 2005, countries and regions were traditionally very autonomous within GSK Consumer Healthcare.

With the exception of a central marketing group known as 'Category Management,' little else was organized across regions. Under this system, a small team in the center tried to leverage marketing learning across the business. While they had some authority to innovate, they lacked the necessary resources, money or authority to take a lead. At that point, regions and countries were driving the GSK innovation agenda. The consequence: Immense fragmentation. Growth levels remained at a modest 3 percent.

FAST FORWARD: THE 'FUTURE GROUP'
Clearly, GSK required a new approach to innovation in order to drive growth. In 2005, the organization launched a new, more centralized global marketing and R&D organization dubbed the 'Future Group.' As a confederation of seven GSK Consumer Healthcare global brands, the Future Group was responsible for taking the lead on driving the growth and innovation agenda.

The Future Group vision and business promise was to step-change growth, sustaining it at a higher level than the average growth rate of GSK's 'local jewel' brands – and, the group hoped, ultimately overtaking them in terms of scale and contribution.

With this objective in mind, GSK took pains to create its Future Group Teams to ensure they represented a true mix of brand and market expertise. The company co-located Future Group brand and R&D teams. They also gave them strong incentives to work collaboratively to ensure a fusion of consumer insight and technology.

In order to monitor and guide the Future Group success, the Global Marketing Excellence team conducted a *PulseCheck*, comprising a quantitative online survey across the complete brand community, as well as in-depth interviews with key stakeholders around the drivers of global marketing effectiveness.

SAY YOU WANT AN EVOLUTION?
Two years after GSK formed the Future Group, it became clear to all that the team was doing a great job of developing and launching global innovation. In 2007, *PulseCheck* results found that over two-thirds of local markets wanted the Future

Group to take on an even greater role. They wanted stronger strategic thinking, and a more holistic approach to global brands.

Many stakeholders wanted there to be increased alignment between global and local objectives – and uncovered opportunities to more comprehensively fuse global and local strategic planning.

In turn, the model evolved by making global brand teams responsible for total global brand equity, including overall communication. The Future Group gave especial attention to communicating and embedding the changes in scope across the organization, both to ensure clarity and to minimize 'turf' debates. In 2009, when the results suggested a degree of 'overreach,' with the Future Group venturing too far into local execution, the group took quick corrective action to recalibrate and re-state the edges of the central team's remit.

LET'S STAY TOGETHER
Another key learning point from the 2007 PulseCheck was that as an organization, GSK recognized it had to be more explicit about acknowledging and celebrating the complementary roles the local and global marketing teams played in order to extract maximum results from both fronts.

Much of this had to do with how global, regional and local teams interacted and behaved on a day-to-day basis. However, the Future Group also made sharing strategic brand directions and plans a key focus of its annual GO meeting that brought together all the Markets and Future Group teams – some 300 people in all.

GSK also implemented structural changes in order to help improve collaboration within the Future Group. In 2007, the company decided to truly 'co-locate' all the different highly matrixed functions within the same physical space, thereby creating Global Brand 'Innovation Hubs.'

Future Group commercial teams, R&D and Future Group leadership eliminated their offices and began working together at one big 'kitchen table.' The result was a more fun, inspiring work environment and more importantly, more 'constructive eavesdropping' and in-person conversations, rather than email traffic.

Around the same time, GSK began bringing in more people from the markets and putting them into the Future Group, while exporting people from the Future Group into local markets. By walking in another person's shoes, the organization immediately strengthened trust, understanding and the best kind of interdependency between local and global.

GSK Panadol

The *PulseCheck* also highlighted situations where there was room for collaborative improvement between a Future Group team and the markets. For one of the global brands, the responses to the survey question, 'It is clear to everybody where my individual responsibilities start and end,' showed a significant drop between 2008 and 2009.

Based on these results, the team quickly scheduled a work session with the markets to drive alignment around roles and responsibilities. These work sessions focused on identifying key deliverables, as well as the 'critical value' that global, regional or local teams needed to contribute. This approach of engaging and embedding the broad principles of global and local roles and responsibilities – in effect, bringing the RACI document to life – proved immensely effective.

Another Future Group team interpreted the 2009 *PulseCheck* findings as a call to action to improve 'Core Team' ways of working between the global brand team and the top-5 core markets. Moving fast, the team redefined the Team role, responsibilities, deliverables, membership criteria and meeting structure in order to build a more empowered team with a stronger sense of ownership – ultimately resulting in greater alignment around the global brand vision and strategy, and increased effort and focus on the activities that delivered the vision.

WINNERS NEVER QUIT
To ensure it continues to drive growth, the Future Group has kept on modifying its global marketing operating model. For example, in 2007, the group created a new specialist Expert Marketing team, which it authorized to develop central strategy and communication packages for healthcare professionals, including dentists and pharmacists. That way, markets found it easier to focus on activation. A new specialist Project Management resource was charged with managing any new issues, and ensuring that projects came in on time. A global innovation network helped share and drive new ideas, and also build capability across the company.

CODA
GSK Consumer Healthcare's growth track record makes for compelling reading. Historically, before the company established the Future Group model, it was accustomed to two to three percent growth. Since the company instituted the new global operating model, overall growth has soared – up to 14 percent in 2007, and seven percent during the challenging economic conditions in 2009.

The results of the *PulseCheck* also confirmed the success of the Future Group. Across GSK, we saw significantly higher confidence in the quality of the global brand innovation pipeline. Better yet, countries trust the Future Group to deliver on promises (a 15 base-point improvement).

Though the Future Group marketing operating model has evolved over the last five years, the strategy of driving the growth of its global brands has remained consistent. The ambition and drive for results remain resolutely at the heart of the team. During this time, the annual *PulseCheck* assessments have not only helped monitor and guide the Future Group's success. They've also played an equally essential function: to reflect clearly in the results the ongoing efforts of the organization's global and local teams.

About the Authors

MARC DE SWAAN ARONS

Marc is an acknowledged thought-leader in the burgeoning arena of global marketing leadership. He is co-founder and Chairman of EffectiveBrands, the global marketing consultants. Marc has worked directly with some of the world's most prominent Chief Marketing Officers and global brand leaders, and is a frequent keynote speaker at business schools, companies and industry conferences. His work has appeared in general press and industry journals including Forbes, Sprout, Advertising Age, Chief! Marketer, Marketing Week and BrandWeek.

Marc co-founded EffectiveBrands in 2001 following a successful career with Unilever. He has been listed among the top-10 marketers for the last three years in TvM, and in 2008 he was awarded the *Asian Global Marketing Award*. At EffectiveBrands, Marc spearheads the *Leading Global Brands* study, an ongoing learning project with contributions from over 250 global brands and 2,500 global brand leaders.

Educated in the U.K. and the Netherlands, Marc holds a Business Economics degree from the Erasmus University, and serves as a volunteer on the Advisory Board of *GoodWeave*, which works toward ending child slavery in the carpet industry. He lives with his family in New York City. **marc@effectivebrands.com**

FRANK VAN DEN DRIEST

As co-founder of EffectiveBrands, Frank is well known for his work in developing leading global brand strategy and deployment programs. Having worked in executive management roles for BBDO, GfK, and the PositioningGroup, Frank gained a wealth of experience in defining the most successful paths from insight to growth, and has an enviable track record of delivering results. Being a true entrepreneur, Frank also co-founded a *Zimbabwean Art* trading company, that also established a chain of high-end galleries.

Frank has lectured at various MBA programs and led many in-company global brand excellence programs. Frank has been a highly successful sparring partner and coach to many CMOs and global brand leaders, all in pursuit of building the elusive archetype of the *global marketing machine*. He is a non-executive board member of Brandnew.design, an international design agency and 'sounding board member' to multiple start-ups.

Frank holds a degree in Communication Sciences from the University of Amsterdam, and also studied at the Hebrew University in Jerusalem. He lives with his family near Amsterdam. **frank@effectivebrands.com**

About EffectiveBrands

EffectiveBrands is the only global marketing consultancy focused specifically on unlocking the value of global brands and global marketing organizations.

Founded in 2001, EffectiveBrands helps global marketing leaders increase global brand effectiveness with programs and practical tools that build global marketing *strategy*, *structure* and *capability* for profitable growth.

The EffectiveBrands team consists of over 50 international and experienced global marketing consultants and support staff spread across offices in New York, London, Amsterdam, Singapore, Paris and Tokyo.

Our insights and practical solutions are predicated on in-depth global marketing experience, as well as our proprietary *Leading Global Brands* study. As of 2010, over 250 global brands, 2,500 global marketing leaders and 21,000 global brand marketers and their colleagues contributed to this study.

www.effectivebrands.com / info@effectivebrands.com

PULSECHECK™

PURPOSEFUL POSITIONING™

BRAND LIVE!™

ONE STRATEGY™

Key global & local business and stakeholder understanding 5C Analysis Brand roots & health analysis	Brand ID! definition Portfolio architecture	Internal engagement – marketing mix review & optimisation	Global – local prioritisation & alignment

VISION, MISSION & VALUES →

COMPANY 2 -3 YR BUSINESS OBJECTIVES →

CATEGORY 2 -3 YR BUSINESS & BRAND GOALS →

REQUIRED STRATEGIC INPUT

**HE EMPOWERED
MARKETING
ORGANISATION™**

**GLOBAL
MARKETING
EXCELLENCE™**

**RESULTS
FACTORY™**

Fit for purpose
marketing
structure &
operating
model
development

Marketing
capability
Program
development

Knowledge &
learning
infrastructure

Real time local
deployment of
global
marketing
strategy

Brilliant
activation
planning

MPANY
GANIZATIONAL
RATEGY

COMPANY
TRAINING
STRATEGY

LOCAL MARKET
TARGET &
ANALYSIS

The Leading Global Brands study

Anyone working in global marketing will know that there is little or no specific support available to help better understand what it takes to build winning global marketing strategy, structure and capability. There is no book to buy, no peer council to join, and until a decade ago, no specialized consultancy to ask for support.

THE OPPORTUNITY

Over the last ten years a record number of brands have 'gone global'. Never before has so much practical experience and learning been generated. Many brands have been very successful in growing quickly across geographies and cultures. But at least as many other brands have made painful mistakes and have had to redo or retreat from their global efforts.

THE 'LIVING' PROJECT

This is not an area where marketing theory has much value. Today's marketers have no time or need for three-dimensional theoretical models that explain made-up scenarios. To truly understand the pitfalls to avoid and to build on the experience of the most successful global brands, EffectiveBrands set out to learn from the people that have been fighting these battles on the frontlines. Instead of simply conducting 'research' that would someday be published and forgotten, we have for the last eight years, focused on developing an ongoing, practice-based study designed to apply insights and learning in real-time to the work we do with our clients on a daily basis.

THE PARTICIPANTS

Since the start of this ongoing study, more then 250 global brands, 2,500 global brand leaders, and 21,000 global marketers and their colleagues have contributed to the study.

Participating Brands

3M	AQUAFRESH	BISTEFANI	CAPTAIN COOK
	ARISCO	BLUE BAND	CARESS
A	ASTRA, LA DANESA	BOMBAY SAPPHIRE	CARGILL
A1	ASTRAZENECA	BONA	CARLSBERG
ABN AMRO	ATOPICA	BONELLA	CARREFOUR
ABSOLUT VODKA	AVA	BOSTON COLLEGE	CARTE D'OR
ACCENTURE	AVIANCE	BOVRIL	CHANTILLY
ACHMEA / EUREKO	AVIVA	BP	CHARLES SCHWAB
ACTIVIA	AXE	BREATHE RIGHT	CATERPILLAR
ADEZ	AYALA GROUP	BREEZE	CHEVRON
AHOLD	AYUSH	BRILHANTE	CHICLETS
AIM		BROOKE BOND	CHICORY
AKZONOBEL	**B**	BROWN & POLSON	CHIRAT
ALA	BABA	BRU	CHRYSALIS
ALACTA	BACARDI	BRUMMEL & BROWN	CICA
ALGIDA FINDUS	BAILAN	BRUNCH	CIF
ALLI	BAIN & CO.	BRUT	CITRA
ALSA	BANGO	BUAVITA JUICES	CLEAN & CLEAR
ALTIS SOFT	BANK OF AMERICA	BUSHELLS	CLEAR SHAMPOO
ALTRIA CLIENT SERVICES	BBH		CLINIC PLUS
AMAZE	BECEDA	**C**	CLORETS
AMERICAN EXPRESS	BECEL	CADBURY SCHWEPPES	CLOSE-UP
AMERICAN RED CROSS	BEDO	CALCIUM SANDOZ	COCA-COLA
AMINO	BEIERSDORF	CALIPPO	COCCOLINO
AMODENT	BELIVOIR	CALVÉ	COLMAN'S
AMORE	BENEFIBER	CALVIN KLEIN	COMFORT
ANDRÉLON	BERTOLLI	CAMEL	CONIMEX
ANHEUSER-BUSCH	BESEDA	CAMPBELL'S	CONTINENTAL
ANNAPURNA SALT	BEST BUY	CAMPINA	COORS LIGHT
AOL	BIFI	CANDADO	CORAL
AON CORP.	BING	CANON	COREGA
APPLE INC.	BIO LUVIL	CAPITAL ONE	CORNETTO

IMPULSE

INDUS VALLEY INTERNA-

TIONAL

ING

INTEL CORP

INTERCONTINENTAL

HOTELS

INTERPUBLIC GROUP

INTUIT

J

J.C. PENNEY

JAM BRANDS

JAN SMIT

JOHNNIE WALKER

JOKO

K

KALIAKRA

KANTAR

KASIA

KB HOME

KBS+P

KEY

KFC

KIMBERLY-CLARK

KISSAN

KLEENEX

KLM

KLONDIKE

KLORINI

KNORR

KNORR TRAITEUR

KNORR VIE

KNORROX

KOTEX

KPN

KRAFT

KUNER

KUSCHELWEICH

L

LA LLAVE

LA PERFECTA

LABOR RELATIONS

LACTUM

LADY'S CHOICE

LAKMÉ

LAMISIL

LANGNESE

LÄTTA

LAUNDRY

LAWRY'S

LE SANCY

LEASEPLAN

LEGO SYSTEMS

LEGOÛT

LEVER 2000

LEVERHOME

LEVI STRAUSS & CO.

LIBERTY MUTUAL

LIFEBUOY SHAMPOO

LIFESCAN

LIGERESA

LINIC

LIPTON

LIRIL

LISTERINE

LIVING HYGIENE

LIZ CLAIBORNE INC.

LIZANO

LLOYDS BANKING GROUP

LOBLAW COMPANIES

LOCAL JEWELS

LOGITECH

LOWE & PARTNERS

LU

LUKULL

LUVIL

LUX

LUX PROGRESS

LVMH

LYNX

LYONS

LYSOFORM

M

M&M'S

M.A.D. BRAND CARE

MAGNUM

MAGNUM AMBIENT

MAILLE

MAIZENA

MALLOA

MARMITE

MARRIOTT

MARS

MARTINI

MASTERBRAND

MASTERCARD

MATA

MAX

MAXIMOUSSE

MAZOLA

MC-COLLINS

MDC PARTNERS

MEAD JOHNSON

MEDIA (ONE)

MENTADENT

MEXX

MIFFY

MIKO

MILDA

MILLWARD BROWN

MIMOSIN

MINERVA

MINI PAKS

MIRASOL

MISTOLIN

MOD'S HAIR

MOENCH

MOLSON

MONDAMIN

MONITOR

MOO

MOTI

MRMLOGIQ

MRS.BALL'S

N

NATURA

NBC UNIVERSAL

NESTLÉ

NICORETTE

NICOTELL

NIELSEN IAG

NIKE

NINTENDO

NOKIA

NORTHWESTERN MUTUAL

LIFE

NOVAMEDIA

NOVARTIS

NUVARING

O

OGILVY & MATHER

OLA

OMO

ONE

OPAL

ORANGE

OSWALD

P

P&G

PANADOL

PEA RL DUST

PEARS

PEDIGREE

PEPERAMI

PEPSI

PEPSODENT

PERNOD RICARD

PERSIL

PFANNI

PFIZER

PHASE

PHILIPS

PHILIPS

(ORAL HEALTHCARE/

SONICARE)

PINGÜINO

PINUK

PITNEY BOWES

PIZZA HUT

PLANTA

POLIDENT

POLIGRIP

POMAROLA

PONDS

PONDS PROFESSIONAL

POPSICLE

POT NOODLE

PROMISE

PRONTO

PUMMARO

PURE IT

PURO

Q

Q-TIPS

QUIX

R

R/GA MEDIA

RABOBANK

RADIANT

RADION

RAGU

RAGULETTO

RAMA

RAZAR

RBS

REACH

RED ROSE

REMBRANDT

REXONA

RIN

RINSO

ROBERTSONS HERBS

AND SPICES

ROBIJN

ROGERS COMMUNICATION

RONDO

ROYCO

ROZANA

RUFFINO

S

SAAB GRIPEN

SABMILLER

SAGA

SAKIMS

SALADA

SANA

SANTA ROSA

SAP

SARA LEE

SARIWANGI

SAS INSTITUTE

SCA

SCHLUMBERGER

SEDA

SEDAL

SELECTA ICE CREAM

SENSEO

SENSODYNE

SHEDDS

SHIELD

SHISEIDO

SHOTS

SICLE

SIGNAL

SIKKENS AND DULUX

SKIP

SKIPPY PEANUT BUTTER

SLIM FAST

SMALL & MIGHTY

SMART CHOICE

SMIRNOFF

SMOKING CONTROL

SNICKERS

SNUGGLE

SOBE

SOFFICINI

SOLERO

SOLO

SONY

SONY ERICSSON

SOYA SAUCE

SPARES

SPENCER STUART

SPREED

STARBUCKS

STARLUX

STERLING

STORK

STREETS

SUAVE

SUMAIZ

SUN

SUNIL

SUNLIGHT

SUNSILK

SUPERPELL

SUPERSHOTS

SURF

SURF EXCEL

SUSTAGEN

SVELTO

SWIRLS

T

TAAZA

TACO BELL

TAG HEUER

TANGUERAY

TARO SNACKS

TÉ CLUB

TELMA

THAT'S AMORE

THE BODY SHOP

THE EMPOWERMENT

INSTITUTE

THERAFLU

THERMASILK

THOMSON REUTERS

TIAA-CREF

TIFFANY & CO

TIMOTEI

TIO RICO

TODAS

TOM TOM

TOSHIBA

TRIAMINIC

TRIDENT

TROFAI

TULIPAN

U

UAL CORP

UNCLE BEN'S

UNILEVER

UNILEVER COSMETICS

INTERNATIONAL

UNILEVER

FOOD SOLUTIONS

UNITEDHEALTH GROUP

UNOX

USA CORP

V

VAPORESSE

VAQUEIRO

VASELINE

VASENOL

VERIZON

VIA

VIENNETTA

VIM TOILET/VIM FLOOR

CARE

VINOLIA

VIRGIN

VISA

VISO

VITA

VITALITY

VITAM

VÍVERE

VODAFONE

VOLTAREN

W

WALL'S

WALMART

WESTERNGECO

WHEEL

WILDE

WINDMILL

WISH BONE

WISK

WRIGLEY

X

XEDEX

XTRA

Y

YUMOS

Z

ZED

ZHONG HUA

ZURICH FINANCIAL SERVICES

ZWAN